WITH THE MASTER ON THE MOUNT

A Ladies' Bible Study of the Sermon on the Mount

By
Susan J. Heck

With the Master on the Mount
A Ladies' Bible Study of the Sermon on the Mount
By Susan J. Heck

Cover design by Amelia Schussman

ISBN 978-1-936141-45-6

Printed in the United States of America

Dedication

To Dr. John MacArthur

A devoted servant of God whose life has exhibited salt and light
by faithfully preaching the Word of God.
His "good works" of preaching truth have impacted many
and glorified our Father in heaven.

Endorsements

This Bible study provides clarity for the student of The Sermon on the Mount—clarity in the essential message of Jesus' sermon, in sound doctrine, and in relevant application for the Christian woman today. Susan knows how to help women examine their hearts in order to challenge them to live in full obedience to Jesus Christ. Those who are hungry to understand the truths in Jesus' great sermon will not be disappointed. I highly recommend it to you!

Dr. John D. Street
Chair, Graduate Department of Biblical Counseling
The Master's University & Seminary
President, ACBC Board of Trustees

We are so thankful for Susan Heck and her commitment to faithfully studying, memorizing and teaching the Scriptures in such an indepth manner. Our family has personally been blessed through Susan's ministry in the USA and here in India. The women in our church have now studied all of the "With the Master" series and look forward to working through this new book. In this study *With the Master on the Mount*, Susan will take you to the heights of Jesus' teaching through a study of His Sermon on the Mount. You will be encouraged towards obedience as you evaluate your life through the study questions. Susan's commitment to Scripture memorization comes out through her grasp of the text and exhortations to hide specific verses in your heart. As you take in this verse by verse study of a much treasured text, you will be transformed by Christ in attitude and action!

Sammy and Nicole Williams
Cornerstone Community Church, India

Are you a kingdom citizen? Or are you a religious hypocrite? Are you a wise man, building your house on the Rock? Or are you a foolish man, building your house on the sand? Although this study will undoubtedly lead to serious self-examination, it is written in a way that is warm, as Susan calls her readers "friends," and personally identifies with those being convicted of sin. Susan often points out that Jesus is describing what the lifestyle of every genuine believer looks like and although she encourages her readers to study and even memorize this Sermon, most of all, she encourages us to LIVE it. There are numerous reasons that I can highly recommend this book: alliterative outlines are excellent and accurate, substantive summaries of each chapter also suggest personal application, study questions at the end of each chapter lead to additional Scripture references, clear exposition emphasizing context, and thorough teaching regarding Matthew 7:12 (the Golden Rule). I spiritually profited from reading *With the Master on the Mount* and I sincerely believe you will too.

Fonda Mauser, personal friend and mentor of Susan's for over 30 years.

Table of Contents

Chapter 1

The Blessed Beatitudes (Part 1)

Matthew 5:1-6

> When we hear of men living in sin and yet claiming to be Christians, we are disgusted with their pretenses, but we are not deceived by their professions. In the same manner, we care little for those who are *orthodox Christians in creed*—if it is clear that they are *heterodox in life.* He who believes the truth, should himself be true. How can we expect others to receive our religion—if it leaves us foul, false, malicious, and selfish? *We sicken at the sight of a dirty dish*, and refuse even good meat when it is placed thereon. So pure and holy is the doctrine of the cross, that he who *hears* it aright will have his ear cleansed, he who *believes* it will have his heart purged, and he who *preaches* it should have his tongue purified. Woe unto that man who brings reproach upon the gospel by an unholy walk and life![1]

Charles Spurgeon, after whom we named our son, wrote these words more than 150 years ago, yet his words remain true today. My friends, we are living in an age of apostasy. The signs are everywhere that we are living in the age of the great falling away, of which Paul speaks in 2 Thessalonians, a clear indication of the Lord's soon return!

My heart is grieved as I watch many professing believers make a mockery of the Savior whom they claim to profess as Lord. Their personal lives are a sham; their public lives are a disgrace; and very few professing Christians seem to care. But there is One who does care. And He cares so much that He left us a profound sermon about it so that we would be left with no doubt as to what He expects from those who profess to be His children! The "One" I am speaking of

---

1 Charles Spurgeon, "Orthodox in Creed — But Heterodox in Life!" *Flowers from a Puritan's Garden* (1883) www.GraceGems.org (gracegems.org/Spurgeon/flowers_ from_a_puritans_garden.htm).

is Jesus, and the profound sermon I am referring to is the Sermon on the Mount.

John R. W. Stott says of this sermon, "The Sermon on the Mount is probably the best-known part of the teaching of Jesus, though arguably it is the least understood, and certainly it is the least obeyed."[2] The Sermon on the Mount begins with Matthew, chapter 5, and ends with chapter 7. Three chapters, just 110 verses, but what powerful words are spoken from our Lord! Four hundred years of silence had passed since the last Old Testament book, the last prophetic word from the LORD—the book of Malachi—had been recorded, and now, in Jesus' Sermon on the Mount, God is speaking through His Son.

Before we begin to examine this portion of God's Word, let's briefly review what has transpired in the first four chapters of Matthew's Gospel. The first chapter of the Gospel of Matthew begins with the genealogy of Jesus Christ (1:1-17). What is interesting about this particular genealogy is that it includes five women, which is unusual in that most biblical genealogies include only men. What is even more unusual about this genealogy is that all five of these women would have been considered to have some blight on their character: Tamar, Rahab, Ruth, Bathsheba and Mary. After Matthew writes concerning the genealogy of Jesus, he then writes about the announcement to Joseph of the birth of Jesus. This would have been shocking to Joseph as he was at that point engaged to Mary but not yet married to her (1:18-25).

Chapter two of Matthew's Gospel begins with the birth of Jesus and the account of the wise men worshiping the Christ-child. Joseph is then told to flee Egypt due to Herod seeking to kill baby Jesus. Following Herod's death, Joseph takes Mary and young Jesus and returns to Israel, and they settle in Nazareth to live (2:1-23). In chapter three, we are introduced to the ministry of John the Baptist, whose purpose in coming on the scene is to announce the coming

---

2 John R. W. Stott, *The Message of the Sermon on the Mount* (Downers Grove: Inter-Varsity Press, 1978), 15.

of the Lord and then begin his public ministry of preaching. His message is simple: "Repent, for the kingdom is at hand!" Jesus comes to John to be baptized; John protests but eventually consents and baptizes his Lord (3:1-16).

At this point, Jesus is about to begin His public ministry, but before He does, chapter four records that He is led by the Spirit into the wilderness to be tested by the devil. After this testing by the evil one, Matthew records the touching account of angels coming to minister to Jesus (4:1-11). Jesus then hears of John being in prison (John was in prison because he was outspoken about Herod's adulterous relationship) (4:12-17). Jesus then begins His public ministry with a message that was identical to John's: "Repent, for the kingdom of heaven is at hand!" Jesus calls Peter and Andrew to follow Him, along with James and John (4:18-22). Then, we read in 4:23-25, "And Jesus went about all Galilee, teaching in their synagogues, preaching the gospel of the kingdom, and healing all kinds of sickness and all kinds of disease among the people. Then His fame went throughout all Syria; and they brought to Him all sick people who were afflicted with various diseases and torments, and those who were demon-possessed, epileptics, and paralytics; and He healed them. Great multitudes followed Him—from Galilee, and from Decapolis, Jerusalem, Judea, and beyond the Jordan." This brings us to chapters 5-7, the portion of Scripture known as the Sermon on the Mount.

Jesus has just begun His public ministry with the gospel of the kingdom: "Repent, for the kingdom of heaven is at hand!" Since the kingdom of heaven is indeed at hand, we ought to ask ourselves what this means. Just what does it take to get into the kingdom of heaven? What does a genuine kingdom citizen look like? And what does repentance look like? Jesus will answer all these questions in the Sermon on the Mount. And His message, as the rest of the Gospel of Matthew demonstrates, would shake the Jewish world to its core because they thought that the kingdom was to be ushered in by political or military force.

It's worth noting that what Jesus is describing in this sermon is what every kingdom citizen looks like, not some super-Christian. If our lives do not measure up to what Jesus teaches in these chapters, then we would do well to do some serious self-examination. This sermon also does not describe some personal effort to attain righteousness on our own, like the self-righteousness of the Pharisees, but a righteousness that is brought about in us as the result of a right relationship with God. One man has said of it, "Jesus repeated his sayings many times as all great teachers and preachers do, but this sermon has unity, progress, and consummation. It does not contain all that Jesus taught by any means, but it stands out as the greatest single sermon of all time, in its penetration, pungency, and power."[3] Another says, "It is violent, but its violence can be our ongoing liberation! It is the antidote to the pretense and sham that plagues Christianity."[4] These men penned it well because Matthew tells us what happened when Jesus finished this sermon in Matthew 7:28-29: "And so it was, when Jesus had ended these sayings, that the people were astonished at His teaching, for He taught them as one having authority, and not as the Scribes." These people were struck dumb—exepleessonto is the Greek term—and it means that they were dumbfounded, they were struck out of their mind! They could not believe what they were hearing![5] With these things in mind, let's

---

3 Robertson's Word Pictures, *PC Study Bible, Version 5* (from Robertson's Word Pictures in the New Testament, Electronic Database. Copyright © 1997, 2003, 2005, 2006 by Biblesoft, Inc. Robertson's Word Pictures in the New Testament. Copyright © 1985 by Broadman Press.) Many have pointed put that the Sermon on the Mount was Jesus' often-preached stump message, because Luke 6:17-45 records a similar sermon. Sometimes that is called the Sermon on the Plain and could have been written within a day or so of the Sermon on the Mount, as if Jesus preached on the mountain and then descended to the plain to preach a similar sermon.
4 R. Kent Hughes, *Need Title* (Wheaton: Crossway Books, Inc., 2001), 16.
5 As a matter of fact, the Greek word Matthew selects, ekeplasonto, is used in the imperfect tense, to stress the sense that point after point during the Lord's sermon the people were astonished. His point is not that after the message the people took a deep breath and said, "Whoa!" But, rather, after each principle, after each statement, after each illustration, the people were struck out of mind! It blew their minds throughout the message. Hendriksen explains this unique effect upon the original audience on the mount: "The people listening to Jesus that day must have been spellbound from the very beginning. They must have been enthralled by the very opening sentence, for Jesus was telling them things which on the surface seemed absurd." (William Hendriksen, *Exposition of the Gospel of Matthew* (Baker Book House, 1973, 264.)

turn our attention to the first 6 verses of Matthew 5.

Matthew 5:1-6

> And seeing the multitudes, He went up on a mountain, and when He was seated His disciples came to Him. ²Then He opened His mouth and taught them, saying: ³"Blessed are the poor in spirit, for theirs is the kingdom of heaven. 4Blessed are those who mourn, for they shall be comforted. ⁵Blessed are the meek, for they shall inherit the earth. ⁶Blessed are those who hunger and thirst for righteousness, for they shall be filled."

As we examine Matthew 5:1-6, we will consider:

Three Beginning Blessings (vv 1-2)
Four Blessed Beatitudes (vv 3-6)

Beginning Blessings

Matthew 5:1-2

> And seeing the multitudes, He went up on a mountain, and when He was seated His disciples came to Him. Then He opened His mouth and taught them, saying:

We begin with Matthew's opening words in verse 1: *And seeing the multitudes, He went up on a mountain, and when He was seated His disciples came to Him.* What *multitudes* is Matthew speaking about? He is speaking of the multitudes mentioned in 4:25, those from Galilee, Decapolis, Jerusalem, Judea, and beyond the Jordon. There are many instances in Matthew's Gospel where it is recorded that when Jesus saw the multitudes He was moved with compassion. Matthew 9:36 says, "But when He saw the multitudes, He was moved with compassion for them, because they were weary and scattered, like sheep having no shepherd." Matthew 14:14 states, "And when Jesus went out He saw a great multitude; and He was moved with compassion for them, and healed their sick." Matthew 15:32 records, "Now Jesus called His disciples to Himself and said, 'I have compassion on the multitude, because they have now continued with me three days and have nothing to eat. And I do not want to send them away hungry, lest they faint on the way.'" In each of these instances, Jesus, seeing the multitudes, decided to act on what He saw, whether it was healing, feeding or helping them spiritually. Here, in Matthew 5:1, it doesn't specifically state that Jesus had compassion, but you know He did. These were multitudes that knew nothing of the gospel of the kingdom. His seeing these multitudes led Him to do something, and that something was to open His mouth and preach. The word *seeing* means that He was aware; He perceived and He considered. *This is the first beginning blessing—Jesus saw them.*

Seeing the multitudes led Christ to do something. He didn't decide to go take a nap or go fishing because He was already weary from the day. I fear many of us see crowds of people with spiritual needs but we quickly drown out our conviction by busying ourselves or dulling our consciences with social media or television. But not our Lord; He did something. He went up on the mountain and He sat down. *This is the second beginning blessing—He sat down.* You might be wondering, why is this sitting such a blessing? Jesus' sitting was a blessing because it was the normal teaching position for the Jew. A teacher would sit with his legs crossed and those listening would do the same. In fact, if Christ had stood to teach or had walked as He taught, His listeners would have considered His teaching to be informal, but the position of sitting would have indicated a formal and honored position. In American culture, we would think the opposite. To sit and teach would be informal, but to stand would be a formal way of teaching. So, when Christ sat down, it meant He was intending to teach them.

Now the text says *He went up on a mountain.* We're not sure what mountain this was, as it isn't indicated in the text. It was probably not a huge mountain or the crowds wouldn't have been able to see Him or hear Him. It also mentions in this verse that *His disciples came to Him* after He was seated. They knew this meant He was going to teach and they didn't want to miss it! This reminds me of Mary, in Luke's account, where it says, "Now it happened as they went that He entered a certain village; and a certain woman named Martha welcomed Him into her house. And she had a sister called Mary, who also sat at Jesus' feet and heard His word. But Martha was distracted with much serving, and she approached Him and said, 'Lord, do You not care that my sister has left me to serve alone? Therefore tell her to help me.' And Jesus answered and said to her, 'Martha, Martha, you are worried and troubled about many things. But one thing is needed, and Mary has chosen that good part, which will not be taken away from her'" (Luke 10:38-42). Mary sat at the feet of Jesus to learn. The disciples sat at the feet of Jesus to learn. That is what a disciple is—a learner, a pupil. The Greek word for *disciple* is the noun <u>mathetes</u>, and it occurs 264 times in the New Testament, exclusively in the Gospels and Acts. It speaks of attachment to someone for the purpose of learning, coming from the Greek verb <u>manthano</u>, which means "to learn." Yet it also indicates a level of sincerity, because it is certainly possible to attach yourself to someone for the purpose of learning, but not necessarily be committed to that person. Even Judas is called a disciple in Matthew 10 and John 12. But although Judas had attached himself to Jesus to learn from Him, Judas hadn't dedicated himself to the Lord as a genuine, sincere disciple of Him. In John 8:31, Jesus described genuine discipleship by contrasting them with superficially-attached believers, when He said, "If you abide in my word, you are truly my disciples" (John 8:31). To continue in Jesus' word is to believe it and obey it in one's life. The Lord Himself makes it clear that there are those who are disciples indeed, and there are spurious disciples, those who are disciples in name only. There are true disciples who are committed to Jesus, and there are false disciples, who attach themselves to Him to learn from Him, but not for the purpose of obeying Him or remaining committed to Him. The disciples sat at the feet of Jesus to learn. That is what a disciple is—a learner, a pupil. A disciple is one who attaches themselves to another person for the purpose of growing towards Christlikeness. A disciple is someone who imitates their master. My dear friend, we are the pupils, we are the learners, and we would do well to join the disciples and learn at the feet of our Master as He opens His mouth and teaches this wonderful Sermon on the Mount! This is exactly what He does, as we see in verse 2.

In verse 2, we read that *He opened His mouth and taught them.* Jesus opens His mouth. This is an interesting phrase because up until now, according to Matthew's Gospel, Jesus hasn't spoken much except to tell John to baptize Him, to speak the Word to Satan when Satan tempted Him in the wilderness, to tell the people to repent, and to tell a few of the disciples to follow Him. But now He opens His mouth to teach. *This is the third beginning blessing—He spoke, He opened His mouth.* Paul asks in Romans 10:14, "How shall they hear without a preacher?" All public teaching begins with opening one's mouth. It behooves us, as followers of the Lord Jesus Christ, to open our mouths and speak God's Word to others. Women use their mouths for a lot of things, most of it being idle chatter, but to use our mouths to instruct others in the things of our Lord—oh, what joy, my friend!

Here, Jesus opens His mouth, and this is the beginning of His sermon. So, we turn from the three beginning blessings—that Jesus saw, He sat, and He spoke—to, now, the blessed beatitudes. We will only look at four beatitudes in this lesson and finish the last four in our next lesson.

Blessed Beatitudes

Matthew 5:3-6

> "Blessed are the poor in spirit, for theirs is the kingdom of heaven. Blessed are those who mourn, for they shall be comforted. Blessed are the meek, for they shall inherit the earth. Blessed are those who hunger and thirst for righteousness, for they shall be filled."

This is the beginning of what is known as the beatitudes. The first blessed beatitude that Jesus mentions is *blessed are the poor in spirit*. He begins by saying *blessed are the poor in spirit, for theirs is the kingdom of heaven.* Since Jesus uses the word *blessed* in each one of these beatitudes, we should define it. The word means happy, fortunate, and supremely blessed. This state of blessedness is not dependent on circumstances or people. It is odd that we think of happiness in our culture as laughing or joking or always smiling, yet we know that Jesus was happy and we don't see Him doing those things in the pages of the New Testament. His happiness was manifested by a calmness and a joy that He possessed all throughout life, even in the face of death!

So, who is it that is blessed? Jesus says it is those who are *poor in spirit. Poor* describes a beggar who is crouching in a corner. This one is so physically poor that he is utterly dependent on another for sustenance. But Jesus is not speaking here of one who is physically poor, because He says this one is poor *in spirit*, which is an indication of one's soul. So, this means that the person who is poor in spirit is one who is utterly dependent on God because she realizes she possesses nothing in and of herself. This is the person who realizes that she is spiritually bankrupt without the redeeming grace of Christ. There is no pride, no hint of self-reliance; rather, she is completely helpless and hopeless. "John Wesley said of the poor in spirit, 'He has a deep sense of the loathsome leprosy of sin which he brought with him from his mother's womb, which overspreads his whole soul, and totally corrupts every power and faculty thereof.'"[6] What a contrast this is to the Jewish world of Jesus' day! In Matthew 23, Jesus pronounced a series of woes on the Jews because they were full of pride and wanted to be seen and admired by men. This is also a contrast to American culture, as we would consider ourselves blessed and happy if all was well with all our surroundings, our circumstances, and our relationships.

Now, why is it that the poor in spirit are blessed? Jesus says *for theirs is the kingdom of heaven*, which literally reads "theirs and theirs only is the kingdom of heaven." Jesus makes it clear to the Jews who were listening that day that the kingdom He is referring to is not of this world. The Jews were hoping Messiah would usher in

6 Ibid, 19

a political or military kingdom, but Jesus isn't concerned with these issues at all. He's come to do the will of the Father. He lived for the kingdom to come and so should we.

It is not by "chance" that being poor in spirit is the first beatitude that Jesus mentions, because if we do not recognize our destitute, depraved state we cannot enter into the kingdom of God. Unless we realize that we are without hope and throw ourselves upon His mercy we cannot enter into His kingdom. Without this beatitude in place we will in no way be able to live out the rest of the Sermon on the Mount because we will have no power to do so.

Let's move on to the second blessed beatitude. Jesus says *blessed are those who mourn, for they shall be comforted*. Those who are happy or fortunate are those who mourn. John Stott has said of this, "One might translate this second beatitude 'Happy are the unhappy' in order to draw attention to the startling paradox it contains."[7] *Those who mourn* refers to those who grieve or wail like they are mourning for the dead. And what are they wailing about? Their spiritual poverty, the fact that they are nothing without their Savior, the fact that their heart is desperately wicked. It is like Isaiah said, in Isaiah 6:5, "Woe is me, for I am undone! Because I am a man of unclean lips, and I dwell in the midst of a people of unclean lips; for my eyes have seen the King, The Lord of hosts." When Isaiah considered himself in the presence of God, he saw himself for what he was—sinful! This is an appropriate beatitude to follow after the first, being poor in spirit, because once I recognize how destitute and bankrupt I am, I bewail my sinfulness, I mourn over my sin.

I remember how true this was in my own life when God saved me; I wept over my sin for the first time, even though I had been "saved and baptized" three times before. All those other times that I had supposedly gotten "saved" I had never mourned over my sin or even really seen myself as a sinner. We live in an age where we minimize our sin and we rarely confess it, much less mourn over it.

---

7 John R. W. Stott, *The Message of the Sermon on the Mount* (Downers Grove: Inter-Varsity Press, 1978), 40.

But a genuine Christian mourns over the fact that she is a sinner and she mourns over her sin. The Greek rendering of the word *mourn* indicates a continual mourning over our sins. A good question for us to ask ourselves is: "When did I last grieve over my sin? When did I last grieve over my pride, my loose tongue, my anger, my selfishness?" A kingdom citizen mourns over her sins. She doesn't buy into the modern psychology of our day that minimizes and rationalizes sin. Instead, she owns up to it, confesses it, mourns over it, and repents of it. Jesus' half-brother James echoes what Jesus says here, in James 4:8-10, "Draw near to God and He will draw near to you. Cleanse your hands, you sinners; and purify your hearts, you double-minded. Lament and mourn and weep! Let your laughter be turned to mourning and your joy to gloom. Humble yourselves in the sight of the Lord, and He will lift you up." Jesus says in Luke 6:25b, "Woe to you who laugh now, for you shall mourn and weep.

May I also say that we ought to mourn over the sins of others, as well? We don't laugh at the sin of others; we don't minimize it, and we certainly don't join the crowd, even the "Christian" crowd that tells us we need to lighten up. We are told that we need to accept homosexuality as a lifestyle, we need to live together and not get married, and we need to accept the anger and unrighteousness of others. My friend, we would do well to get back to the biblical doctrine of sin and see what Jesus says and not what the church or even our well-meaning friends say.

Jesus says that those who mourn over their sin *will be comforted.* They and they alone will be *comforted*, which means that they will be consoled. The world doesn't know that kind of comfort; they don't know what it means to have the guilt of their sin removed. Instead, their sin heaps heavy on them, and they react in anger and all types of wickedness, as described in Romans 1. But just as we continually mourn over our sins, so we are continually comforted. What a blessed beatitude! King David knew this state of blessedness, and he certainly needed the comfort of the Lord's forgiveness after his sins of adultery with Bathsheba and orchestrating her husband Uriah's murder on the front lines of battle. In Psalm 32:1, David says, "Blessed is he whose transgression is forgiven, whose sin is covered." The songwriter put it well: "Nothing in my hand I bring, simply to Thy cross I cling; Naked, come to Thee for dress, Helpless, look to Thee for grace; Foul, I to the fountain fly; Wash me, Saviour, or I die."[8] This, again, would be a rebuke to the Jewish leaders of the day who prided themselves in their spirituality. They didn't mourn over sin. Jesus illustrates this well in Luke 18:9-11:

> Also He spoke this parable to some who trusted in themselves that they were righteous, and despised others: "Two men went up to the temple to pray, one a Pharisee and the other a tax collector. The Pharisee stood and prayed thus with himself, 'God, I thank You that I am not like other men—extortioners, unjust, adulterers, or even as this tax collector. I fast twice a week; I give tithes of all that I possess.'" And the tax collector, standing afar off, would not so much as raise his eyes to heaven, but beat his breast, saying, "God, be merciful to me a sinner!" I tell you, this man went down to his house justified rather than the other; for everyone who exalts himself will be humbled, and he who humbles himself will be exalted.

The third blessed beatitude is found in verse 5: *blessed are the meek, for they shall inherit the earth.* Those who are fortunate are those who are meek, Jesus says. *Meek* indicates that they are humble, patient, and gentle. The word has been used to describe an animal that has been tamed, one that isn't wild or out of control. Meek people don't think of themselves at all but, instead, look to the interests of others. This is the opposite of someone who is spiritually proud. My friend, God opposes the proud and gives grace to the humble. Again, there is a natural flow from being poor in spirit to recognizing our depravity, which then causes us to mourn over our sin, and as we do that we have no pride left in us. To think that God would save any of us should humble us! To think that we have been chosen before the foundation of the world to be His own should humble us! How can we be arrogant about anything?! Humility is a virtue that the Jews did not seek after; instead, they prided themselves in their keeping of the law. They thought that by doing so they would be granted entrance into heaven. But Jesus tells them in Matthew

---

8 Augustus Toplady, *Rock of Ages* (1776).

23:12, "And whoever exalts himself will be humbled, and he who humbles himself will be exalted." The proud will never embrace the gospel, for it is their very pride that keeps them from the cross. They are too proud to give up their reputation, their friends, their sin, their selfish lifestyle. Pride has ruined many a man and woman, and it is pride that sends a person to hell if they will not bow their knee to Christ. But one day, yes, one day too late, they will bow the knee, but only once, for after that they shall be cast in the lake of fire!

Jesus goes on to say that those who are meek *will inherit the earth*. The Jews took special pride in the land that had been promised to them, and to *inherit the earth* would indicate God's blessing on their life. The Promised Land became emblematic of heaven. But Jesus is saying that it isn't the proud Jew who will inherit the everlasting Promised Land, but those who are meek.

The fourth blessed beatitude is found in verse 6. Jesus says *blessed are those who hunger and thirst for righteousness, for they shall be filled*. This fourth beatitude has to do with those who hunger and thirst for righteousness, that is, they are blessed, they are happy. The Greek rendering of this text communicates not that we are hungry and thirsty for partial righteousness but for all the righteousness there is. It's not like saying I am hungry for some food or thirsty for some drink, but I am hungry for all the food and all the water there is. Does this describe you, my friend? I hope that you will consider the study questions at the end of this chapter and are able to try the experiment of going without food or water for a few hours to get a glimpse of what Jesus is saying here. We must eat and drink to sustain our physical lives, so why would we think it is any different in the spiritual realm? Many seem satisfied with a small crumb or a drop of water. Jesus would have something to say to those who think this way. He says that genuine followers of Him know nothing of this type of "Christianity." A genuine disciple wants to replace all her unrighteousness with all the righteousness she can get. *Righteousness* is the act of doing what is right. A genuine believer has been declared righteous in God's eyes, but she still longs for more and more practical righteousness in her own life and the lives of others.

Again, this beatitude follows well after the others. As we realize our destitute state of being poor in spirit, it results in us mourning over our sin, and that results in an attitude of humility, which then leads us to hungering and thirsting for all the righteousness there is.

Now what happens to the person who hungers and thirsts for righteousness? Jesus says *they shall be filled. To be filled* means to be gorged, to supply food in abundance. Jesus makes this clear in John 6:35, when He says, "I am the bread of life. He who comes to Me shall never hunger, and he who believes in Me shall never thirst." In the physical realm when we crave a certain food, after we eat it we are satisfied. When we're thirsty and have a drink, we're satisfied. But you know what? We get hungry and thirsty again and have to repeat the whole process over and over again. So it is in the spiritual realm. We cannot depend on yesterday's spiritual nourishment to help us today. We must hunger and thirst for all the righteousness there is, today and tomorrow and the next week and the next month and the next year, until we are in glory where we will be satisfied forever! This, again, would be a stark contrast to the Jews who prided themselves on their outward righteousness. Jesus says to them in Matthew 23:27-28, "Woe to you, Scribes and Pharisees, hypocrites! For you are like whitewashed tombs which indeed appear beautiful outwardly, but inside are full of dead men's bones and all uncleanness. Even so you also outwardly appear righteous to men, but inside you are full of hypocrisy and lawlessness."

Summary

In this beginning of our study of the Sermon on the Mount, we have discovered three *Beginning Blessings*, (vv 1-2): Jesus saw the crowds; He sat down to teach them; and He spoke. My friend, do you stop long enough to see the crowds of people that are lost and without hope? Do you see them at the mall, at the grocery store, at the park, on the highway, and even in your church? Do you take your eyes off yourself long enough to see men and women who are lost and going to hell and need a Savior? Do you close your heart to them? Do you get busy with the trivialities of life to drown out your conviction? Or do you do as Jesus did and open your mouth and speak the truth to them?

We have also seen the first four of the *Blessed Beatitudes*, (vv 3-6). Do the words "poor in spirit" describe you? Are you relying on your religious works for salvation, or have you come to see yourself as spiritually bankrupt? Has there been a time when you mourned over your sin and do you still mourn when you sin, or do you justify your sin and minimize it? Are you meek, or are you prideful, thinking your way is the only way? Do you hunger and thirst for righteousness? For what are you hungry and thirsty? Food and water? More time in social networking? More time to watch movies, TV, or attend more concerts and sporting events? Are you hungry for more money so you can buy new and bigger and better material things? Jesus says those who belong in His kingdom see themselves as desperate, they mourn, they are meek, and they hunger and thirst for all the righteousness they can get. To these and to these alone, Jesus says they will be happy, they will inherit heaven, and they will be filled!

The quote from Charles Spurgeon with which I began this lesson ended with this prayer: "Lord, evermore make us vessels fit for your own use, and then fill us with the pure juice of the grapes of sound doctrine and wholesome instruction. Do not allow us to be such *foul cups* as to be only fit for the wine of Sodom!"[9] It is my desire as we study with the Master on the Mount that you will soberly examine your life to make sure it matches up with what Jesus describes of those who belong to Him. If you find that your life doesn't compare, I pray that you will see how desperate you are, that you will mourn over your sin, humble yourself, and hunger and thirst for the true righteousness that comes from Christ alone! Let us sit with the disciples at the feet of Jesus and listen to our blessed Master's Sermon on the Mount!

---

9 Charles Spurgeon, "Orthodox in Creed — But Heterodox in Life!" *Flowers from a Puritan's Garden* (1883) www.GraceGems.org (gracegems.org/Spurgeon/flowers_ from_a_puritans_garden.htm).

Questions to Consider
The Blessed Beatitudes (Part 1)
Matthew 5:1-6

1. (a) What facts do you already know about the Sermon on the Mount, found in the Gospel of Matthew, chapters 5-7? (b) Read Matthew 5-7 and write down at least 10 things you don't understand from these chapters. (Save this for the last lesson in hopes that you will understand them by then!)

2. Please memorize Matthew 5:3, 4, 5, 6, or 7. I would highly encourage each one of you to memorize the Sermon the Mount. It flows well and it is a powerful portion of God's Word that will change your life!

3. (a) The first beatitude mentioned is that those who are poor in spirit are blessed. In what ways do Jesus' words in Matthew 23 contrast with this beatitude? (b) Did those people mentioned in Matthew 23 enter into the kingdom of heaven?

4. (a) What are the traits of a person who is truly mourning over their sin, according to 2 Corinthians 7:10-11? (b) How would you compare these traits with the typical, modern day "Christian's" attitude towards sin? (c) How do you personally deal with sin in your own life? Do you minimize it, or do you confess it, mourn over it, and forsake it? (d) In what specific ways can we make sure that we are dealing with our sin in a biblical way instead of the world's way?

5. (a) According to Philippians 2:5-8 and 1 Peter 2:21-24, how did our Lord exemplify meekness? (b) Why is it imperative that we follow our Lord's steps in being meek, according to Psalm 25:9; Isaiah 29:19; Zephaniah 2:3; James 1:21; and James 4:6-10?

6. (a) How do Psalm 42:1-2; Psalm 63:1-5; and Jeremiah 15:16 help you understand the fourth beatitude of hungering and thirsting for righteousness? (b) According to Psalm 107:9; John 4:13-14; John 6:35, 51; and John 7:37-38, how are we filled?

7. (a) Endeavor this week to go without food and water for at least 4-5 hours. Make note of your physical passions of hunger and thirst. (b) After partaking of food and water, how did you feel? (c) How does this physical illustration help you to better understand the spiritual beatitude in Matthew 5:6?

8. (a) Do you think your life is obedient to the instructions in the Sermon on the Mount? (b) What changes do you need to make? Please write a prayer asking the Lord to help you make those changes during this study.

Chapter 2

The Blessed Beatitudes (Part 2)

Matthew 5:7-12

The summer before I wrote this lesson, I was encouraged by my husband to read a book by J.C. Ryle, entitled *Light from Old Times*. It was a sober read, recounting the stories of martyrs burned at the stake in the 1500s during the reign of Queen Mary. All of them were beaten and tortured for preaching the gospel. For many, the fires that surrounded them would go out and then have to be relit, while their arms and legs were falling off. Many of their wives and children would watch from afar while their fathers and husbands were burned to death. I found myself convicted as I read things like the following:

> Rogers went to death "as if he was walking to his wedding."[10]

> "Good people I have taught you nothing but God's Holy Word, and those lessons that I have taken out of the Bible; and I am come hither to seal it with my blood." He would probably have said more, but like all the other martyrs, he was strictly forbidden to speak, and even now was struck violently on the head for saying these few words. He then knelt down and prayed, a poor woman of the parish insisting, in spite of every effort to prevent her, in kneeling down with him. After this, he was chained to the stake, and repeating the 51st Psalm and crying to God, "Merciful Father, for Jesus Christ's sake, receive my soul into Thy hands," stood quietly amidst the flames without

---

10 J.C. Ryle, *Light from Old Times* (Moscow: Charles Nolan Publishers, 2000), 40.

crying or moving till one of the guards dashed out his brains with a halberd.[11]

"O England, England, repent thee of thy sins! Beware of idolatry; beware of false Antichrist! Take heed they do not deceive you!" After that he turned to the man Leaf, who suffered with him, and said, "Be of good comfort, brother, for we shall have a merry supper with the Lord this night." After that he spoke no more that man could hear, excepting that he embraced the reeds, and said, "Strait is the gate, and narrow is the way, that leadeth to eternal life, and few there be that find it." "He embraced the flames," says Fuller, "as a fresh gale of wind in a hot summer day." And so, in the prime of life, he passed away.[12]

That was the 1500s, but even in our day men and women are killed for their faith. One pastor in Romania recalls being in solitary confinement with chunks of his flesh being cut from his body and receiving no food. Yet amidst that suffering, he recounts that the joy of the Lord would so overtake him that he would dance with joy in his prison.[13]

To you and me, these things might sound foreign. But for those of us who are God's children, it may not be long before this type of suffering is not so foreign, but common-place. Some of us will be persecuted, yes, even killed for righteousness' sake. This, my friend, is one of the eight beatitudes Christ taught in the Sermon on the Mount. Perhaps it isn't our favorite beatitude, but for the genuine kingdom citizen it is as cherished as the other seven. Let's consider them together.

---

11 Ibid, 43-44.
12 Ibid, 46.
13 R. Kent Hughes, *The Sermon on the Mount* (Wheaten: Crossway Books, 2001), 70.

Matthew 5:7-12

Blessed are the merciful, for they shall obtain mercy. [8]Blessed are the pure in heart, for they shall see God. [9]Blessed are the peacemakers, for they shall be called sons of God. [10]Blessed are those who are persecuted for righteousness' sake, for theirs is the kingdom of heaven. [11]Blessed are you when they revile and persecute you, and say all kinds of evil against you falsely for My sake. [12]Rejoice and be exceedingly glad, for great is your reward in heaven, for so they persecuted the prophets who were before you. (Matthew 5:7-12)

As we began our study of the Sermon on the Mount in our last lesson, we discovered three Beginning Blessings: Jesus <u>saw the crowds</u>, He <u>sat down</u> (to teach them), and He (opened His mouth and) <u>spoke</u>. We then looked at the first four beatitudes and learned that they are listed in a proper order. As we realize our destitute state of being poor in spirit, that results in our mourning over sin, which results in our having an attitude of humility. In that humility, we realize how desperate we are for more righteousness, and so we hunger and thirst for all the righteousness there is. These first four beatitudes relate to our relationship with God, and the last four beatitudes speak of our relationship to others. In this lesson, we will examine these last four *Blessed Beatitudes*, (vv 7-12). Let's begin with the first one.

Blessed are the merciful, for they shall obtain mercy.
(Matthew 5:7)

As Jesus continues on with the last four beatitudes, He reminds his audience that they are happy and fortunate if they possess these beatitudes. He moves now to the fifth beatitude and it has to do with our relationship with others: *blessed are the merciful*. Essentially, those who are happy are those who are merciful. The word *merciful* means one who shows pity or compassion, and it carries the idea of a woman who is in labor, being in severe pain. Those who are merciful enter into the pains of others and then endeavor to alleviate those sufferings, if at all possible.

Again, we need to remind ourselves that Jesus is not describing here something that we hope to be, but rather what genuine Christians, in fact, look like. John echoes the same thing in 1 John 3:17, "But whoever has this world's goods, and sees his brother in need, and shuts up his heart from him, how does the love of God abide in him?" In other words, the love of God does not dwell in that man; he is lost, even though he might think himself saved. Jesus' half-brother James says the same thing in James 2:14-17:

> What does it profit, my brethren, if someone says he has faith but does not have works? Can faith save him? If a brother or sister is naked and destitute of daily food, and one of you says to them, "Depart in peace, be warmed and filled," but you do not give them the things which are needed for the body, what does it profit? Thus also faith by itself, if it does not have works, is dead.

James says if you can harden your heart to the needs of others, do not fool yourself, my friend, your faith is dead.

Now, this mercy includes not only compassion for those who are suffering, but also forgiveness for those who have sinned against us. It makes sense that when the first four beatitudes are in place—being poor in spirit, mourning over our sin, humility, and hungering and thirsting for righteousness—we will then show mercy toward others because we have been shown mercy by God. We want to minister to others' needs because our greatest need, forgiveness of sin and life eternal, has been granted to us! We will have no problem forgiving others because we have been forgiven much!

Jesus goes on to say that those who show mercy *will obtain mercy*, which means they will obtain compassion by divine grace. The Greek word for *mercy* in this phrase refers to God's divine compassion for us, whereas the first word for mercy, in the previous phrase, refers to our human compassion toward others. When we look at Matthew 6 later in our study of the Sermon on the Mount, we will see Jesus clearly teach that only those who forgive will be granted mercy. In Matthew 6:14-15, Jesus says, "For if you forgive men their trespasses, your heavenly Father will also forgive you. But if you do not forgive men their trespasses, neither will your Father forgive your trespasses." And His half-brother James again says in James 2:13, "For judgment is without mercy to the one who has shown no mercy. Mercy triumphs over judgment." Jesus and James are basically saying that if you show no mercy, you will be granted no mercy. And, my friend, examined within its larger context, it is clear that Jesus' statement here is referring to one's eternal state! This would have shocked Jesus' Jewish audience, and He will again rebuke them, later in Matthew 23:23-24, when He says to them, "Woe to you, Scribes and Pharisees, hypocrites! For you pay tithe of mint and anise and cumin, and have neglected the weightier matters of the law: justice and mercy and faith. These you ought to have done, without leaving the others undone. Blind guides, who strain at a gnat and swallow a camel!" They performed all the outward religious requirements, but they showed no mercy. We might say, "I tithe, I attend church, I go to ladies' Bible study," while we fail to show mercy to others. We who profess Christ and yet remain insensitive to the needs of others are, in reality, headed for eternal damnation. Micah 6:8 states, "He has shown you, O man, what is good; and what does the Lord require of you but to do justly, to love mercy, and to walk humbly with your God?" Are you merciful? Are you reaching out to those in need? Do you forgive others for the wrongs they have done to you? Do you hold grudges? Jesus continues on with the sixth beatitude.

> Blessed are the pure in heart, for they shall see God.
> (Matthew 5:8)

The sixth beatitude is this: *happy are those who are pure in heart*. The word *pure* means to be holy, to be free from every taint of evil; it has the idea of being single of heart. In other words, we have a single focus and are not divided in our devotion. James 4:8 reiterates this same truth: "Draw near to God and He will draw near to you. Cleanse your hands, you sinners; and purify your hearts, you double-minded." The Psalmist also knew this to be true, as he says in Psalm 24:3-4, "Who may ascend into the hill of the Lord? Or who may stand in His holy place? He who has clean hands and a pure heart, who has not lifted up his soul to an idol, nor sworn deceitfully." The Psalmist knew that without purity of heart he could not worship the Lord. You might be wondering how this relates to our relationship with others. Simply put, the inward will manifest itself in the outward. Jesus put it well in Matthew 15:19, "For out of the heart proceed evil thoughts, murders, adulteries, fornications, thefts, false witness, blasphemies." When our heart is pure it will manifest itself in having thoughts, feelings, emotions, and actions that are pure. So, we could ask ourselves questions like, "What are my motives in doing this or saying this? It is pure? Is it for the glory of God? Is it for the sake of the person or for the sake of me or pleasing men?" If our hearts are clean, then our lives will be clean, as well.

The wonderful joy of those who are pure in heart is that *they shall see God*. The word *see* means to gaze with wide open eyes. Now, maybe you're wondering how we can see God when John is clear in 1 John 4:12 that no one has seen God at any time. Well, John explains this very thing in John 1:18, where he says, "No one has seen God at any time. The only begotten Son, who is in the bosom of the Father, He has declared Him." God can be seen in the person of His Son Jesus Christ. We see God now in the sense that we see Him through His Word and through creation and other ways, but seeing Him face to face is something that will not transpire until we reach glory. Listen to John again in 1 John 3:2-3, "Beloved, now we are children of God; and it has not yet been revealed what we shall be, but we know that when He is revealed, we shall be like Him, for we shall see Him as He is. And everyone who has this hope in Him purifies himself, just as He is pure." It's interesting that John equates seeing God with purity of heart, just like Jesus does in the Sermon on the Mount. One man says,

> If we grasped this, it would revolutionize our lives. You and I
> are meant for the audience chamber of God; you and I are being
> prepared to enter into the presence of the King of kings. Do you
> believe it, do you know it as true of you? Do you realize that a
> day is coming when you are going to see the blessed God face-
> to-face? Not as in a glass, darkly, but face-to-face. Surely the

moment we grasp this, everything else pales into insignificance. You and I are going to enjoy God, and to spend our eternity in His glorious and eternal presence.[14]

For the prideful Jew, this beatitude would be bleak. They prided themselves in their outward rituals, like the ceremonial washing of hands and cleaning of cups; they knew nothing of an inward cleansing of the heart. Jesus tells them their hearts are revealed in what they think, what they say, and what they do. Listen to His words in the following passages: Matthew 9:4, "Why do you *think evil* in your hearts?" Matthew 12:34-37, "Brood of vipers! How can you, *being evil,* speak good things? For out of the abundance of the heart the *mouth speaks.* A good man out of the good treasure of his heart brings forth good things, and an evil man out of the evil treasure brings forth evil things. But I say to you that for every idle word men may speak, they will give account of it in the day of judgment. For by your words you will be justified, and by your words you will be condemned." And Matthew 23:27-28, "Woe to you, Scribes and Pharisees, hypocrites! For you are like whitewashed tombs which indeed appear beautiful outwardly, but *inside are full of dead men's bones* and all uncleanness. Even so you also outwardly appear righteous to men, but *inside you are full of hypocrisy and lawlessness*" (all emphases mine).

What about your heart? Is it pure? Maybe you don't know if it is or not. Well, consider your thoughts, your actions, and your words— even today—were they pure? The answer to that question will give an indication of the condition of your heart. Jesus moves on the seventh beatitude, that of being a peacemaker.

> Blessed are the peacemakers, for they shall be called sons of God. (Matthew 5:9)

The seventh blessed beatitude is this: *happy are those who make peace.* Being a peacemaker is the natural result in those who are poor in spirit, who mourn over their sin, who are meek, who hunger

---

14 D. Martyn Lloyd-Jones, *Studies in the Sermon on the Mount* (Grand Rapids: Eerdman's Publishing Co., 1984), 97.

and thirst for righteousness, who show mercy and react to others from a pure heart. When you see yourself in the light of God's holiness, and then start acting on it, you aren't interested in stirring up trouble. When you remember the depravity of your own heart and from where you've come, you don't stir up conflict but rather solve it. Proverbs 16:7 explains that "When a man's ways please the Lord, He makes even his enemies to be at peace with him."

A peacemaker strives to solve conflicts, not to stir them up; they strive for unity. But they also want others to be at peace with one another, so a peacemaker will pursue others in order that those they pursue can be at peace as well, by holding them accountable to be reconciled to and make restitution with others. It is interesting that purity of heart comes before peacemaking. James, again, echoes his brother Jesus in James 3:17-18, "But the wisdom that is from above is first pure, then peaceable, gentle, willing to yield, full of mercy and good fruits, without partiality and without hypocrisy. Now the fruit of righteousness is sown in peace by those who make peace." Purity comes before peace. Impurity breads strife, as James says in the immediately preceding verses, James 3:14-16, "But if you have bitter envy and self-seeking in your hearts, do not boast and lie against the truth. This wisdom does not descend from above, but is earthly, sensual, demonic. For where envy and self-seeking exist, confusion and every evil thing are there." Paul states in Hebrews 12:14, "Pursue peace with all people, and holiness, without which no one will see the Lord."

Now this does not mean that we ought to pursue peace at the expense of purity or truth. Jesus says in Matthew 10:34-39:

> Do not think that I came to bring peace on earth. I did not come to bring peace but a sword. For I have come to "set a man against his father, a daughter against her mother, and a daughter-in-law against her mother-in-law"; and "a man's enemies will be those of his own household." He who loves father or mother more than Me is not worthy of Me. And he who loves son or daughter more than Me is not worthy of Me. And he who does not take his cross and follow after Me is not worthy of Me. He who finds

his life will lose it, and he who loses his life for My sake will find it.

Though we may try very hard to be a peacemaker, sometimes peace is impossible. Paul says in Romans 12:18, "If it is possible, as much as depends on you, live peaceably with all men." And I have lived long enough now to know that this is a very true statement. Some people just don't want to be at peace with you! That's why Paul continues on with Romans 12:19-21, "Beloved, do not avenge yourselves, but rather give place to wrath; for it is written, 'Vengeance is Mine, I will repay,' says the Lord. Therefore 'If your enemy is hungry, feed him; if he is thirsty, give him a drink; for in so doing you will heap coals of fire on his head.' Do not be overcome by evil, but overcome evil with good."

The good news is that if we are peacemakers *we shall be called sons of God. Son* is a word which pertains to the relationship of a child to his or her parent. Since God is the God of all peace, it makes sense that His children will exhibit peace as well. Again, the Jewish world wasn't interested in making peace; they wanted to usher in the kingdom with military or political force. What about you? Are you a trouble-maker? Do people run when they see you coming or avoid your calls because they know you are intent on stirring up strife? Or do you look for ways to make peace and to bring peace?

Jesus finishes with the eighth beatitude, and this one would be perhaps the most shocking of all not only to the audience sitting at His feet, but also to those who are even now reading and hearing these words!

> Blessed are those who are persecuted for righteousness' sake, for theirs is the kingdom of heaven. (Matthew 5:10)

You might be thinking, "Now, wait a minute … Jesus just said that I should be a peacemaker, and yet now I'm going to be persecuted for being a peacemaker and trying to do what's right?" Yes, that's right! This is, perhaps, a beatitude that you'd prefer not to have in the

Bible, but nonetheless it is as important as the other seven. It is also a principle that has pushed many a nominal Christian to leave the faith they thought they possessed. But Jesus warned of that in the parable of the soils in Matthew 13. There, Jesus spoke of the one for whom the seed was sown on stony soil and who immediately received it with joy, but when tribulation and persecution came, he was out of there! That one loved the Jesus-loves-me-this-I-know stuff, but the persecution thing, well, that's a bit rough, and he certainly did not sign up for that!

But Jesus says here that you are happy if you *are persecuted.* *Persecuted* means to pursue, to chase, to drive away. And we are persecuted *for righteousness' sake,* because we do what is right. If you are I are hungering and thirsting for all the righteousness there is, and if we are practicing righteousness by living out the other seven beatitudes, then it makes sense that we will be persecuted for living righteously, doesn't it? Those who hunger and thirst for all the righteousness there is will stand out as strange to those who are in the world and even to many who are in the church. Peter reiterates this to the suffering Christians of his day, in 1 Peter 4:14-16, "If you are reproached for the name of Christ, blessed are you, for the Spirit of glory and of God rests upon you. On their part He is blasphemed, but on your part He is glorified. But let none of you suffer as a murderer, a thief, an evildoer, or as a busybody in other people's matters. Yet if anyone suffers as a Christian, let him not be ashamed, but let him glorify God in this matter." Some of us suffer because of our own sin, but to suffer for doing what is right, that is good. In 1 Peter 3:17, Peter says, "For it is better, if it is the will of God, to suffer for doing good than for doing evil." Paul says in Philippians 1:29, "For to you it has been granted on behalf of Christ, not only to believe in Him, but also to suffer for His sake." Jesus tells His disciples, in John 15:18-21, in the Upper Room right before He goes to the cross,

> If the world hates you, you know that it hated Me before it hated you. If you were of the world, the world would love its own. Yet because you are not of the world, but I chose you out of the world, therefore the world hates you. Remember the word that

> I said to you, "A servant is not greater than his master." If they persecuted Me, they will also persecute you. If they kept My Word, they will keep yours also. But all these things they will do to you for My name's sake, because they do not know Him who sent Me.

My friends, we are persecuted when we act like Christ; people hate that we act like Christ. In fact, later on, in John 16:2, Jesus will tell His disciples that the time will come when those who are killing them will think they are doing God a service!

The glorious benefit, though, is that those who are persecuted are not just happy, but theirs alone *is the kingdom of heaven*. The first beatitude ended with this phrase as well, theirs and theirs alone is the kingdom of heaven! It's as if all the other beatitudes are sandwiched in between the first and the last. In verse 11, Jesus expounds on this beatitude a little more. He says:

> Blessed are you when they revile and persecute you, and say all kinds of evil against you falsely for My sake. (Matthew 5:11)

Jesus mentions twice here that we are blessed. Doing so could mean that He is emphasizing this point, because it would have been such a shocking statement to the Jews who heard it. They considered prosperity to be a blessing, but certainly would not have said that of suffering. Of course, there is nothing new under the sun; this also is a massive heresy in our day, the idea that Jesus died to make us wealthy and healthy but not to suffer.

Jesus says the persecution will be manifested *when they revile and persecute you, and say all kinds of evil against you. Reviling* would be insulting and rebuking you in your face. To *say all kinds of evil* would include saying things that are not true and malicious. Jesus Himself was called crazy and was even accused of having a demon (John 8:48 and 10:20). But Jesus again emphasizes that this suffering is for His sake, for righteousness' sake. This is because we belong to God, because we are His children. It is a privilege to suffer for our Lord and to identify with Him in this way! As if all this is not shocking enough, Jesus finishes by telling us what our attitude should be as we suffer.

> Rejoice and be exceedingly glad, for great is your reward in heaven, for so they persecuted the prophets who were before you. (Matthew 5:12)

Instead of retaliating against those who persecute us, we are to rejoice. Instead of resenting those who persecute us, we are to rejoice. This is where we practice that mercy beatitude! Peter tells us how Jesus did this, in 1 Peter 2:21-24, "For to this you were called, because Christ also suffered for us, leaving us an example, that you should follow His steps: 'Who committed no sin, nor was deceit found in His mouth'; who, when He was reviled, did not revile in return; when He suffered, He did not threaten, but committed Himself to Him who judges righteously."

The first response Jesus says we are to have is to *rejoice*, which means to be cheerful and calmly happy. We see this in Acts 5:41, when the apostles were beaten for sharing the gospel, "So they departed from the presence of the council, rejoicing that they were counted worthy to suffer shame for His name." Second, Jesus calls us to be *exceedingly glad*, which means to leap for joy.

You might be wondering, "Why should I have these attitudes?" Jesus says, first, because *great is your reward in heaven*. My friend, you don't just inherit the kingdom of heaven, but you also have a great reward. The Greek word for *great reward* means pay for services. Now, I don't know what this is, but Paul says that eye has not seen nor ear has heard what God has prepared for those who love Him, so it will be glorious, whatever it is (1 Corinthians 2:9)!

Secondly, Jesus says you can have these attitudes because you are not the first to suffer, *for so they persecuted the prophets who were before you*. We could take a whole lesson just talking about the sufferings of the prophets and the apostles, but suffice it to say that Moses, Samuel, Jeremiah, Ezekiel, Daniel, Nehemiah, Stephen,

Peter, Paul, James, and many others were persecuted because of their faith. So, we are in good company! And when we read the end of the great faith chapter in Hebrews, Paul gives us a chilling summary. He says in Hebrews 11:35-40:

> Others were tortured, not accepting deliverance, that they might obtain a better resurrection. Still others had trial of mockings and scourgings, yes, and of chains and imprisonment. They were stoned, they were sawn in two, were tempted, were slain with the sword. They wandered about in sheepskins and goatskins, being destitute, afflicted, tormented—of whom the world was not worthy. They wandered in deserts and mountains, in dens and caves of the earth. And all these, having obtained a good testimony through faith, did not receive the promise, God having provided something better for us, that they should not be made perfect apart from us.

My friend, Jesus says in Luke 6:26, "Woe to you when all men speak well of you, for so did their fathers to the false prophets." And He rebukes the Jewish hypocrites regarding this, in Matthew 23:29-39:

> Woe to you, Scribes and Pharisees, hypocrites! Because you build the tombs of the prophets and adorn the monuments of the righteous, and say, "If we had lived in the days of our fathers, we would not have been partakers with them in the blood of the prophets." Therefore you are witnesses against yourselves that you are sons of those who murdered the prophets. Fill up, then, the measure of your fathers' guilt. Serpents, brood of vipers! How can you escape the condemnation of hell? Therefore, indeed, I send you prophets, wise men, and Scribes: some of them you will kill and crucify, and some of them you will scourge in your synagogues and persecute from city to city, that on you may come all the righteous bloodshed on the earth, from the blood of righteous Abel to the blood of Zechariah, son of Berechiah, whom you murdered between the temple and the altar. Assuredly, I say to you, all these things will come upon this generation. O Jerusalem, Jerusalem, the one who kills the prophets and stones those who are sent to her! How often I wanted to gather your children together, as a hen gathers her chicks under her wings, but you were not willing! See! Your house is left to you desolate; or I say to you, you shall see Me no more till you say, "Blessed is He who comes in the name of the Lord!"

Jesus was certainly far from being "seeker friendly" in His day! It is said that Charles Spurgeon's wife took these eight beatitudes and wrote them on a piece of paper and put them over her husband's bed so that every morning and every night he would see them. She didn't want him to forget that the persecution he endured was because of his righteous life. What a great wife! (Job's wife needed to take some lessons from her!) Mrs. Spurgeon knew that 2 Timothy 3:12 was true of her husband Charles, and it is true for all of God's kingdom citizens: "Yes, and all who desire to live godly in Christ Jesus will suffer persecution." Are you being persecuted because you belong to Christ? If you're not suffering for Christ's sake, my friend, then you aren't living the kind of righteous life before the world that will incur suffering!

Summary

What a great beginning to the great Sermon on the Mount! Eight blessed beatitudes that should possess each child of God. Do they possess you? Do they describe you? What's so interesting about these, besides the fact that they build on one another, is that the first four are fleshed out in the last four. For example, *being poor in spirit* (v 3) leads us to *being merciful* (v 7). *Mourning over our sin* (v 4) leads to *purity of heart* (v 8). *Being meek* (v 5) leads us to *being a peace maker* (v 9). *Hungering and thirsting for all the righteousness there is* (v 6) leads to *suffering for righteousness sake* (v 10). These 8 beatitudes are indeed blessed, for those who know God. Sadly, however, those who are hypocrites won't consider these beatitudes as blessed; rather, they will view them as burdens to which they can't possibly attain. But, my friend, these blessed beatitudes are fundamental both to the life of a kingdom citizen and to the rest of the Jesus' Sermon on the Mount.

If these eight blessed beatitudes do not describe you, then may I say in all sincerity that you need to do some serious self-examination to make sure that you fully understand the gospel—not the cheap gospel of our day, but the real gospel that Jesus preached: "Repent, for the kingdom of God is at hand!"

Questions to Consider

The Blessed Beatitudes (Part 2)
Matthew 5:7-12

1. (a) As you read over the eight beatitudes in Matthew 5:1-12, what would you say Jesus is trying to communicate to the multitudes? (b) Which of these beatitudes is most difficult for you, and why?

2. Memorize Matthew 5:11.

3. (a) Who did or did not show mercy in Genesis 50; Matthew 18:21-35; and Luke 10:25-37? (b) Write down at least one valuable lesson from each of these accounts that you can use in your own life or the life of someone else.

4. (a) According to Psalm 18:26; Psalm 24:3-4; Proverbs 21:8; Proverbs 22:11; Titus 1:15; and 1 Peter 1:22-23, why is it essential that we be pure in heart? (b) What happens to those whose hearts are not pure, according to Proverbs 11:20; Proverbs 12:8; and Hebrews 3:12? (c) How do you keep your heart pure? Perhaps stop and pray with David, "Create in me a clean heart, O God, and renew a steadfast spirit within me" (Psalm 51:10).

5. (a) What is the Christian's mandate in Hebrews 12:14? (b) With that in mind, how would you endeavor to help the men in Acts 15:36-41 and the two women mentioned in Philippians 4:2-3? (c) What things have you found helpful in your own life in trying to be a peacemaker, especially in your home?

6. (a) What types of persecution are mentioned in the following passages? 2 Samuel 16:5-14; 1 Kings 18:4; Jeremiah 37:13-38:6; Acts 5:40-42; Acts 7:54-8:3; 2 Corinthians 11:22-33? (b) If it is stated, note the attitude that is found in each of these. (c) How does this compare to our persecutions for the sake of Christ? (d) How do you personally prepare yourself spiritually for persecution? (e) How are you instructing or have you instructed your children regarding persecution for being a follower of Christ?

7. What changes do you need to make as a result of these two lessons on the beatitudes? Please write a prayer to the Lord for these needs.

Chapter 3

The Christian's Impact on the World
Matthew 5:13-16

June 26, 2015 will go down in history as a monumental day. The Supreme Court of the United States of America voted to allow couples of the same sex to get "married." Men are now legally allowed to "marry" men; women are now legally allowed to "marry" women. This decision for our country was decided by two men and three women. The ruling was both shocking and grieving, and we who are kingdom citizens have since found ourselves asking many questions. One of those questions is this: "How did we get here in our culture?" Some of us answer that question by acknowledging that God is Sovereign and that He has a plan beyond our understanding.

While those of us who are reformed believers would certainly hold that such an answer is true, will we also then use it as a cloak for our lackluster Christianity? Have we failed in being effective in a lost world? Have we failed in being salt and light in a world that is filled with darkness and becoming more evil all the time? Are we in some measure responsible for the moral decay of our society because we have not been salty enough and shiny enough to stop the moral decay and rot? I must answer that question by saying vehemently, "Yes!" Christians are to be in the world but not of the world; yet, we are failing to make an impact on our world. Christ left us here to go and make disciples and to be His representatives, and we do that in two ways according to the text of Matthew 5:13-16, by being salt and light. Let's listen to Jesus and what He says on the mount:

Matthew 5:13-17

You are the salt of the earth; but if the salt loses its flavor, how shall it be seasoned? It is then good for nothing but to be thrown out and trampled underfoot by men. [14]You are the light of the world. A city that is set on a hill cannot be hidden. [15]Nor do they light a lamp and put it under a basket, but on a lampstand, and it gives light to all who are in the house. [16]Let your light so shine before men, that they may see your good works and glorify your Father in heaven.

We have been considering in our last two lessons the eight beatitudes Jesus gave as He began His Sermon on the Mount. As we discovered, these beatitudes are not things that we as Christians seek after, but rather what we are. We also learned that each of these beatitudes builds upon the others. As kingdom citizens live out these beatitudes, the result will be that we are salt and light because we will stand in stark contrast to a dark world. As we consider Matthew 5:13-16 in this lesson, we will see:

> *The Christian's Two-fold Impact on the World* (vv 13-15)
> *The Christian's Failure to Impact the World and Its Result* (v 13)
> *The Christian's Faithfulness to Impact the World and Its Result* (v 16)

It is interesting that Jesus uses the examples of salt and light to describe His children because salt and light would be things that all who were listening to Him would have used in their homes. We, too, in the 21st century can understand these illustrations because we also use salt and light on a daily basis. In fact, when I sat down to write this lesson there was a light on in the room, and I just salted my eggs before consuming them! Let's consider the first way we as Christians impact our world, from verse 13.

The Christian's Two-fold Impact on the World

Matthew 5:13-15

You are the salt of the earth; but if the salt loses its flavor, how shall it be seasoned? It is then good for nothing but to be thrown out and trampled underfoot by men. (Matthew 5:13)

The first way we as believers impact our world is by being salt. Jesus says *you are the salt of the earth*. The word *you* means you yourselves. It's a word that forces us to take a look at ourselves, not at our neighbor or our husband, but ourselves. Notice it is not you will be salt or you will grow into being salt. You *are* the salt, you are currently right now the salt of the earth. *The earth* is a term that would represent the entire world, which motivates us to consider that we are salt whether we are at home or in a foreign land, whether we are in private or in public. We should be salt at all places and at all times. By the way, this is not a command; this is a statement, this is what kingdom citizens look like. Those who are living the beatitudes just mentioned are salt (and light.) Being salt and light is something the world is not; but it is something that those who belong to Christ, and only those who are in Christ, are indeed.

In the ancient world salt was a valuable commodity and people valued it far more than we do today. Often people were even paid their wages in salt. In addition to salt's obvious use in flavoring foods, there are numerous other things for which salt is useful. Salt is good for preserving things, and the biblical world would understand this. Because they did not yet have refrigeration systems, they would preserve their meats by using salt. With this in mind, we could say that by being salt we preserve the world from corruption like salt preserves meat from corruption. Jesus' immediate audience lived around the Sea of Galilee, where the fishing trade was dominant, so this idea of preservation for the purpose of holding back corruption is the favorite among commentaries of the Sermon on the Mount.15 Simply put, citizens of God's Kingdom hold back the natural decay of a rotting, fallen world. Salt also makes one thirsty, it could be said of believers that by being salt we should make the world thirsty for the things of Christ. Salt also makes one thirsty, so we could say

---

15 John R. W. Stott is an example: "The world also manifests a constant tendency to deteriorate. The notion is not that the world is tasteless and that Christians can make it less insipid...but that it is putrefying. It cannot stop itself from going bad. Only salt introduced from outside can do this. The church, on the other hand, is set to hinder the process of social decay.... This means that, when each community is itself and is true to itself, the world decays like rotten fish or meat, while the church can hinder its decay." cf. John R. W. Stott, *The Message of the Sermon on the Mount* (Downers Grove: Inter-Varsity Press, 1978).

that by being salt we should make the world thirsty for the things of Christ. In addition to these uses, salt also contains healing agents, and so we could infer from that that by being salt we bring spiritual healing to lost people.

The Christian's Failure to Impact the World and Its Result

Matthew 5:13b

... but if the salt loses its flavor, how shall it be seasoned? It is then good for nothing but to be thrown out and trampled underfoot by men. (Matthew 5:13)

In the context of the Scriptures we are considering, we know that Jesus is using salt to refer to something that gives flavor. He says, *but if the salt loses its flavor, how shall it be seasoned?* If we, as Christians, are not making an impact by preserving the world from corruption then we have lost our flavor. If we are not standing in stark contrast to the world's values and morals—which means that we must speak out against them—then we have lost our flavor. If we are not making an impact by our lives, making others thirsty to know why we are different, then we have lost our flavor. If our words and our actions don't bring healing to a lost and dark world, then, my friend, we have lost our flavor! For salt to *lose its flavor* means that it is dull, bland, foolish. For us to have lost our flavor means that we're no longer making an impact but are looking like our lost neighbors. Spiritually speaking, we are dull, we're foolish; there's nothing different about us. And may I say that is what many churches look like right now?! You can't tell the difference between a typical church in America and a movie theater.

Our works should make others take notice and say, "I want what you have. How do I get it?" Even our speech should be salty; Paul says in Colossians 4:6, "Let your speech always be with grace, seasoned with salt, that you may know how you ought to answer each one." We lose our flavor when we become influenced by the world, when we fail to be disciplined in the means of grace, when we lose our passion and zeal, and when we stop using our mouths to share the gospel. Jesus says if we lose our flavor, we can't *be seasoned* again, but we are *good for nothing.*[16]

Jesus says that if we have lost our flavor, then we are *good for nothing.* My friend, being good for nothing is a serious statement. Do you hear what Jesus is saying? Good for nothing! What do you do with those things that are good for nothing, that have no value anymore? You throw them out! This is exactly what Jesus says next, that flavorless salt is *good for nothing but to be thrown out and trampled underfoot by men. Thrown out* means to be violently thrust out. And *trample* means to trodden down, to reject with disdain. In biblical times, salt was not as pure as today because they did not have the purification methods that we utilize. Sometimes, salt was mixed with dirt and vegetation and would become useless. When it became useless they would throw it out on the road or the ground and it would disappear as men would walk on it. It had lost its effectiveness for being used for flavoring or preserving or healing. If "believers" don't make others thirsty for God, if they don't add flavor to a tasteless society, if they don't preserve their society from moral decay, then they are good for nothing. But Jesus says something even more alarming in Luke 14:34-35; He says, "Salt is good; but if the salt has lost its flavor, how shall it be seasoned? It is neither fit for the land nor for the dunghill, but men throw it out. He who has ears to hear, let him hear!" Salt that has lost its flavor is not even fit to kill weeds or be put in a manure pile; so it is with a "Christian" who has lost her flavor. It is impossible for salt to regain its saltiness after it has been lost.

Now, I admit this has some serious implications, since Jesus says His children are salt and light. If we are not salt and light, it would prove we were never in the faith but are, instead, like the Pharisees

---

16 It has been said that in the land of Judea there is a place called the Valley of Salt. When one breaks off a piece of the rock, the part that has been exposed to the elements, it has lost its salty flavor. However, the part of the rock that had been connected to the rock retains is flavor. So, it is with a believer, when we stay connected to the rock we retain our flavor.

Jesus mentions later in His sermon, who had an outward show of religion but not the real thing. The failure to impact our world results, tragically, in the reality that we are good for nothing! Our brother Paul knew the implication of this even in his own life, which is why he writes in 1 Corinthians 9:27, "But I discipline my body and bring it into subjection, lest, when I have preached to others, I myself should become disqualified." Paul says again in Hebrews 6:4-6, "For it is impossible for those who were once enlightened, and have tasted the heavenly gift, and have become partakers of the Holy Spirit, and have tasted the good word of God and the powers of the age to come, if they fall away, to renew them again to repentance, since they crucify again for themselves the Son of God, and put Him to an open shame." Even brother Peter writes in 2 Peter 2:21-22, "For it would have been better for them not to have known the way of righteousness, than having known it, to turn from the holy commandment delivered to them. But it has happened to them according to the true proverb: 'A dog returns to his own vomit,' and, 'a sow, having washed, to her wallowing in the mire.'" And Jesus Himself gives a similar warning later in His sermon in Matthew 7:19: "Every tree that does not bear good fruit is cut down and thrown into the fire." And He moves on in His Sermon on the Mount to the second way genuine believers impact the world, in verse 14.

The Christian's Two-fold Impact on the World

Matthew 5:13-15

> You are the light of the world. A city that is set on a hill cannot be hidden. Nor do they light a lamp and put it under a basket, but on a lampstand, and it gives light to all who are in the house. (Matthew 5:14-15)

The Christian's two-fold impact on the world is to be both salt and light. The rendering here is the same as in verse 13. It means *you, yourselves, are the light of the world.* Again, this is not something we grow into or that we become, but we are at this moment the light of the world. We know Jesus calls Himself the light of the world in John 8:12, so it makes sense that His children will resemble Him as also being lights of the world. *Light* means to make manifest or to shine. We know that light dispels darkness, so we would say that Christians shine in a dark world, and as we do so we chase away the darkness. Our lives should be an affront to the world.

Jesus further illustrates this by saying that *a city that is set on a hill cannot be hidden. Cannot* means that it is impossible; it is impossible to conceal a city that is *set on a hill.* Many cities in biblical times were set on hills, so the multitude that Jesus was preaching to would understand the imagery here. And interestingly enough, as Jesus was teaching, He was doing so from a hill. I have a family member who once lived in the hills of Monterey, California. You can't hide that house; it can be clearly seen from the road below. Jesus uses this illustration to drive His point further home: a genuine kingdom citizen does not hide their faith. People don't have to wonder if a person is a believer or not, because it will be as obvious as a city set on a hill. Everyone can see it. And if you have ever driven long distances at night, you've probably found it a comfort to see off in the distance the lights of an approaching city. Cities that are set on hills are obviously more easily noticed than cities set elsewhere. We can conclude from this that as God's children live out the light of the gospel in a real sense—not a pharisaical sense—they bring comfort to a dark world, just as a city on the hill brings comfort in the night. We dispel the darkness and we bring comfort. Over the years, I have thought it to be most interesting how unbelievers who are in a crisis often seek out believers for help and prayer. In an odd way, it seems comforting to them.

Jesus continues to illustrate the importance of being light by yet another illustration in verses 15. Just as a city that sits on a hill cannot be concealed, so a light within a house is not intended for hiding but for *giving light to all those who are in the house.* This might be difficult for us to understand but not so much for the audience listening to Jesus. The biblical world did not have electricity as we do, which powers street lights and other light sources. The night hours would have been very dark. Most homes had one lampstand or a single candlestick for the whole house. A *lamp* was a vessel that had a wick in the middle of it, and a bushel or a *basket* was a utensil used for measuring grain. Obviously, they would not *light a lamp and then put it under a basket*, but they would put it on the one *lampstand* that was in the house, so that it would *give light to all who are in the house*. Neither would we turn on a lamp in our house and then hide it under the bed; that would be ludicrous. We have lights in our home so that they can give off light to those who are in the house. The woman mentioned in Proverbs 31:18 did not let her lamp go out at night. Why? Because if someone needed to get up at night they would be able to see so that they wouldn't stumble or fall. Most of us have some type of light that we leave on at night, so that if a member of our household gets up at night they can see where they are going. As God's children, we give light to a dark world. Wise old Solomon once wrote in Proverbs 4:18-19, "But the path of the just is like the shining sun that shines ever brighter unto the perfect day. The way of the wicked is like darkness; they do not know what makes them stumble." We, too, do not let our light go out but we keep it burning, as Jesus illustrated in His parable of the ten virgins, in Matthew 25:1-13:

> Then the kingdom of heaven shall be likened to ten virgins who took their lamps and went out to meet the bridegroom. Now five of them were wise, and five were foolish. Those who were foolish took their lamps and took no oil with them, but the wise took oil in their vessels with their lamps. But while the bridegroom was delayed, they all slumbered and slept. And at midnight a cry was heard: "Behold, the bridegroom is coming; go out to meet him!" Then all those virgins arose and trimmed their lamps. And the foolish said to the wise, "Give us some of your oil, for our lamps are going out." But the wise answered, saying, "No, lest there should not be enough for us and you; but go rather to those who sell, and buy for yourselves." And while they went to buy, the bridegroom came, and those who were ready went in with him to the wedding; and the door was shut. Afterward the other virgins came also, saying, "Lord, Lord, open to us!" But he answered and said, "Assuredly, I say to you, I do not know you." Watch therefore, for you know neither the day nor the hour in which the Son of Man is coming.

The point of this parable is that we ought to be ready for the Lord's return. But in illustrating this we see that the five foolish virgins were also those whom the Lord says He did not know. They didn't keep their lamps lit; they were not light. My friend, we cannot say we know Christ and fail to be light. We cannot say we know Jesus and hide the gospel from others. We cannot say we love the Lord and live foolishly. It is only the lost world that loves darkness. Jesus says in John 3:19-21, "And this is the condemnation, that the light has come into the world, and men loved darkness rather than light, because their deeds were evil. For everyone practicing evil hates the light and does not come to the light, lest his deeds should be exposed. But he who does the truth comes to the light, that his deeds may be clearly seen, that they have been done in God." It has been said that in biblical times some people would put a candle under a bushel and then when all in the house were fast asleep they would arise to do their evil—murder, steal, etc. But those who love the light want only to represent the light, which is the Lord Jesus. Their desire is to share the Light of The World. This should cause us to pause and consider if we are light, especially when we consider that recent statistics say that only 61 percent of professing believers share their faith. Even though 3 out of 4 of us think we should, in reality, most of us don't. God is sovereign in salvation, that is true, but man is also responsible, and that is true as well. And, my sister, those who profess to be Christians and are failing to be salt and light will be held accountable one day! [17]

We who are Christians impact our world in a two-fold way, by being salt and light. Failure to do so manifests who we really are—good for nothing—which is tragic. But being faithful to be salt and light manifests itself in something wonderful, and it is the natural <u>conclusion of</u> being light in a dark world. What is that natural

[17] In summary, Pastor MacArthur writes, "Whereas salt is hidden, light is obvious. Salt works secretly, while light works openly. Salt works from within, light works from without. Salt is more the indirect influence of the gospel, while light is more its direct communication. Salt works primarily through our living, while light works primarily through what we teach and preach. Salt is largely negative. It can retard corruption. Light is more positive. It not only reveals what is wrong and false but helps produce what is righteous and true." cf. John MacArthur, Jr. *The MacArthur New Testament Commentary: Matthew 1-7* (Chicago: Moody Press, 1985), 244.

conclusion? Jesus tells us in verse 16.

The Christian's Faithfulness to Impact the World and Its Result

Matthew 5:16

> Let your light so shine before men, that they may see your good works and glorify your Father in heaven. (Matthew 5:16)

Jesus says to *let your light so shine before men that they may see your good works and glorify your Father in heaven*. Notice, again, that it is *your light* which you must let shine. Too often, we are like Peter, failing to look at ourselves but instead looking at our neighbor. This is illustrated in John 21:18-22, where Jesus tells Peter:

> Most assuredly, I say to you, when you were younger, you girded yourself and walked where you wished; but when you are old, you will stretch out your hands, and another will gird you and carry you where you do not wish." This He spoke, signifying by what death he would glorify God. And when He had spoken this, He said to him, "Follow Me." Then Peter, turning around, saw the disciple whom Jesus loved following, who also had leaned on His breast at the supper, and said, "Lord, who is the one who betrays You?" Peter, seeing him, said to Jesus, "But Lord, what about this man?" Jesus said to him, "If I will that he remain till I come, what is that to you? You follow Me."

Jesus tells Peter not to be concerned about John, but to be concerned about Peter. It's as if Jesus is saying, "Peter, you follow me, and leave John up to Me." Each one of us is individually responsible for letting our *light shine*, which means to radiate brilliantly. We are not going to heaven on the coattails of another. Each of us individually will stand before the Lord, and we won't be holding the hand of our mate or our friend or our child.

So, we are to let our light shine *before men*. It was said of John the Baptist, in John 5:35, "He was the burning and shining lamp, and you were willing for a time to rejoice in his light." Does that describe you? Are you a burning and shining lamp? Paul tells the church at Philippi, "Do all things without complaining and disputing, that you may become blameless and harmless, children of God without fault in the midst of a crooked and perverse generation, among whom you shine as lights in the world" (Philippians 2:14-15). This is in reference to our speech and to making sure that we are manifesting light to a corrupt world by not murmuring and complaining!

In order for us to let our light shine before men, we must get out of our comfort zone and be busy for Him. We can't isolate ourselves in our homes with all our tech stuff and think we are being light by posting some poem or Scripture verse on our Facebook page to our 6000 friends. We have to get out, meet people, and invest time and energy into relationships. My friend, the time is short, and if you and I are going to make a difference we must do it now.

You might be asking, "Why should I let my light shine before men?" Jesus says we are to let our light shine before men so that, first, they can *see our good works*. This would include those things that the Spirit of God produces in us which manifest that we belong to Him. This would include the fruit of the Spirit, the sharing of the gospel and living out the gospel, along with living out the Word of God. Hopefully, you will see some of those "good works" that we as women are to produce in the Questions to Consider.

As men and women see our good works, the glory doesn't go to us but to the one who gives us the ability to do anything, and that is our Father. This is the second reason that we should let our light shine before men: that others may *glorify our Father in heaven*. Jesus mentions that our *Father* is *in heaven* 10 times in the Sermon on the Mount, this being the first mentioning—perhaps as a reminder that kingdom citizens here live for a kingdom to come! The wonderful result of faithfully following Christ in living our life as salt and light is that the Father in heaven is glorified. As the Psalmist says in Psalm 115:1, "Not unto us, O Lord, not unto us, but to Your name give glory." When we are faithful to impact our world, the great result is that we glorify our Father who is in heaven. We put Him on display and, hopefully, by our good works we make the lost world thirsty to know what makes us different from them, so that they too can come to glorify Him. In 1 Peter 2:12, Peter says, "having your conduct honorable among the Gentiles, that when they speak against you as evildoers, they may, by your good works which they observe, glorify God in the day of visitation." Jesus says in John 15:8, "By this My Father is glorified, that you bear much fruit; so you will be My disciples." Both of these verses speak to the fact that our works glorify our Father by putting Him on display to a lost world. In the physical sense, when a light goes on or a lamp is lit, it doesn't draw attention to itself but it illumines others. The same is true with us; we don't do our good works to draw attention to ourselves but to draw attention to another, our Father in heaven. To *glorify* Him means to honor or magnify Him. When the Supreme Court made their decision on June 26, 2015, I remember having an intense discussion with someone about it. In that discussion, I made mention that our Father in heaven had been dishonored in a tremendous way by the court's decision, that our world had taken something that God intended to be good—marriage between a man and a woman—and had made it an abomination and blasphemous.

Summary

The Christian's Two-Fold Impact on the World (vv 13-15) is to be salt and light. Does this describe you? Are you a deterrent to the moral decay of the world? Does your life bring healing and comfort to those around you? Do you make others thirsty for God? What about being a light to the world? Does anyone outside of your immediate family know you are a Christian? What impact are you making on your world? Are you a shining light to a lost and dying world or are you being influenced by the world? *The Christian's Failure to Impact the World and Its Result* (v 13b) is this: If we fail to impact our world, the tragic result is clear: we are good for nothing. The world is getting worse and worse, as Christ predicted, but our response is not to throw our hands up and hide in a corner but to be faithful to the end. It will be tragic indeed to proclaim the name of Christ and yet never live as Christ, only to find on that day that Jesus says to you, "I never knew you" (Matthew 7:23). *The Christian's Faithfulness to Impact the World and Its Result* (v 16) is this: If we are faithful to impact our world by our good works by being salt and light, then the wonderful result is that we glorify our Father who is in heaven, with Whom we will spend all eternity. Is your life bringing glory to God? How are you putting Him on display?

Interestingly enough, just about two years before the Supreme Court's decision, on June 30, 2013, one of the faithful voices of our day, John MacArthur, said the following in a question and answer session at his church.

> The evangelical church has become tolerant. Tolerant of what? You name it and I will tell you what the next one will be—homosexuality. We have been softened up. We have given up the fight. We have basically rolled over in the name of love and now I pick up an article and it says, and I'm sure Jerry Falwell would roll over in his grave, that a student at Liberty Seminary is an open homosexual, that there are gay groups on Christian college campuses, that the church needs to accept homosexuals and accept even homosexual marriage. This is going to come like a flood .... This is going down fast. How do I feel about that? I expect the world to act like the world. What I don't expect is the church to act like the world... What I'm concerned about is what the church does. What we do in the name of Jesus Christ. And when we so hurriedly abandon the biblical pattern and when a Christian institution with tens of thousands of students says we want to work with the students here who have gender identity issues, the church is caving in.[18]

18 John MacArthur, "Strange Fire Q & A, Part 1" *Grace to You*, June 30, 2013 (www. gty.org/library/sermons-library/70-34).

Will you determine to not cave in? Will you be zealous for the sake of Christ and His kingdom? Will you be one of the few faithful ones left when the Son of Man comes? The end of the world will go down as a monumental event, much more monumental than the Supreme Court decision of June 26, 2015. It will be a much more serious decision than same-sex marriage. The decision will be that the earth will be burned up. This decision will not be made by the Supreme Court of the United States but by One Man, the Supreme Ruler of all the earth, God our Father. No longer will men marry men, or women marry women, but each of these who have not repented will be cast into the lake of fire forever along with all who have never repented of their sins and given their life over to the Lordship of Christ! The time is short, my friend. Do not waste another day being dull in your flavor and dim in your light. Have salt within yourself and let your light shine!

Questions to Consider
The Christian's Impact on the World
Matthew 5:13-16

1. (a) Read Matthew 5:13-16. Why do you think Jesus uses the example of believers being salt and light after giving the beatitudes in the previous verses? (b) What comes to your mind when you hear the words salt and light? (c) Why do you think Jesus uses these two words to describe what His children should look like?

2. Memorize Matthew 5:16.

3. In what ways can we be salt and light, according to Romans 13:11-14; Philippians 2:14-15; Colossians 4:6; and 1 Thessalonians 5:5-10?

4. (a) Jesus tells us that we are the light of the world. Paul tells believers to walk as children of light in Ephesians 5:8. Read Ephesians chapter 5 and write down all the ways God's children should be shining forth as lights to a dark world. (b) Are you shining forth in these ways?

5. (a) In what ways do you see Christians today being salt and light? (b) In what ways are we failing to be salt and light? (c) In what ways should we as *women* be showing forth our good works so that we are salt and light, according to Proverbs 31:10-31; Titus 2:2-5; 1 Timothy 2:8-15; and 1 Timothy 5:9-10? (d) Do these things describe your life? (e) Where can you improve?

6. (a) This week try to eat a certain food with salt and then without salt. Which one tastes better, and why? (b) How does this illustrate to you the importance of being salt in the world? (c) Secondly, find a place in your home or elsewhere that is completely dark. Allow yourself a few minutes in that darkness, and then turn on a light (flashlight, cell phone, etc.). How does this illustration help you better understand what Jesus said about us being the light of the world?

7. (a) How have you been impacted by this lesson? (b) What changes will you make by God's grace to be more salty and shiny? (c) Please write a prayer to God asking for His help!

Chapter 4

The Relationship of Christ and His Followers to the Law

Matthew 5:17-20

Throughout church history, unfortunately, an errant way of thinking sometimes gains influence. Even now, such an errant way of thinking is impacting the evangelical world. The teaching is antinomianism, and it basically says that those who are redeemed are not obligated to keep the moral law of God's Word. After all, they say, Christ came to fulfill the law; therefore, there is no need for us to obey the law. One of this movement's biggest proponents not long ago tweeted, "'Just as I am without one plea' is just as true for sanctification as it is for justification." At first you might think that doesn't sound so bad, but what is being insinuated by this statement is that after salvation there is no need to press on in sanctification; we can just do our own thing. In fact, a few months after this first tweet, this same man tweeted, "One thing is certain. I am hyper about grace!" This man is Tullian Tchividjian, who sadly also tweeted on June 21, 2015, "Welcome to the valley of the shadow of death ... grace reigns here." Why did he tweet that? Well, on that very same day, *Christianity Today*, a popular Christian news magazine, wrote the following:

> Popular pastor and author Tullian Tchividjian has resigned as senior pastor of Coral Ridge Presbyterian Church. A grandson of Billy Graham, Tchividjian cited "ongoing marital issues" as the reason for his departure from the PCA congregation in Fort Lauderdale, Florida. He said that his wife had an affair, and in response, he sought comfort in a friend and their relationship turned "inappropriate." Tchividjian's name was removed from the church's

website on Sunday as rumors of his resignation began flying on social media. [19]

Is the teaching of antinomianism biblical? What should be our response to God's law? Do we have any moral obligation to it? What did Jesus mean in the Sermon on the Mount when He said that He came to fulfill the law? Well, let's consider these few verses together as we consider Christ's and His followers' relationship to the law. Jesus says in Matthew 5:17-20:

Matthew 5:17-20

Do not think that I came to destroy the Law or the Prophets. I did not come to destroy but to fulfill. [18]For assuredly, I say to you, till heaven and earth pass away, one jot or one tittle will by no means pass from the law till all is fulfilled. [19]Whoever therefore breaks one of the least of these commandments, and teaches men so, shall be called least in the kingdom of heaven; but whoever does and teaches them, he shall be called great in the kingdom of heaven. [20]For I say to you, that unless your righteousness exceeds the righteousness of the Scribes and Pharisees, you will by no means enter the kingdom of heaven. (Matthew 5:17-20)

As we consider Jesus' words in Matthew 5:17-20, we will see:

Christ's Relationship to the Law (vv 17-18)

The Christian's Relationship to the Law (vv 19-20)

In our last lesson, we learned that the Christian has a two-fold impact on the world, as salt and light. We learned that failure to impact the world labels us as good for nothing. Faithfulness in doing so, however, brings glory to our heavenly Father. If you and I are to be faithful representatives of Christ by being salt and light, then we must represent Him as He is spelled out in the Word of God—as the perfect Son of God—and not water down His glorious gospel

19 Bob Smietana and Morgan Lee, "TullianTchividjian Resigns after Admitting 'Inapropriate Relationship'" *Christianity Today*, July 31, 2015 (www.christianitytoday. com/gleanings/2015/june/tullian-tchividjian-resigns-after-admitting-inappropiate-re. html).

or make Him out to be something He is not. We must give out the Word in all its fullness, and we must live out the Word in all that it requires. As Jesus begins this next portion of His sermon, He makes an amazing claim: He fulfilled the law and the prophets!

Christ's Relationship to the Law

Matthew 5:17-18

> Do not think that I came to destroy the Law or the Prophets. I did not come to destroy but to fulfill. (Matthew 5:17)

Jesus says *do not think. Do not* is an absolute denial. Don't even entertain this thought, Jesus is saying. What is it they are not to think? *That He came to destroy the Law or the Prophets.* What does it mean *to destroy*? It means to dissolve or demolish something by completely destroying it. When Christ came to earth as a man, He did not come with the intention of demolishing the Law or the Prophets. Now, what would be included in *the Law and the Prophets*? The word for *law* simply means commandments or instructions. This would be the directives God had given to His people to govern their lives. Included in this would be the moral law, judicial law, and ceremonial law.

- The moral laws included the Ten Commandments.

- The judicial laws gave guidance regarding how to govern their lives together, specifically in what they were to do and not do in relationship to one another.

- The ceremonial laws provided details regarding how the nation of Israel was to perform sacrifices to God.

Christ came to fulfill all of these. And we must remember when we are reading the Old Testament and we come across these difficult chapters that make no sense or have little meaning to us, that these have been fulfilled by Christ. One man helps us here: "Because

Matthew does not qualify his use of the Law, we are safe to say that it was God's whole law—the commandments, statutes, and judgments; the moral, judicial and ceremonial—that Jesus came not to abolish but to fulfill. It was also the other Old Testament teachings based on the law; and all their types, patterns, symbols, and pictures that He came to fulfill. Jesus Christ came to accomplish every aspect and every dimension of the divinely authored Word."[20]

Jesus also says He fulfilled not only the law but *the Prophets*. This is a reference to the Old Testament and specifically to what was said in it about Christ in the prophecies concerning Him. Also included in the prophets would be the reiteration of the moral law of God, which the prophets repeatedly spoke of and warned the nations concerning. When Jesus came, He warned the nation of Israel of much that the Old Testament prophets had previously warned them of. This gives huge weight to the argument that we should give heed to the Old Testament. One man says, "The moment you begin to question the authority of the Old Testament, you are of necessity questioning the authority of the Son of God Himself, and you will find yourself in endless trouble and difficulty."[21] And Jesus says He did not come to destroy *but to fulfill. Fulfill* means to satisfy, to complete, to fill up, and it has the idea of filling a vessel to the top. Christ fulfilled the law by completely obeying the law, which culminated in His death on the cross. Jesus emphasizes the fulfilling of the law in verse 18.

> For assuredly, I say to you, till heaven and earth pass away, one jot or one tittle will by no means pass from the law till all is fulfilled. (Matthew 5:18)

Jesus says *assuredly*, which means verily, surely; it is a strong word of affirmation. He says *assuredly, I say to you, till heaven and earth pass away, one jot or one tittle will by no means pass from the law till all be fulfilled.* The Greek word here for *fulfilled* is different than the word used in verse 17. Instead of meaning to fill up or complete, as

20 John MacArthur, *The MacArthur New Testament Commentary: Matthew 1-7* (Chicago: Moody Press, 1985), 255.
21 D. Martyn Lloyd-Jones, *Studies in the Sermon on the Mount* (Grand Rapids: Eerdmans Publishing Co., 1960), 164.

in verse 17, the word here means to bring to pass or end. Everything that God has ever written will be fulfilled. Every prophecy, every requirement of us, and even the judgment to come, it will all happen just as He said. Even the minutest things that may seem insignificant will all be fulfilled; they will all come to pass. In fact, Jesus uses the words *jot* and *tittle* to emphasize that nothing will be undone. All will be fulfilled. The jot is the 8th letter of the Greek alphabet; it is as we would say, one iota. This would be quite small and would be similar to the dot above our letter "i" in English. Tittle actually means little horn. A tittle is a small, angled line that completes a letter, like an "R" in English. We might not think these are important, but that is exactly Jesus' point; even the smallest letters are vital because the slightest change in a letter can change the whole meaning of a word. And we know *heaven and earth* will eventually *pass away*, because Peter tells us in 2 Peter 3:10-13:

> But the day of the Lord will come as a thief in the night, in which the heavens will pass away with a great noise, and the elements will melt with fervent heat; both the earth and the works that are in it will be burned up. Therefore, since all these things will be dissolved, what manner of persons ought you to be in holy conduct and godliness, looking for and hastening the coming of the day of God, because of which the heavens will be dissolved, being on fire, and the elements will melt with fervent heat? Nevertheless we, according to His promise, look for new heavens and a new earth in which righteousness dwells.

As significant as that event will be, Jesus says in Luke 21:33, "Heaven and earth will pass away, but My words will by no means pass away." And in Luke 16:17, "And it is easier for heaven and earth to pass away than for one tittle of the law to fail."

So, what is Christ's relationship to the law? He fulfilled it! Because heaven and earth will not pass away till all the law is fulfilled, the implications to Christ's followers are serious, according to verse 19. And here, Jesus moves from talking about His relationship to the law to what His followers' relationship to the law should be, in verses 19 and 20.

The Christian's Relationship to the Law

Matthew 5:19-20

> Whoever therefore breaks one of the least of these commandments, and teaches men so, shall be called least in the kingdom of heaven; but whoever does and teaches them, he shall be called great in the kingdom of heaven. (Matthew 5:19)

Jesus says *whoever*; there is no exception for anyone to break even the littlest commandment. *Whoever therefore* does this, Jesus says, *shall be called least in the kingdom of heaven*. When Jesus says *therefore*, it is important, as it means because of what He has just said. Because He is the fulfillment of the law, then the law is vitally important; because every jot and tittle of the law will be fulfilled, then the law is absolutely important. Therefore, we must not break God's law, even the least commandment. A *commandment* was something that had divine authority. The word *break* means to destroy, to violate, or to disobey. The *least commandment* would refer to the ones which they thought were the smallest. The religious leaders of the day would divide the commandments into the greater and the lesser ones, and if you broke the lesser commandments, well, it was no big deal, or so they taught. In fact, later in Matthew's gospel, one of the Pharisees tried to trip up Jesus with a question. In Matthew 22:34-40, we read, "But when the Pharisees heard that He had silenced the Sadducees, they gathered together. Then one of them, a lawyer, asked Him a question, testing Him, and saying, 'Teacher, which is the great commandment in the law?' Jesus said to him, 'You shall love the Lord your God with all your heart, with all your soul, and with all your mind.' This is the first and great commandment. And the second is like it: 'You shall love your neighbor as yourself.' On these two commandments hang *all* the Law and the Prophets" (emphasis mine). Since the Pharisees had divided the commandments up into greater and lesser categories, they wanted Jesus to tell them which was the greatest of all the commandments! They didn't know what to do with His answer, so much so that Mark and Luke tell us no one asked Him any more questions! Jesus wasn't duped by their trick question. All of His commandments are important, and He wasn't going to "divide" them up, even though the religious leaders had done so.

I think we are just as guilty as the Pharisees. For example, we might say if you tell a premeditated lie that's big, but if you tell a little white lie, well then, no worries. Or, if you commit adultery, that's huge, but if you just think about committing adultery and lust over someone else's spouse, it's not a big deal. I just heard a podcast the other day in which the speaker was saying that some Christians now think it is okay to have same sex attraction just so long as they're not having the sex! That is ludicrous! Of course, Jesus thinks a tad bit differently, as we will see as we continue on in the lessons to come in Matthew 5. I fear that we are not much different than the Scribes and Pharisees of Jesus' day, picking and choosing what we will obey and what we won't obey. Some of us have even bought into the hyper-grace movement and its antinomianism. Jesus' half-brother James picks up on this in his epistle, in James 2:10-12, "For whoever shall keep the whole law, and yet stumble in one point, he is guilty of all. For He who said, 'Do not commit adultery,' also said, 'Do not murder.' Now if you do not commit adultery, but you do murder, you have become a transgressor of the law. So speak and so do as those who will be judged by the law of liberty." We are not going to be judged by our laws or our friends' and family's laws but by God's law, the law of liberty. We must be careful, as so many today are minimizing the law of God, saying, "Grace, grace!" They are effectively rewriting Romans 6:1 to say, "Shall we sin that grace may abound! *Yes indeed!*" Beware, my friend! God doesn't change the nature of who He is to suit our sinfulness. (Just as a side note: *This* is why it is imperative that we be in a church that teaches the whole counsel of God from Genesis to Revelation, which is all of God's revealed Word. We should not be satisfied to sit week after week in a church that does topical preaching and avoids the hard sayings of Jesus or the ones that are difficult to interpret. We cannot ignore even the least commandments of God.)

It's bad enough that we would break any of God's commandments, even *the least of them*, but then to teach others to do the same, why, this is unthinkable! Jesus says if you *teach men so*, you will be the *least in the kingdom of heaven*. Now, perhaps you're unsure about this idea. A number of places in Scripture, actually, seem to indicate the idea of there being lesser and greater rewards in heaven. In Matthew 20, when the mother of Zebedee's sons asks Jesus if her two sons could sit by Him in heaven, one on the right hand and the other on the left hand, Jesus replies to her request in verse 23b by saying, "but to sit on My right hand and on My left is not Mine to give, but it is for those for whom it is prepared by My Father." In 1 Corinthians 3:9-15, Paul indicates that there will be degrees of rewards at the judgment seat, which would indicate lesser and greater rewards in heaven:

> For we are God's fellow workers; you are God's field, you are God's building. According to the grace of God which was given to me, as a wise master builder I have laid the foundation, and another builds on it. But let each one take heed how he builds on it. For no other foundation can anyone lay than that which is laid, which is Jesus Christ. Now if anyone builds on this foundation with gold, silver, precious stones, wood, hay, straw, each one's work will become clear; for the Day will declare it, because it will be revealed by fire; and the fire will test each one's work, of what sort it is. If anyone's work which he has built on it endures, he will receive a reward. If anyone's work is burned, he will suffer loss; but he himself will be saved, yet so as through fire.

No wonder the apostle John says in 2 John 8, "Look to yourselves, that we do not lose those things we worked for, but that we may receive a full reward." Part of this looking to ourselves would include not only how we live but also what we teach others. James says in James 3:1, "My brethren, let not many of you become teachers, knowing that we shall receive a stricter judgment." This leaves us with a sobering responsibility as teachers, mothers, grandmothers, and friends to watch what we teach others; Jesus clearly indicates in Matthew 10:25 that a disciple will be like his teacher.

Jesus now uses a word of contrast, *but*, and says *but whoever does and teaches them, he shall be called great in the kingdom of heaven*.

So instead of breaking a little ole' commandment, I obey all the commandments. I do them. Again, as Jesus half-brother says in James 1:22-25, "But be doers of the word, and not hearers only, deceiving yourselves. For if anyone is a hearer of the word and not a doer, he is like a man observing his natural face in a mirror; for he observes himself, goes away, and immediately forgets what kind of man he was. But he who looks into the perfect law of liberty and continues in it, and is not a forgetful hearer but a doer of the work, this one will be blessed in what he does." Paul reiterates this same truth in Romans 2:13: "for not the hearers of the law are just in the sight of God, but the doers of the law will be justified."

So, we must do the Word—obey the Word—but we must also pass it on to others; as Jesus says, we must *teach* others. Jesus rebukes the religious leaders of the day, in Matthew 23:1-3, for their neglect of this, "Then Jesus spoke to the multitudes and to His disciples, saying: 'The Scribes and the Pharisees sit in Moses' seat. Therefore whatever they tell you to observe, that observe and do, but do not do according to their works; for they say, and do not do.'" This was their grave error—they could give out the goods, the laws, but they did not live them out. (Romans 2 also refers to this hypocrisy.) The one who *does and teaches* the commandments of God, Jesus says will be called *great*—or mighty—*in the kingdom of heaven*. To further illustrate what He means, Jesus ends His thoughts by saying something shocking!

> For I say to you, that unless your righteousness exceeds the righteousness of the Scribes and Pharisees, you will by no means enter the kingdom of heaven. (Matthew 5:20)

Jesus tells those who are listening to Him that their *righteousness* must *exceed the righteousness of the Scribes and Pharisees* if they want to enter into heaven. The term *righteousness* means conduct or holiness and the word *exceed* means to be in excess, to abound more. So, unless their conduct exceeds that of the religious leaders of the day they *will by no means*—which is an absolute denial—enter into the kingdom of heaven. This would be a shocking statement to the audience listening, as well as to the religious leaders of the day. *The Scribes and Pharisees* were considered the religious leaders of the day and were viewed as the greatest, and now Jesus tells them they are not! In fact, the word *Pharisee* means separatist. These people were set apart and were considered the most holy of all men! They prided themselves in keeping all 248 commandments and all 365 prohibitions in the Old Testament Scriptures. What is Jesus saying? He is saying that it is not by works of righteousness which we have done but according to His mercy that we are saved (Titus 3:5). He is saying that it is by grace that we are saved and not by our religious works, lest we should boast (Ephesians 2:8-9). Outward religion will not get anyone into heaven because Christ is calling for an inward change of the heart. A kingdom citizen is motivated by love; a Pharisee is motivated by duty. After the Lord saved me, one of the first things that changed in me was that all those religious things I had been doing from a heart of duty became motivated by a heart of delight. God changed my heart. Only the redeeming grace of Christ and the blood of Jesus can change a human heart. It's interesting that Jesus tells His audience in the previous verse that they must not only teach His Word, but do it; they must live it out. This was the problem of the Pharisees—they loved to tell you what to do, but they didn't do it themselves. Their religion was only outward, but Jesus is calling for an inward change of the heart that produces an outward change. He's not calling for an evil heart that can fake an outward religion. That kind of righteousness is not the righteousness of God.

Paul, having been a Pharisee himself before the Lord saved him, describes such pharisaical religion in Romans 10:1-3, "Brethren, my heart's desire and prayer to God for Israel is that they may be saved. For I bear them witness that they have a zeal for God, but not according to knowledge. For they being ignorant of God's righteousness, and seeking to establish their own righteousness, have not submitted to the righteousness of God." Paul knew personally the deception of a religious imposter! But because of the grace of God, Paul had experienced the promise of the new covenant mentioned in Ezekiel 36:26-28, "I will give you a new heart and put a new spirit within you; I will take the heart of stone out of your flesh and give you a heart of flesh. I will put My Spirit within you and cause you to walk in My statutes, and you will keep My judgments and do them."

In Luke 18:18-23, we also have the sad account of the rich young ruler.

> Now a certain ruler asked Him, saying, "Good Teacher, what shall I do to inherit eternal life?" So Jesus said to him, "Why do you call Me good? No one is good but One, that is, God. You know the commandments: 'Do not commit adultery,' 'Do not murder,' 'Do not steal,' 'Do not bear false witness,' 'Honor your father and your mother.'" And he said, "All these things I have kept from my youth." So when Jesus heard these things, He said to him, "You still lack one thing. Sell all that you have and distribute to the poor, and you will have treasure in heaven; and come, follow Me." But when he heard this, he became very sorrowful, for he was very rich.

This man kept the commandments, he was exemplary externally, but he lacked love for God which resulted in loving others by giving to them in their need. My friend, this should cause us to think about our own personal lives, and to reflect on all the outward religious things we do, and to examine ourselves as to why we do those things. Are we growing in love for God and others, or are we just getting more and more outwardly religious? In our lessons to come we will see some shocking examples of what Jesus means when He says our righteousness must exceed that of the Pharisees.

So, what is the Christian's relationship to the law? He must do it and teach it. Now, we must make clear that the Christian is not under the judicial and ceremonial laws of the Old Testament, as those were given for the nation of Israel. They were done away with when Christ died on the cross, as Mark indicates in Mark 15:38, when he states that the veil in the temple was torn in two, which indicated that the ceremonial laws had been done away with. But we are still under the moral law of God. In fact, nine out of the Ten Commandments are repeated in the New Testament. God's moral law never changes, even though the state of Oklahoma, where I live, has repeatedly endeavored to remove The Ten Commandments from its capital lawn. Regardless of what the state of Oklahoma does, God's laws are still in effect! Removing them from one's sight does not make them null and void.

Summary

What is *Christ's Relationship to the Law* (vv 17-18)? He came to fulfill it! When you read the Old Testament, do you see Christ in its pages? Do you read it just as enthusiastically as you would your favorite New Testament book? When you come to those difficult parts of the Old (and even the New) Testament, do you ask the Lord to open your eyes so that you can behold wondrous things from out of His law?

What is *The Christian's Relationship to the Law* (vv 19-20)? To do it and teach it! First, how does it fare with you in regard to your obedience to the Word of God? Are you haphazard in your obedience? Do you pick and choose what is comfortable for you to obey? Do you have someone with whom you can share your real struggles so that they can pray and encourage you toward love and good deeds? My friend, these are dark times and we cannot afford to waste them with apathetic attitudes toward holy living. Second, are you taking what you know from Scripture and passing it on to others? Your children? Your friends? To whom are you passing the baton of truth?

When Jesus ends the Sermon on the Mount, He will have some pointed things to say that tie up His whole sermon but are especially pertinent to this passage we have just studied. He says in Matthew 7:24-29:

> Therefore whoever hears these sayings of Mine, and does them, I will liken him to a wise man who built his house on the rock: and the rain descended, the floods came, and the winds blew and beat on that house; and it did not fall, for it was founded on the rock. But everyone who hears these sayings of Mine, and does not do them, will be like a foolish man who built his house

on the sand: and the rain descended, the floods came, and the winds blew and beat on that house; and it fell. And great was its fall.

And then verses 28-29 of Matthew 7 record this: "And so it was, when Jesus had ended these sayings, that the people were astonished at His teaching, for He taught them as one having authority, and not as the Scribes." They were shocked out of their minds; they were struck dumb, as the Greek rendering indicates. Why? Because Jesus' words and Jesus' life were not as the religious leaders of the day. Jesus lived and taught a righteous life; the Scribes and Pharisees taught and lived self-righteous lives. What about you? Let us endeavor not to break even one of the least commandments. Let us be faithful to do and to teach the whole counsel of God. Let us be zealous for true righteousness, not for the self-righteousness of the Scribes and the Pharisees.

Questions to Consider

The Relationship of Christ and His Followers to the Law
Matthew 5:17-20

1. Read Matthew 5:17-20. If Christ came to fulfill the law, as mentioned in verse 17, then why is it imperative that His followers obey the law, as mentioned in verse 19?

2. Memorize Matthew 5:20.

3. (a) Jesus said He came to fulfill the Law and the Prophets. What are some of the ways that Old Testament prophecy was fulfilled when Christ came, according to Matthew 1:19-23; 2:1-6; 2:14-23; 4:12-16? (b) How does this encourage you especially as it relates to some prophecies that have not yet been fulfilled or that you do not understand?

4. (a) What is the "righteousness" of the Scribes and Pharisees, according to Matthew 23? (b) What is true righteousness, according to this passage? (c) What do you think that Jesus meant when He said in Matthew 5:20 that unless our righteousness exceeds that of the Scribes and Pharisees we will not enter into heaven? (d) Prior to his salvation, what did the apostle Paul consider to be righteous living, according to Philippians 3:1-11? (e) What kind of righteousness did he possess after salvation?

5. How does Romans 2 relate to what Jesus says in Matthew 5:17-20? (b) What are the dangers of teaching others things that you yourself do not do, according to Romans 2? (c) In what ways are we guilty of doing this in our lives? (d) How do we make sure that we live out what we say?

6. (a) How do we discern between self-righteousness and true righteousness? (Use Scripture to back up your answer, if you're able.) (b) Are you depending on your own righteousness for salvation?

7. (a) In what ways does Christendom today manifest the "righteousness of the Scribes and Pharisees"? (b) How can followers of Christ avoid this pitfall? (c) How can we manifest genuine righteous living?

8. Those who are God's children have been redeemed from the curse of the law, according to Galatians 3:13! Write a prayer of thanksgiving to the Lord for what He has done for you in redemption.

Chapter 5

The Dangerous Sin of Anger!
Matthew 5:21-26

Recent statistics tell us that about 16,000 murders are committed in the United States each year. That number doesn't include the roughly 41,000 suicides—which is also murder, by the way, since it is taking one's own life—that also occur in the US each year. When you combine these figures, you have about 60,000 murders in the United States each year. Compared to the population of the United States, roughly 318 million, that might not seem like a huge number. But I wonder how many of the 318 million people who live in this country would admit to ever being angry—or annoyed, exasperated, impatient, irritated, which are all expressions of anger. I imagine, most Americans, if they were honest, would at least admit to moments of anger. But few would admit that their anger would qualify as being equal with the 60,000 murders which take place in our country each year. But as kingdom citizens who belong to another country, we have a King who has something quite startling to say as He speaks on the mount regarding the dangerous sin of anger. Let's listen in!

Matthew 5:21-26

You have heard that it was said to those of old, 'You shall not murder, and whoever murders will be in danger of the judgment.' ²²But I say to you that whoever is angry with his brother without a cause shall be in danger of the judgment. And whoever says to his brother, 'Raca!' shall be in danger of the council. But whoever says, 'You fool!' shall be in danger of hell fire. ²³Therefore if you bring your gift to the altar, and there remember that your brother has something against you, ²⁴leave your gift there before the altar, and go your way. First be reconciled to your brother, and then come and offer your gift. ²⁵Agree with your adversary quickly, while you are on the way with him, lest your adversary deliver you to the judge, the judge hand you over to the officer, and you be thrown into prison. [26]Assuredly, I say to you, you will by no means get out of there till you have paid the last penny.

We considered in our previous lesson the theme of Christ's and His followers' relationship to the law. We saw that Christ's relationship to the law was to fulfill it. His followers' relationship to the law is to do it and to teach it. Jesus ended this topic by declaring to His listeners that their righteousness must exceed that of the Scribes and Pharisees in order for them to be granted entrance into the kingdom of heaven. I'm certain that these words left many of His listeners with their mouths wide-opened and in shock, just as I'm certain it has left many of us in shock as well. Now, in the verses that follow, Jesus will expound on what He means, and it is shocking indeed. In this lesson, we will see:

The Dangerous Sin of Anger (vv 21-22)

The Divine Solution for Anger (vv 23-26)

Let's begin by looking at the dangerous sin of anger, in verse 21.

The Dangerous Sin of Anger

Matthew 5:21-22

You have heard that it was said to those of old, "You shall not murder, and whoever murders will be in danger of the judgment." (Matthew 5:21)

To those seated on the mount, Jesus says *you have heard that it was said to those of old, "You shall not murder."* When Jesus says *of old* He is referring to that which is written in the Old Testament. Even before the Ten Commandments were given to Moses (interestingly enough, also on a mount), God had made it clear to Noah what the penalty for murder was, in Genesis 9:6, "Whoever sheds man's blood, by man his blood shall be shed; for in the image of God He made man." The commandment is also repeated in the Ten Commandments, which were given to Moses; Exodus 20:13 states, "You shalt not murder."

Exodus 21:12 also repeats the commandment: "He who strikes a man so that he dies shall surely be put to death." Leviticus 24:21 is also clear about it: "And whoever kills an animal shall restore it; but whoever kills a man shall be put to death." Most people living in the time in which Jesus was speaking did not have a copy of the Scriptures, so they were dependent on hearing the Word of God from their religious leaders. The religious leaders of the day taught this and lived it, as they were exemplary in both the teaching and the keeping of the Old Testament law.

What does it mean to *murder*? It means to take the life of another with ill-will intent. This is, obviously, premeditated murder. God clarifies in Numbers 35 (as you will see in the Questions to Consider) that there is premeditated murder and there are also murders that are accidental. The one who murders intentionally is to be put to death; the one who murders by accident is to be brought before a judge to determine what the outcome of his actions should be. In addition to these, there were also God-ordained murders, in the sense that God appointed war in a number of Old Testament passages (see Exodus 17:16; Numbers 31:7; 1 Samuel 23:2).

Jesus says that if you intentionally murder someone you are *in danger of the judgment*. This means you are guilty and subject to just punishment. In biblical times, if someone killed another person they were to be judged for their crime. Deuteronomy 16:18-20 says, "You shall appoint judges and officers in all your gates, which the Lord your God gives you, according to your tribes, and they shall judge the people with just judgment. You shall not pervert justice; you shall not show partiality, nor take a bribe, for a bribe blinds the eyes of the wise and twists the words of the righteous. You shall follow what is altogether just, that you may live and inherit the land which the Lord your God is giving you." Even in the New Testament, there was a judicial system set up for those who committed murder. One man helps us here: "This was the tribunal that had cognizance of cases of murder, etc. It was a court that sat in each city or town, and consisted commonly of seven members. It was the lowest court among the Jews, and from it an appeal might be taken to the

Sanhedrin."[22] In our society, if we murder someone intentionally we might be executed; we might spend some time in prison, and be let out in a few years; or we might be found not guilty by a jury trial and let go. But, no matter what an earthly nation's judicial system does, premediated murder in God's eyes is not something to be taken lightly. No matter what a nation may do, in God's eyes a murderer is in danger of judgment, in danger of hell! John makes this clear in 1 John 3:15: "Whoever hates his brother is a murderer, and you know that no murderer has eternal life abiding in him." Paul makes this clear, as well, in Galatians 5:19-21, when he says, "Now the works of the flesh are evident, which are: adultery, fornication, uncleanness, lewdness, idolatry, sorcery, hatred, contentions, jealousies, outbursts of wrath, selfish ambitions, dissensions, heresies, envy, *murders*, drunkenness, revelries, and the like; of which I tell you beforehand, just as I also told you in time past, that those who practice such things will not inherit the kingdom of God" (emphasis mine).

Of course, many of us are like the religious leaders of Jesus' day in that most of us would never think of killing someone intentionally. But outward laws were not meant only to govern outward behavior; they were intended to govern the inward heart, as well. We might be thinking that we are off scott-free because we've never murdered. This is exactly what the Jewish leaders thought; murder was a big no-no to them! But Jesus is saying something a bit different, and it just might cause some of us concern, and rightly so. He says,

> But I say to you that whoever is angry with his brother without a cause shall be in danger of the judgment. And whoever says to his brother, "Raca!" shall be in danger of the council. But whoever says, "You fool!" shall be in danger of hell fire. (Matthew 5:22)

The word *but* is a word of contrast. Jesus says, "This is what you've heard, that you shall not murder, *but* I'm telling you something different." Jesus makes it clear that He is the authority and not the religious leaders of their day. (By the way, He is also the authority in

---

22 Barnes' Notes, Electronic Database Copyright © 1997, 2003, 2005, 2006 by Bible-soft, Inc. All rights reserved.

our day as well, and we would do well to filter *all* biblical teaching through the grid of His Word.) Jesus had just told them that He had come to fulfill the law and not to destroy it. Therefore, He is able—with all authority—to expound on the law that was from God. Jesus' teaching did not contradict the law but, rather, completed it.

With that in mind, Jesus says *whoever is angry with his brother without a cause shall be in danger of judgment.* And Jesus specifies what this anger is: it is anger *without a cause. Anger* refers to being provoked, being exasperated, being enraged. Your anger, in this case, is without a reason. It might be as simple as a husband who doesn't do something when and how you want it done so you become provoked or irritated with him. A child who is having trouble getting the concept of potty-training and you lose all rationale with him or her. This is anger without a cause, mind you, not anger with a cause. There is such a thing as righteous anger and will see examples of that in the Questions to Consider.

But if one is angry without a cause, they also, just like the one who murders, are *in danger of the judgment.* This would have been absolutely shocking to the religious leaders of Jesus' day, and they would've wondered what judgment Jesus was talking about, since there was no law regarding judgment for anger. Jesus is raising the bar and squaring off with the religious hypocrites of the day. Murder is equal to unrighteous anger and both can lead to eternal judgment. Isn't that just what Paul said in Galatians 5:19-21 regarding those who would not enter into the kingdom of heaven?! In the list Paul gives, he certainly includes murder, but he also lists outburst of wrath as a sin worthy of hell-fire!

Jesus goes on to say *whoever says to his brother, "Raca!" shall be in danger of the council.* The word *raca* means empty one, worthless fellow, shallow brains. *The council* is a reference to the Jewish Sanhedrin. One man helps us to understand this; he says, "Every town in Palestine with a population of 120 or more had a Sanhedrin (a court of 23 men.) This Sanhedrin had the power to pronounce the sentence of capital punishment."[23] This would be the highest of the Jewish courts, but Jesus isn't setting up a human court as the judge. He's referring to His *council*, which is the only council which shall stand.

Jesus goes even further to say *but whoever says, "You fool!" shall be in danger of hell fire.* To call someone a *fool* means to call them stupid, blockhead, and moron. You might be thinking, "Wait a minute, Jesus called the Pharisees, 'blind fools,' so is Jesus condemning Himself?" What Jesus did was quite different. He was rebuking the false teachers of His day, the religious hypocrites, and we have ample biblical precedent in the Scriptures to allow for this. What Jesus is condemning in this verse is the response of unrighteous anger to personal offenses or people who irritate us or who are not like us. When we become frustrated or put out with others, it is nothing more than pride and anger, no matter what we might call it! This should cause us to pause before we use our mouths to belittle others. Jesus says in Matthew 12:36, "But I say to you that for every idle word men may speak, they will give account of it in the day of judgment." And by the way, we as parents need to help our children use their mouths for things that are edifying and not allow them to speak unkind and foolish things to others, even their siblings. Even the inward thoughts of anger or irritation are seen by our Lord. This should motivate us all to change the way we think. Nothing is hidden before His eyes.

The words *hell fire* would have been understood by those who were listening to Jesus as a reference to what was then known as the Valley of Gehenna. The Jews would have understood this imagery as symbolic of a place where the fire never went out. In the Valley of Gehenna, they would burn rubbish, dung, and dead animals. Jesus, however, is not referring to the fire that never goes out in the Valley of Gehenna, but the fire that never goes out in a place called Hell. My friend, anger is serious and could be a matter of life or death in an eternal sense!

---

23 Jay Adams, *The Christian Councilor's Commentary: The Gospels of Matthew and Mark* (Woodruff: Timeless Texts, 1999) 46.

Before we go on, I want to be clear that Jesus is not saying anger leads to murder, though sometimes it does, as in the case of Cain and Abel. Instead, Jesus is saying that anger is murder! Jesus is equating anger with murder, a sin which brings eternal punishment. Neither the Jewish court, nor the Jewish Sanhedrin, can send anyone to hell for anger, but Jesus can.

How dangerous is the sin of anger? It is very dangerous. All three of these—anger without a cause, anger that leads to calling someone "Raca," and anger which prompts us to call someone "fool"—are all equated with unrighteous anger, and all have the potential to put us in danger of the judgment, the council of God, and hell fire. [24] It is a sin that Jesus equates with murder, and it is a sin worthy of hell. That's pretty dangerous, I'd say. No wonder Jesus says in Luke 21:19, "By your patience possess your souls."

But Jesus gives us hope. He turns now to teach on the divine solution for anger, in verses 23-26. Instead of becoming angry, I am to take care of the offense. Instead of murdering someone, literally or in my heart, I am to take care of the offense. And Jesus illustrates His divine solution with two illustrations. The first one has to do with religious matters and the second has to do with legal matters.

The Divine Solution for Anger

Matthew 5:23-26

Therefore if you bring your gift to the altar, and there remember that your brother has something against you, (Matthew 5:23)

Because of the seriousness of anger, we are to do something about it. Here is example number one, and it has to do with worship. Jesus

---

24 Notice in this first illustration about the law, that Jesus was reclaiming the original intent of the Law by pointing out that the "greater stands for the lesser," i.e., when God said "thou shalt not kill," the command extends even to mental or inward thoughts of anger or outward insults. In a similar way, when God says "thou shalt not commit adultery," the command extends even to the mental thought of lust, etc. The "greater stands for the lesser" as the Law includes the whole of the outward actions plus the inner motives.

says *if you bring your gift to the altar, and there remember that your brother has something against you*. Now, a *gift* would be an offering or a sacrifice that one would bring to the altar. The *altar* was at the front of the temple and their offering was a symbol of their worship to God. In our day, we would say, "If we are heading off to church and enter the doors to worship God, and I remember that brother or sister so-and-so has something against me ...." So, I'm on my way to church and realize I have an offense with a brother or a sister, or he or she has some offense with me, what should I do? Jesus tells us what to do in the next verse.

> leave your gift there before the altar, and go your way. First be reconciled to your brother, and then come and offer your gift. (Matthew 5:24)

Jesus says don't offer your gift at the altar, *leave it there before the altar, and go your way.* We must remember that God is Spirit and they that worship Him must worship in spirit and in truth. We cannot come to church to worship God and hold anger in our hearts toward a brother or sister, or have some unresolved offense. If we do so, our worship is in vain. Instead, Jesus says, *first be reconciled.* So, we leave the gift and go and find the brother or sister with whom we need to reconcile. The word *brother* is adelphos, so this is a Christian brother to whom Jesus is referring. To *reconcile* means to settle differences, to change thoroughly. So, you do this first, then you go back and offer your gift at the altar. We would say we leave the church parking lot or the auditorium, go and reconcile with our brother, and then come back to church if church is still going on. If not, we come the next time the doors are open. I remember one time years ago my husband was teaching on this passage and one of the leaders of the church got up and left the auditorium. He knew he needed to go and make something right with another person. That, my friend, is being a doer of the Word! Dear sister, this is why we must endeavor to live as our brother Paul did, that is, to keep short accounts with God and man (Acts 24:16). Don't put off reconciliation! If you know you have offended someone, take care of it. If someone has offended you, don't call and complain to your best friend, or to your pastor or your pastor's wife, but you take care of it yourself, and you don't wait for a week to do so.

These words would have been a rebuke to the Pharisees; they would have been exemplary in paying their tithes of mint, anise and cumin, but they omitted the real things like justice, mercy and faith (Matthew 23:23). We are much like them at times. We, too, come to church with our pious looks, sing some worship songs, give our ten percent offering, shake some hands, and head out the door and think we've worshipped God, yet we had an argument with our husband on the way to church or have ought with someone and we've not yet taken care of it. The Old Testament is replete with warnings regarding this. Consider Isaiah 1:15-17, "When you spread out your hands, I will hide My eyes from you; even though you make many prayers, I will not hear. Your hands are full of blood. Wash yourselves, make yourselves clean; put away the evil of your doings from before My eyes. Cease to do evil, learn to do good; seek justice, rebuke the oppressor; defend the fatherless, plead for the widow." Or Jeremiah 7:9-11, "'Will you steal, murder, commit adultery, swear falsely, burn incense to Baal, and walk after other gods whom you do not know, and then come and stand before Me in this house which is called by My name, and say, "We are delivered to do all these abominations"? Has this house, which is called by My name, become a den of thieves in your eyes? Behold, I, even I, have seen it,' says the Lord." In Psalm 66:18, we read, "If I regard iniquity in my heart, The Lord will not hear." God is clear in His Word that to obey Him is better than offering Him some sacrifice (1 Samuel 15:22). I know of marital relationships where there is feuding all week long, and yet they put on their religious face for Sundays and think they're worshiping God. I know of women who are at odds with others, or even avoid others at church, or don't care for a certain person in the church, and yet they think they've come on Sunday to worship. My friend, if this describes you, then worship is far from what you are doing on the Lord's Day; hypocrisy would be a better description, because that's what Jesus says it is.

Putting off reconciliation is dangerous, as Jesus mentions in our next verse, and here He uses yet another illustration, that of going to court. The first illustration involved a conflict with another Christian brother or sister, but this second illustration involves not a brother but an unbeliever. We're not off the hook, whether we are at odds with believers or unbelievers!

> Agree with your adversary quickly, while you are on the way with him, lest your adversary deliver you to the judge, the judge hand you over to the officer, and you be thrown into prison. (Matthew 5:25)

This second example has to do with legal matters, while the first pertained to religious matters. Jesus says *agree with your adversary quickly. Agree* means to reconcile, which we defined earlier. The *adversary* in this case was someone who was an opponent, someone, perhaps, that I might be suing or going to court with. *Quickly* means to reconcile right away, without delay. It is interesting that in both examples, religious and judicial, we are told to reconcile quickly. Wise Solomon spoke of this in Proverbs 25:8-10, "Do not go hastily to court; for what will you do in the end, when your neighbor has put you to shame? Debate your case with your neighbor, and do not disclose the secret to another; lest he who hears it expose your shame, and your reputation be ruined." Jesus says I am to reconcile with him *while* I am *on the way with him*. In other words, settle the matter before you go to court. According to Roman law, two individuals who were going to court could settle a matter before they got there, but they could not reconcile once they entered into the court. So it would be in their better interest to take care of the matter before they were delivered to the judge. Once your adversary *delivers you to the judge*, the judge *hands you over to the officer*, and then the officer *throws you into prison*. This is the simple progression of what happens if you don't settle matters out of court. It is very similar to our judicial system. You go to court before a judge and have a trial. When you're found guilty, you're handed over to the officer present and he throws you into prison.

Jesus uses this illustration to further illustrate what He has said. Settle the matter now, and do it quickly; otherwise, it will be settled in heaven by the Judge of all the earth. If you're found guilty, you may be thrown into prison, which, in this case, would be eternal hell. Revelation 21:8 is pretty clear about this: "But the cowardly, unbelieving, abominable, murderers, sexually immoral, sorcerers, idolaters, and all liars shall have their part in the lake which burns with fire and brimstone, which is the second death." In the 40-plus years that my husband and I have been married, we have endeavored on numerous occasions to be obedient in reconciling with others. Many times, the other parties will not adhere, but we do everything, as Paul says, to try to live peaceably with all men (Romans 12:18). I remember telling one lady, as I was trying to reason with her, that it would be better to settle our differences in this life than to stand before God on Judgment Day and settle them then. Jesus ends this illustration by saying,

> Assuredly, I say to you, you will by no means get out of there
> till you have paid the last penny. (Matthew 5:26)

Assuredly, I say to you, says Jesus, this indeed will happen. *You will by no means get out of there till you have paid the last penny.* The word for *penny* here means farthing, which was the smallest of Roman coins. If a person was put into prison, he could not get out until he had paid his debt off, even to the smallest coinage. Jesus is not saying that once we are condemned we can bargain our way out of hell, but He is emphasizing the seriousness of anger and the seriousness of reconciling quickly!

So what is the divine solution for anger? The solution is to reconcile, and to reconcile quickly. If not, ongoing habits of anger put you in serious danger of eternal punishment. This was the same solution that was told of old in Leviticus 19:17, "You shall not hate your brother in your heart. You shall surely rebuke your neighbor, and not bear sin because of him." We will see in a few verses from now, that Jesus will tell those on the mount to get serious about sin, to pluck their eye out, to cut off their arm, to do whatever it takes to get rid of sin! If anger is a problem for you, then do what you must to get rid of it. Pray, fast, be accountable to someone, and memorize the Word. If we are going to put off the sin of anger, we must replace it something, and that something is contentment!

Summary

I appeal to you, as sisters in Christ, do not underestimate the sin of anger. It is deadly serious! So, I ask you, have you ever wanted to murder anyone? I pray that you haven't, and I would venture to say that most of you have not. But have you ever been angry with anyone? Have you been frustrated with anyone? Have you been irritated with anyone? Have you been annoyed with anyone? If you are answering yes in your heart, then you have been angry and you have been guilty of murder, according to Jesus. Do you now at this moment have any offense with anyone, believer or unbeliever? If so, please take care of it this day. We must never put off reconciliation with a believer or with an unbeliever. We must take care of it quickly. Putting off reconciliation breeds gossip, bitterness and criticism. And, by the way, avoidance is not reconciliation.

The day I was finishing up this lesson, the Spurgeon "Thought for the Day" was front page on my Bible Study software. Spurgeon can certainly say it better than I!

> Anger is not always or necessarily sinful, but it has such a tendency to run wild that whenever it displays itself, we should be quick to question its character, with this enquiry, "Doest thou well to be angry?" It may be that we can answer, "YES." Very frequently anger is the madman's firebrand, but sometimes it is Elijah's fire from heaven. We do well when we are angry with sin, because of the wrong which it commits against our good and gracious God; or with ourselves because we remain so foolish after so much divine instruction; or with others when the sole cause of anger is the evil which they do. He who is not angry at transgression becomes a partaker in it. Sin is a loathsome and hateful thing, and no renewed heart can patiently endure it. God himself is angry with the wicked every day, and it is written in His Word, "Ye that love the Lord, hate evil." Far more frequently

it is to be feared that our anger is not commendable or even justifiable, and then we must answer, "NO." Why should we be fretful with children, passionate with servants, and wrathful with companions? Is such anger honorable to our Christian profession, or glorifying to God? Is it not the old evil heart seeking to gain dominion, and should we not resist it with all the might of our newborn nature. Many professors give way to temper as though it were useless to attempt resistance; but let the believer remember that he must be a conqueror in every point, or else he cannot be crowned. If we cannot control our tempers, what has grace done for us? Someone told Mr. Jay that grace was often grafted on a crab-stump. "Yes," said he, "but the fruit will not be crabs." We must not make natural infirmity an excuse for sin, but we must fly to the cross and pray the Lord to crucify our tempers, and renew us in gentleness and meekness after His own image.[25]

---

25 From Spurgeon's Morning & Evening, PC Study Bible formatted electronic database Copyright © 1999, 2003, 2006 by Biblesoft, Inc. All rights reserved.

Questions to Consider

The Dangerous Sin of Anger!
Matthew 5:21-26

1. (a) According to Matthew 5:21-26, what was the penalty for someone who committed murder? (b) What does Jesus say the penalty is for someone who is angry?

2. Memorize Matthew 5:22.

3. (a) As you read the following passages, put them into a category of righteous anger or unrighteous anger: Genesis 4:4-6; Genesis 30:1-2; Exodus 4:1-14; Exodus 32:19-21; Numbers 25:6-13; 1 Samuel 17:26-29; 1 Samuel 18:8-9; 2 Samuel 6:6-8; Esther 3:1-6; Psalm 7:11; Daniel 3:16-19; Jonah 3:10-4:11; Mark 3:1-5; John 2:13-17; Ephesians 4:26; James 1:19-20. (b) After reading these passages, summarize what righteous anger is and what unrighteous anger is.

4. (a) What did Paul do before salvation, according to Acts 9:1? (b) According to what Paul wrote later after his conversion in Galatians 5:19-21, what would have happened to him had he not repented? (c) What is Paul's response to God's redemptive grace, according to 1 Timothy 1:12-17?

5. (a) What does the Bible say about anger in Psalm 37:8; Proverbs 15:1; Proverbs 16:32; Proverbs 19:11; Ephesians 4:31; Colossians 3:8? (b) How do you personally fight this sin in your life? (c) What should we put on in place of anger? See Galatians 5:22-23 and Colossians 3:12-17 for some ideas.

6. (a) Do you think it is ever right to kill someone? Prove your answer biblically. (For some help, read Numbers 35.) (b) Do you think someone who commits murder against themselves (suicide) will go to heaven?

7. Are you easily frustrated with others? Do you make excuses for your irritation and anger by blaming others? Blaming your hormones? Blaming your circumstances? What would Christ have us do in these situations? Write a request for prayer as you think through these questions.

**Recommended reading: *The Art of Divine Contentment*, by Thomas Watson. We must put off anger; we must put on contentment.

Chapter 6

Passion or Purity?

Matthew 5:27-32

You may have noticed the title to this lesson—"Passion *or* Purity"— and thought, "That sounds familiar." Indeed, it does, if you're familiar with the writings of the late Elisabeth Elliot. Of all that Mrs. Elliot wrote, her book *Passion and Purity* stands out as a must-read for all who desire to be pure in their dating relationships. Her writings, and the principles she distills in them, would do us well to be heeded not only in dating and courting but also in marriage, especially as they relate to lust. She says in her book, "The majority will sacrifice anything—security, honor, self-respect, the welfare of people they love, obedience to God—to passion. They will even tell themselves that they are obeying God (or at least He doesn't mind) and congratulate themselves for being so free, so released, so courageous, so honest and 'up front'… a good and perfect gift, these natural desires. But so much the more necessary that they be restrained, controlled, corrected, even crucified, that they might be reborn in power and purity for God."[26] Notice the words she uses— honor, obedience, control, restrain, crucify—all for purity. These words and thoughts seem so archaic to us in the 21st century. In the area of sexual purity, we have replaced honor with dishonor; obedience with disobedience; control for out-of-control; restrain with unrestraint; and crucify with anything goes! And now, my friend, we are paying for it dearly with the recent U.S. Supreme Court ruling in favor of same sex marriage. We will soon be known for more than the "sexual revolution"; I fear we will be known for the "sexual perversion," as now the door has been opened wide for any kind of sexual expression!

Regardless of what is happening in the world today, those who are

---

26 Elisabeth Elliot, *Passion and Purity* (Tarrytown: Fleming H. Revell Co., 1984), 68.

kingdom citizens are called to crucify the flesh with its passions and desires, as Paul says in Galatians 5:24. Jesus, too, emphasizes this very thing, as He lays out some powerful words on sexual purity for those listening to His Sermon on the Mount, in Matthew 5:27-32. Let's read these words together.

Matthew 5:27-32

> You have heard that it was said to those of old, "You shall not commit adultery." [28]But I say to you that whoever looks at a woman to lust for her has already committed adultery with her in his heart. [29]If your right eye causes you to sin, pluck it out and cast it from you; for it is more profitable for you that one of your members perish, than for your whole body to be cast into hell. [30]And if your right hand causes you to sin, cut it off and cast it from you; for it is more profitable for you that one of your members perish, than for your whole body to be cast into hell. [31]Furthermore it has been said, "Whoever divorces his wife, let him give her a certificate of divorce." [32]But I say to you that whoever divorces his wife for any reason except sexual immorality causes her to commit adultery; and whoever marries a woman who is divorced commits adultery. (Matthew 5:27-32)

Our outline for this lesson will include:

> *The Sin of Adultery* (vv 27-28)
>
> *The Solution for Adultery* (vv 29-30)
>
> *The Sin of Divorce* (vv 31-32)

In our last lesson, we saw the dangerous sin of anger and learned that it is a sin Jesus equates with murder and that it is a sin worthy of hell. We then learned that the divine solution for anger is to reconcile and reconcile quickly. Jesus now turns from teaching about the sin of anger to yet another sin, the sin of adultery. Let's consider what He says about the sin of adultery in verse 27 and 28.

The Sin of Adultery

Matthew 5:27-28

> You have heard that it was said to those of old, "You shall not commit adultery." (Matthew 5:27)

Jesus repeats what He said before in verse 21, that is, *you have heard that is was said to those of old*. Only this time He speaks of adultery and not anger. We learned in our last lesson that this phrase is a reference to what was taught in the Old Testament, along with what was taught by the religious leaders of the day. The command to *not commit adultery* would have been known and taught by the religious leaders. Exodus 20:14 states, "You shall not commit adultery." Adultery was not only forbidden, but the punishment for adultery was death, according to Leviticus 20:10: "The man who commits adultery with another man's wife, he who commits adultery with his neighbor's wife, the adulterer and the adulteress, shall surely be put to death."

Since we are talking about the sin of adultery, we should define it. What is adultery? *Adultery* is any sexual relationship that takes place with someone else besides your spouse. It might be heterosexual adultery, homosexual adultery, or some other perversion, but any sexual relationship that is with someone else besides your spouse is adultery. The Scribes and Pharisees were exemplary in their keeping of the law, and they wouldn't even have given thought to committing adultery. But, my friend, adultery doesn't begin with the act; it begins with something else. Jesus was wise enough to know that and so should we! Notice what He says in verse 28.

> But I say to you that whoever looks at a woman to lust for her has already committed adultery with her in his heart. (Matthew 5:28)

Unlike the self-righteous religious leaders, Jesus is wise enough to know that adultery begins in the heart. (Remember, the first moral illustration, the "greater stands for the lesser.") Adultery can take place by simply looking and lusting. Though there may not be the outward act of adultery, there can still be an inward act of adultery in the mind. Remember this: Man examines outwardly; God examines inwardly. Perhaps the religious leaders forgot this fact or perhaps they chose to ignore it, like many of us do. We think that we can look and lust all we want and that no one knows we desire another person who isn't ours to desire, but God knows, and it is He who will be the Judge on that final day. Most of us know and can recall that one of the Ten Commandments says we should not commit adultery, but we have forgotten the one that says you shall not covet your neighbor's wife and the one that says we should keep our vows (See Exodus 20). When we get married, we make vows (hopefully) that say we will be true to one another in sickness and in health and we will be true to one another till we're parted by death. To not keep that vow is a lie before God and others. I am sure it is not "by chance" that in verses 33-37 Jesus will warn us about breaking vows. Marriage is a vow before God and others.

Jesus raises the bar here, and He lets His audience know that it's not just the act of adultery that will condemn us but it is the look that will condemn us. Jesus says *whoever looks*, meaning that no one is exempt, not even the religious Scribes and Pharisees, and not even women! We're not off the hook just because Jesus refers to men looking at women. Women are quite capable of lusting after men.

Since lust is so awful, just what is it? To *lust* means to set your heart upon something to long for it. It also has the idea of not just taking a look but an ongoing and repeated looking. There is nothing wrong with noticing a nice-looking woman—or a man in our case—but that should be as far as it goes. For example, for King David, there was nothing wrong with him noticing that Bathsheba was beautiful, but that is where it should have stopped. We must look at others as people for whom Christ died, not as objects of our lust. One commentator writes, "The man's very heart and nature must be so changed by divine grace that lustful looks will become impossible for him."[27]

---

27 R. C. H. Lenski, *Commentary on the New Testament: The Interpretation of St.*

Those who are looking and lusting after someone who is not theirs to have (and this includes pornography), Jesus says, *has already committed adultery ... in his [or her] heart*. In other words, you may not have committed the outward act, but you have committed the inward act in your heart, in your thoughts and your feelings. Remember, as a man thinks in his heart so is he (Proverbs 23:7). "Imagination is a God-given gift, but if it is fed dirt by the eye, it will be dirty."[28] In 2 Peter 2:14, Peter says of false teachers that they have eyes full of adultery. They may not commit the act in the flesh, but they commit it in the heart.

As already mentioned, the punishment for adultery was death. The punishment for lust is also death. This statement may be as shocking to you as it was to Jesus' audience. But, remember, Jesus has already said that unless your righteousness *exceeds* that of the Scribes and Pharisees, you will not enter into heaven (Matthew 5:20). Jesus isn't just looking for the outward but for the inward, which is what needs to be changed in us. Once the inner heart is transformed, the outward follows. Lust is serious; it describes our old man, not our new man. Consider these passages (all emphases are mine): Titus 3:3-7,

> For we ourselves were also *once* foolish, disobedient, deceived, serving various lusts and pleasures, living in malice and envy, hateful and hating one another. But when the kindness and the love of God our Savior toward man appeared, not by works of righteousness which we have done, but according to His mercy He saved us, through the washing of regeneration and renewing of the Holy Spirit, whom He poured out on us abundantly through Jesus Christ our Savior, that having been justified by His grace we should become heirs according to the hope of eternal life.

And Ephesians 2:3-5 says,

> ... among whom also we all *once conducted* ourselves in the lusts of our flesh, fulfilling the desires of the flesh and of the

Matthew's Gospel (Peabody: Hendrickson Publishers, 2001), 226.
28 D. A. Carson, *The Expositors Bible Commentary: Matthew, Mark, Luke* (Grand Rapids: Zondervan, 1984), 151.

mind, and were by nature children of wrath, just as the others. *But God*, who is rich in mercy, because of His great love with which He loved us, even when we were dead in trespasses, made us alive together with Christ (by grace you have been saved).

There are so many passages that deal with this, but another one we simply can't wiggle out of is 1 John 2:15-17,

Do not love the world or the things in the world. If anyone loves the world, the love of the Father is not in him. For all that is in the world—*the lust of the flesh*, the lust of the eyes, and the pride of life—is *not of the Father* but is of the world. And the world is passing away, and the lust of it; but he who does the will of God abides forever.

The sin of adultery is serious, as you can see. It includes not just the physical act but the lustful look, as well. Both are considered acts of adultery. So, what should one do if he or she is committing adultery with their body or even in their heart? What action needs to take place? Jesus tells us in the next verse what we must do. Here we have the solution for adultery.

The Solution for Adultery

Matthew 5:29-30

If your right eye causes you to sin, pluck it out and cast it from you; for it is more profitable for you that one of your members perish, than for your whole body to be cast into hell. (Matthew 5:29)

Jesus says instead of lusting with your eyes, pluck out your eye if it's causing you to sin. The word *eye* means a jealous side glance. The phrase *causes you to sin* means to stumble, to entrap, to trip up. So, if your eye is tripping you up, *pluck it out and cast it from you*. This means to tear it out and throw it away. Perhaps you're thinking that this seems a bit extreme. My friend, Jesus means business about sin even though most of us don't! Jesus is not calling for self-mutilation—otherwise we all would be eyeless, limbless, and even brainless—but He is calling for self-mortification. Cutting off members of our bodies does not take care of our hearts. A blind man can still lust, even though he has no eyes. We must mortify the deeds of our flesh. Paul says in Colossians 3:5-7, "Therefore put to death your members which are on the earth: fornication, uncleanness, passion, evil desire, and covetousness, which is idolatry. Because of these things the wrath of God is coming upon the sons of disobedience, in which you yourselves once walked when you lived in them." *Put to death* comes from the word mortify, which means to deaden, to subdue, to be in the process of killing. We are unable to actually kill our fleshly members once and for all, because that would mean that after such an act we would never be tempted by them again. But we do mortify them in the sense that we consider them dying, we consider them to be in the weakened state that no longer dominates us.[29] *Put to death* is the word mortify, which means to deaden, to subdue, to kill. Ladies, we are to make a corpse of our sin; we are to deprive it of its power and strength. The Greek tense here in Colossians indicates that we are to do it now. We do not have the luxury of being apathetic about sin in our lives, and that is Jesus' point here in the Sermon on the Mount. Paul knew the seriousness of this in his own life; he writes in 1 Corinthians 9:27, "But I discipline my body and bring it into subjection, lest, when I have preached to others, I myself should become disqualified." Job, who was the most righteous man in his day, even knew about mortifying his flesh, as he says in Job 31:1, "I have made a covenant with my eyes; why then should I look upon a young woman?" The idea is that we do whatever it takes to be radical about putting off sin. Maybe, for some of you, you need to throw out your television, your smart phone, or your tablet.

---

29 One of the more helpful books on this subject is the classic by Puritan John Owen, *The Mortification of Sin*, where he wisely explains that the imagery means putting the flesh to death, not killing it. When a person is in the process of dying, their strength is weakening and so their flesh is no longer dominating. Hence, in Jesus' analogy here, He is not commanding that if a believer lusts they should literally pluck out their eyes but rather that they should consider those members unable to dominate the thoughts—consider yourself dead to the lure of your eyes.

Maybe you are thinking, "Now, Susan, you're being extreme. Why should I do this? I mean, I kind of enjoy porn and saucy novels and imagining being married to the guy next door or the guy on the big screen. Quit messing with my fun!" Well, Jesus tells you why you must put these things to death and it has to do with your eternal state. He says *it is more profitable for you*, which means it is better for you, *that one of your members perish, than for your whole body to be cast into hell*. It is better for you that one of your bodily functions be destroyed than your entire body be cast into eternal hell. In Matthew 18:9, Jesus says something similar, "And if your eye causes you to sin, pluck it out and cast it from you. It is better for you to enter into life with one eye, rather than having two eyes, to be cast into hell fire." Is the sin you are enslaved to today worth your eternal soul? Oh, that we would have the mindset of Moses, of whom it is said in Hebrews 11:25, that he chose "rather to suffer affliction with the people of God than to enjoy the passing pleasures of sin." Likewise, Jesus mentions another member of our body that we might need to be rid of in verse 30.

> And if your right hand causes you to sin, cut it off and cast it from you; for it is more profitable for you that one of your members perish, than for your whole body to be cast into hell. (Matthew 5:30)

Jesus repeats what He has just said in verse 29, only this time He speaks of the right hand as the part of our body that needs to be put to death. It is interesting that He mentions the eye and then the hand, because it is with our eyes that we do most of our lusting and then with our hands we carry out that lust to take something that is not ours. You will see this in the Questions to Consider at the end of this lesson. The mention of it being the *right eye* and the *right hand* could be because those are the most dominant in most people. The right hand and the right eye are also usually the strongest, perhaps indicating that these two members we hold to be so precious should be eradicated, if need be, in order to preserve our souls. We might lust with our eyes and then use our hands to turn on the TV to watch inappropriate television or movies. We might use our hands to turn the key in the car to go to the theater where there are sexually provocative movies. We might use our hands to search on our phone or computer for porn. Jesus says *cut it off and cast it from you!* And He gives the same reason used for gouging out the eye: that it is better to go heaven with a few limbs missing than to hell with an entire body intact.

We need to be as serious about sexual sin as Joseph was when tempted by Potiphar's wife; he fled and got out. As Spurgeon said, "Better to leave my cloak than lose my character."[30] Paul tells us in Romans 6:12-14, "Therefore do not let sin reign in your mortal body, that you should obey it in its lusts. And do not present your members as instruments of unrighteousness to sin, but present yourselves to God as being alive from the dead, and your members as instruments of righteousness to God. For sin shall not have dominion over you, for you are not under law but under grace." I once read of a woman who was so serious about ridding herself of gossip that she refused to talk on the phone for 3 months till she had mortified that particular deed of her flesh.

The solution for adultery or lust is to put to death whatever the instrument of that sin is. This means you must be serious about your sin and you must be serious about putting it off. You must do whatever it takes. If you are attracted to your boss at work, quit your job. If you are struggling with being attracted to another man at church or some other place, then you avoid that man until you can start looking at him as a brother in Christ and not as an object of your lust. If you have issues with porn or fantasizing at the movies, then stop going to movies and throw all electronic devises in the trash. That's what Jesus is saying!

Some who were sitting on the mount with Jesus, and some of you, might be thinking, "Okay, I see how serious adultery is, I see how serious lust is, so I think I'll just divorce my spouse and marry this other person that I'm finding attractive right now. If I marry him or her that will make everything right." Well, Jesus says something

30 Charles Haddon Spurgeon, *Morning and Evening*; July 25; PC study Software.

drastically different in verses 31 and 32. We now turn to the sin of divorce.

The Sin of Divorce

Matthew 5:31-32

> Furthermore it has been said, "Whoever divorces his wife, let him give her a certificate of divorce." (Matthew 5:31)

Jesus reminds His listeners again of something that was said of old: if you are going to divorce your wife, then give her a certificate of divorce. This was taken from Deuteronomy 24:1 which says, "When a man takes a wife and marries her, and it happens that she finds no favor in his eyes because he has found some uncleanness in her, and he writes her a certificate of divorce, puts it in her hand, and sends her out of his house ...." There were two schools of thought on this passage in the Jewish world of Jesus' day. One said that a husband could divorce his wife if he found anything displeasing or indecent about her. This is how they would interpret the phrase "some uncleanness in her." It could be burning his dinner, speaking to men on the street, wearing her hair down, or a myriad of other ridiculous things (this was the school of Hillel). This is about as ridiculous as our laws today; we can divorce for just about anything. The United States allows divorce for irretrievable breakdown of the marriage, irreconcilable differences, incompatibility, adultery, cruelty, abandonment, mental illness, criminal conviction, drug abuse, impotency, and religious reasons. But there was another school of thought in Jesus' day (the school of Shammai), which said that the reference to a wife being displeasing or indecent had to do with sexual sins or something sexually inappropriate, and that was the only thing for which one could pursue divorce. What is so odd is that both schools of thought missed the whole idea of the Mosaic Law in Deuteronomy 24:1-4. There, we read, "When a man takes a wife and marries her, and it happens that she finds no favor in his eyes because he has found some uncleanness in her, and he writes her a certificate of divorce, puts it in her hand, and sends her out of his house, when she has departed from his house, and goes and becomes another man's wife, if the latter husband detests her and writes her a certificate of divorce, puts it in her hand, and sends her out of his house, or if the latter husband dies who took her as his wife, then her former husband who divorced her must not take her back to be his wife after she has been defiled; for that is an abomination before the Lord, and you shall not bring sin on the land which the Lord your God is giving you as an inheritance." The whole point is in this passage that if you divorce your spouse and marry another person and that person dies, you can't go back to the first spouse as that is an abomination to the Lord. In fact, in Matthew 19:3-10, we have an account of the Pharisees trying to trip Jesus up regarding the laws of divorce.

> The Pharisees also came to Him, testing Him, and saying to Him, "Is it lawful for a man to divorce his wife for just any reason?" And He answered and said to them, "Have you not read that He who made them at the beginning 'made them male and female,' and said, 'For this reason a man shall leave his father and mother and be joined to his wife, and the two shall become one flesh'? So then, they are no longer two but one flesh. Therefore what God has joined together, let not man separate." They said to Him, "Why then did Moses command to give a certificate of divorce, and to put her away?" He said to them, "Moses, because of the hardness of your hearts, permitted you to divorce your wives, but from the beginning it was not so. And I say to you, whoever divorces his wife, except for sexual immorality, and marries another, commits adultery; and whoever marries her who is divorced commits adultery." His disciples said to Him, "If such is the case of the man with his wife, it is better not to marry." (Matthew 19:3-10)

Jesus didn't let the Pharisees off the hook with their silly reasons for divorcing their wives, and neither should we let people off the hook for ridiculous reasons for divorce. Divorce was never God's intention; in fact, we know from Malachi 2:16 that God hates divorce. Jesus says, in Luke 16:18, "Whoever divorces his wife and marries another commits adultery; and whoever marries her who is divorced from her husband commits adultery." So, Jesus sets those straight who are sitting on the mountainside, by saying in verse 32,

> But I say to you that whoever divorces his wife for any reason
> except sexual immorality causes her to commit adultery; and
> whoever marries a woman who is divorced commits adultery.
> (Matthew 5:32)

Simply put, Jesus says, if you divorce your spouse for *any reason
except sexual immorality* you *cause* him or her *to commit adultery*.
The word for *sexual immorality* is the Greek term porneia, from which
we get our English word pornography. This word encompasses any
type of sexual sin: incest, adultery, bestiality, and any other sexually
perverse thing.

Now, Jesus is permitting divorce here, but He is not commanding
it. God hates divorce, as we have already mentioned, and it was
never in His plan for His creation. Just because there is marital
infidelity doesn't mean you automatically pursue a divorce. I would
counsel such a one to remain in the marriage and to begin actively
working on their marriage in hopes of restoring it. But if there is no
repentance on the part of the guilty spouse, then Jesus does permit
divorce. Paul also gives ground for divorce in 1 Corinthians 7:10-
16, when he says,

> Now to the married I command, yet not I but the Lord: A wife
> is not to depart from her husband. But even if she does depart,
> let her remain unmarried or be reconciled to her husband. And a
> husband is not to divorce his wife. But to the rest I, not the Lord,
> say: If any brother has a wife who does not believe, and she is
> willing to live with him, let him not divorce her. And a woman
> who has a husband who does not believe, if he is willing to live
> with her, let her not divorce him. For the unbelieving husband
> is sanctified by the wife, and the unbelieving wife is sanctified
> by the husband; otherwise your children would be unclean, but
> now they are holy. But if the unbeliever departs, let him depart;
> a brother or a sister is not under bondage in such cases. But God
> has called us to peace. For how do you know, O wife, whether
> you will save your husband? Or how do you know, O husband,
> whether you will save your wife?

The ground for divorce here is this: if your unbelieving spouse
wants to leave you, you let him go because God has called you to

peace. But, again, I would encourage you to make every effort to remain married, if at all possible. To what He has just said regarding divorce, Jesus adds that if you marry a person *who is divorced*, then you *commit adultery*. So, if you marry a person whose divorce is not biblically permissible, then you are both committing adultery.

As we bring this lesson to a close, I want to be crystal clear that the sins of adultery, lust and divorce are forgivable. There is no sin that God will not forgive. However, God's Word is clear that those things are from our past. Consider 1 Corinthians 6:9-11: "Do you not know that the unrighteous will not inherit the kingdom of God? Do not be deceived. Neither fornicators, nor idolaters, nor adulterers, nor homosexuals, nor sodomites, nor thieves, nor covetous, nor drunkards, nor revilers, nor extortioners will inherit the kingdom of God. And such *were* some of you. But you were washed, but you were sanctified, but you were justified in the name of the Lord Jesus and by the Spirit of our God" (emphasis mine). Also, Galatians 5:19-21, "Now the works of the flesh are evident, which are: adultery, fornication, uncleanness, lewdness, idolatry, sorcery, hatred, contentions, jealousies, outbursts of wrath, selfish ambitions, dissensions, heresies, envy, murders, drunkenness, revelries, and the like; of which I tell you beforehand, just as I also told you in time past, that those who practice such things will not inherit the kingdom of God."

Summary

So, what about divorce? Is it a sin? We know God hates it and that what He has joined together we are not to put asunder. However, there are some circumstances in which divorce is permissible, according to the Scriptures. One is in the case of sexual immorality and the other is in the case of an unbeliever departing. But, again, I would be cautious about recommending divorce to anyone without first exhausting all possible means of reconciliation.

We cannot afford to dabble in sin; we must kill it the moment it raises its ugly head. Billy Sunday once said, "Listen, I'm against sin. I'll kick it as long as I've got a foot, I'll fight it as long as I've got a fist, I'll butt it as long as I've got a head, and I'll bite it as long as I've got a tooth. And when I'm old, fistless, footless, and toothless, I'll gum it till I go home to glory and it goes home to perdition."[31] I hope that describes your fight against sin this day. As John Owen once said, "Do you mortify? Do you make it your daily work? Be always at it whilst you live; cease not a day from this work; be killing sin or it will be killing you."[32]

---

31 Andrew Himes, *The Sword of the Lord* (Seattle: Chiara Press, 2011), 111.
32 John Owen, *The Mortification of Sin in Believers* (Religious Tract Society, 1842), 9.

Questions to Consider

Passion or Purity?
Matthew 5:27-32

1. (a) Read Matthew 5:27-32. What are the sins that Jesus mentions in this passage? (b) What are the solutions to these sins?

2. Memorize Matthew 5:27-28.

3. (a) What are the ways to avoid adultery according to what Solomon tells his son in Proverbs 5, 6 and 7? (b) How does Solomon describe the adulterous woman in these chapters? (c) What practical things can we do in the 21st century to guard ourselves from the sin of adultery?

4. (a) What happened in each of the following passages when the sin of lusting took place? Genesis 34:1-4; Genesis 39:7-23; 2 Samuel 11:1-5 (b) What should have been done in each of these stories? (c) What should we do when we realize that lust is taking place in our hearts? (This can be sexual lust or other kinds of lust.)

5 (a) What does God think about divorce, according to Malachi 2:15-16? (b) How does this reconcile with what Jesus says in Matthew 5:31-32 and what Paul says in 1 Corinthians 7:10-16? (c) How would you counsel a woman whose husband verbally threatens her or physically abuses her? (d) How would you counsel her if he doesn't provide for her or doesn't lead her spiritually?

6. (a) How do you personally deal with temptation, whether sexual or otherwise? (b) What are some practical things that one can do to guard his or her eyes?

7. First Corinthians 10:12 tells us to take heed lest we fall. Therefore, no one is exempt from sexual temptation. With that in mind, please write a prayer for yourself asking God to protect and help you in this area.

Chapter 7

Truth or Consequences!

Matthew 5:33-37

One of the joys of being on the radio is that I get emails from ladies all over the world. The summer before I wrote this lesson, I received several emails from women in Belgium, Peru, India, and Pakistan, just to name a few. Many of these women live in countries where there are few believers and little, if any, sound teaching. Because of this, many of them have lots of questions. One particular email this past summer caught my eye, as it pertained to one of the verses we are covering in this lesson. The email was quite lengthy and so I won't share it all, but only the portion which pertains to this lesson.

> Well, sorry if I'm writing too much, I will go to the point. I have disregarded many of the prohibitions of my former church as false teachings. But there are some of which I'm not so sure. They considered dyeing hair a sin. I'm not so young now (almost 40) and my hair is still black but is becoming gray. I think in the USA it is different, but here in Lima, Peru, the majority of women dye their hair, unless they are very poor or from some Pentecostal churches, or very, very old. Sometimes I feel a little ashamed. I have to find a new job soon and I think my hair could be an issue. But I don't want to offend my God, nor go against my conscience. I have read arguments in every way about this, and I have been thinking that maybe I could have been too legalistic. Maybe you know some of the arguments. I would mention Matthew 5:36, Proverbs 16:31, and Irenaeus wrote against makeup. Please, you are a Bible teacher and a woman and I think you can help me to clarify this

issue. Sorry again if I take your time for such an issue. God bless you abundantly.

One of the verses this young woman cites, Matthew 5:36, is part of our text for this lesson. What did Jesus mean when He said, "Nor shall you swear by your head, because you cannot make one hair white or black"? Let's read the passage together and discover what Jesus meant by these words.

Matthew 5:33-37

> Again you have heard that it was said to those of old, "You shall not swear falsely, but shall perform your oaths to the Lord." [34]But I say to you, do not swear at all: neither by heaven, for it is God's throne; [35]nor by the earth, for it is His footstool; nor by Jerusalem, for it is the city of the great King. [36]Nor shall you swear by your head, because you cannot make one hair white or black. [37]But let your "Yes" be "Yes," and your "No," "No." For whatever is more than these is from the evil one. (Matthew 5:33-37)

As we consider our topic, *Truth or Consequences*, we will consider a three-fold outline:

The Command to Not Lie (v 33)
Creative Ways of Lying (vv 34-36)
The Consequence of Lying (v 37)

In our last lesson, we discovered the dangerous sin of adultery and lust, as Jesus equates lusting with committing adultery. We then learned that the solution for adultery (or really any sin) is to be radical about it; we must do whatever it takes to mortify the deeds of our flesh. Then, lastly, we considered that divorce also is a sin, unless it is within a context that God allows; that is, in this particular passage, when there has been sexual sin on the part of the spouse. Jesus has been raising the bar and telling His audience that outward sins of murder and adultery are equal to inner attitudes of anger and lust. Jesus says they are all sinful, as the inner man is equally as important as the outer man; the inner heart most often indicates what the outward actions will be. In the verses we will consider in this lesson, Jesus continues on with yet another concerning sin, that of making oaths or promises that you have no intention of keeping. Let's consider, first of all, the command to not lie.

The Command to Not Lie

Matthew 5:33

> Again you have heard that it was said to those of old, "You shall not swear falsely, but shall perform your oaths to the Lord." (Matthew 5:33)

Once again Jesus calls His listeners' attention to something they have heard that *was said to those of old.* He has said this same thing in verses 21 and 27 regarding the sins of murder and adultery. This time, however, He says they have heard that they *shall not swear falsely, but perform [their] oaths to the Lord.* In order to understand what Jesus is saying we need to define what it means to swear falsely as well as define what it means to perform oaths. The phrases *swear falsely* and *perform oaths* come from two different Greek words. To *swear falsely* means to make false vows. In other words, you are saying that you will do something but you have no intention of doing it. Peter is a good example of someone who appears to have sworn falsely. In Matthew 26:35, he promises the Lord that he would never deny Him. But then in Matthew 26:69-75, just 34 verses later, we read: "Now Peter sat outside in the courtyard. And a servant girl came to him, saying, 'You also were with Jesus of Galilee.' But he denied it before them all, saying, 'I do not know what you are saying.' And when he had gone out to the gateway, another girl saw him and said to those who were there, 'This fellow also was with Jesus of Nazareth.' But again he denied with an oath, 'I do not know the Man!' And a little later those who stood by came up and said to Peter, 'Surely you also are one of them, for your speech betrays you.' Then he began to curse and swear, saying, 'I do not know the Man!' Immediately a rooster crowed. And Peter remembered the word of Jesus who had said to him, 'Before the rooster crows, you will deny Me three times.' So he went out and wept bitterly." No doubt Peter had full intentions of keeping his vow to Jesus, but in the end he didn't keep it, and therefore he swore falsely. He lied and said he did not know Jesus when in fact he did. Some people think that swearing falsely is cussing, but that is not the meaning of the word. Interestingly enough, in this passage in Matthew 26, Peter both curses and swears. Cussing, or cursing, is certainly not a good idea, either, but that really has nothing to do with our task in Matthew 5.

Performing oaths means to enclose or bind together. An *oath* then would be something binding, something you could not get out of unless divinely hindered. Making an oath or a covenant with someone is not forbidden in Scripture but actually encouraged. We have the examples of Abraham and his servant in Genesis 24, and David and Jonathan in 1 Samuel 18, along with many others. Additionally, we have the example of Jephthah in Judges 11, who vowed to the Lord that if the Lord would deliver the Ammonites into his hands, he would offer the first thing that came out of his home to meet him. Of course, that ended up being his daughter. Some have said that this was a rash vow, but that's another debate for another time! Even God has made oaths, and I, for one, am glad He has. The writer to the Hebrews states in Hebrews 6:17-20, "Thus God, determining to show more abundantly to the heirs of promise the immutability of His counsel, confirmed it by an oath, that by two immutable things, in which it is impossible for God to lie, we might have strong consolation, who have fled for refuge to lay hold of the hope set before us. This hope we have as an anchor of the soul, both sure and steadfast, and which enters the Presence behind the veil, where the forerunner has entered for us, even Jesus, having become High Priest forever according to the order of Melchizedek." The whole point in all of this is to validate that making oaths and vows is not forbidden, but what is forbidden is doing so falsely, that is, with deception, knowing that you have no intention of keeping your word.

Perhaps you're wondering where this idea is found, when Jesus says *you have heard that it was said to those of old*. This is actually not a direct quote from the Old Testament, like the commands on murder and adultery, but it is an insinuation from some specific Old Testament passages. The first is found in Exodus 20:7: "You shall not take the name of the Lord your God in vain, for the Lord will not hold him guiltless who takes His name in vain." Leviticus 19:11-12 states, "You shall not steal, nor deal falsely, nor lie to one another. And you shall not swear by My name falsely, nor shall you profane the name of your God: I am the Lord." Then, there is Deuteronomy 23:21-23, "When you make a vow to the Lord your God, you shall not delay to pay it; for the Lord your God will surely require it of you, and it would be sin to you. But if you abstain from vowing, it shall not be sin to you. That which has gone from your lips you shall keep and perform, for you voluntarily vowed to the Lord your God what you have promised with your mouth."

The command not to lie is simple. Instead of swearing falsely—not doing what I have promised to do—I am to perform that which I say I will do. I perform my oaths unto the Lord. Now, just as they did with adultery and murder, the Pharisees had some fancy ways of getting out of doing what they said they would do. Jesus confronts them in the next few verses by shattering their creative ways of lying. We, too, have developed some creative ways of not fulfilling what we say we will do. Call it what you like, but it is really lying. We turn in our text from the command to not lie to consider some creative ways of lying. And Jesus doesn't give these as positive examples, but as examples that are not to be followed. Let's consider their first creative deception in verse 34.

Creative Ways of Lying

Matthew 5:34-36

But I say to you, do not swear at all: neither by heaven, for it is God's throne; (Matthew 5:34)

After affirming that they have heard that they are not to swear falsely but to perform their oaths to God, Jesus says, *but*—which is a contrast to what He just said—*I say to you, do not swear at all.* At first, this might seem like a contradiction when Jesus say *do not swear at all.* But this swearing *at all* is defined by the creative ways they found to make oaths. Jesus is not forbidding vows or oaths, but He is forbidding making them with no intention of fulfilling them, or doing some kind of spiritual gymnastics to justify getting oneself out of fulfilling them. And, once again, this swearing is not to be confused with cussing, even though it's a good idea to cut that out of your vocabulary. Some religious sects take this verse and use it as a proof text for why they will not swear in a court of law. Is this what Jesus means? No, otherwise Jesus would have sinned as it states in Matthew 26:62-64, "And the high priest arose and said to Him, 'Do You answer nothing? What is it these men testify against You?' But Jesus kept silent. And the high priest answered and said to Him, 'I put You under oath by the living God: Tell us if you are the Christ, the Son of God!' Jesus said to him, 'It is as you said. Nevertheless, I say to you, hereafter you will see the Son of Man sitting at the right hand of the Power, and coming on the clouds of heaven.'" Additionally, you would have to do away with Deuteronomy 10:20, which says, "You shall fear the Lord your God; you shall serve Him, and to Him you shall hold fast, and take oaths in His name." One commentator helps us here,

> Unfortunately ... by Jesus' time the Jews had built up an entire legalistic system around the Old Testament teaching. In the Jewish code of law called the *Mishnah*, there is one whole tractate given over to the question of oaths, including detailed consideration of when they're binding and when they're not. For example, one rabbi says that if you swear *by* Jerusalem you are not bound by your vow; but if you swear *toward* Jerusalem, then you are bound by your vow. The swearing of oaths thus degenerates into terrible rules which let you know when you can get away with lying and deception, and when you can't. These oaths

no longer foster truthfulness, but weaken the cause of truth and promote deceit. Swearing evasively becomes justification for lying."[33]

Jesus confronts this notion in Matthew 23:16-22, "Woe to you, blind guides, who say, 'Whoever swears by the temple, it is nothing; but whoever swears by the gold of the temple, he is obliged to perform it.' Fools and blind! For which is greater, the gold or the temple that sanctifies the gold? And, 'Whoever swears by the altar, it is nothing; but whoever swears by the gift that is on it, he is obliged to perform it.' Fools and blind! For which is greater, the gift or the altar that sanctifies the gift? Therefore he who swears by the altar, swears by it and by all things on it. He who swears by the temple, swears by it and by Him who dwells in it. And he who swears by heaven, swears by the throne of God and by Him who sits on it." The religious leaders were known for making numerous vows, but they were careful not to swear by God because then, they reasoned, that oath would be binding. They were taking their vows lightly and wiggling out of them by silly rigamaroo ideas that Jesus confronts both in Matthew 23 and here in Matthew 5!

When Jesus says *do not swear at all*, He is referencing the following creative ways they would do that. The Scribes and Pharisees had invented a method, so to speak, whereby they could squirm around their oaths; their oaths would not be binding if they did reference God's name. Because of that thinking, the first creative way the Pharisees would swear was *by heaven*. Why should I not swear by heaven? Because *it is God's throne*. Heaven is the place where God dwells. It is His throne, that is, where He sits. There are many passages which give weight to this fact, but Isaiah 66:1 is clear: "Thus says the Lord: 'Heaven is My throne, and earth is My footstool. Where is the house that you will build Me? And where is the place of My rest?" The religious leaders would say, "Well, I won't swear or make a promise to or by God, but I'll do it by heaven and then if I can't fulfill it I am not bound by my oath." But Jesus says that's crazy

33 D. A. Carson, *The Sermon on the Mount: An Evangelical Exposition of Matthew 5-7* (Grand Rapids: Baker Book House, 1978), 47.

because heaven is where God's throne is. That is where He dwells. To swear by heaven is to swear by Him. In verse 35, Jesus mentions two more creative ways of making oaths, which the Pharisees would use to prevent them from being bound to their oaths.

> nor by the earth, for it is His footstool; nor by Jerusalem, for it is the city of the great King. (Matthew 5:35)

The second creative way was to swear *by the earth*. Why can't one swear by the earth? Because *it is God's footstool*. Again Isaiah 66:1 helps us, "Thus says the Lord: 'Heaven is My throne, And earth is My footstool. Where is the house that you will build Me? And where is the place of My rest?'" What Isaiah said in Isaiah 66 is repeated by Stephen in Acts 7. This is the powerful sermon that got Stephen stoned to death! Acts 7:48-50 is clear: "However, the Most High does not dwell in temples made with hands, as the prophet says: 'Heaven is My throne, and earth is My footstool. What house will you build for Me? says the Lord, or what is the place of My rest? Has My hand not made all these things?'" *The earth* refers to the world or the globe. The *footstool* is the place His foot rests. When you swear by the earth, you are swearing by God, because the earth is the place He rests feet, so to speak. He owns the earth; in essence, swearing by the earth is swearing by Him.

The third creative way of lying was to swear *by Jerusalem*. But Jesus says nope, you can't do that either, *for it is the city of the great King*. Psalm 48:2 says, "Beautiful in elevation, the joy of the whole earth, is Mount Zion on the sides of the north, the city of the great King." This excuse is just as ludicrous as the previous two. Their swearing by this thing or that thing and thinking it wasn't binding was ridiculous because everything belongs to God. So, perhaps one might think, "Maybe I won't swear by anything that belongs to God, but I'll swear by myself." Let's see what Jesus says about that as He gives the fourth creative way the Pharisees lied in their oath-making.

> Nor shall you swear by your head, because you cannot make one hair white or black. (Matthew 5:36)

The reasoning here is the same as the reasoning with the others. God owns your head, too. He created you, so even if you swear *by your head*, well, that belongs to Him as well. Everything is His, so it doesn't matter what you swear by, it's still binding because everything belongs to Him. To swear by one's head was equivalent to swearing by one's life. It would be like saying that if this thing that I'm vowing isn't true, I'll lose my very own life. But since God made you, your life belongs to Him also. So, you can't even swear by yourself!

Why can't I swear by my head? Because I *cannot make one hair white or black*. You might be thinking, "Say, what?!" The biblical world was not like ours is, in the sense that they would have no control over the aging process with things like Botox, face lifts, and the dyeing of hair. (And even though we think we have control over the aging process, we really don't!) Most people in that region of the world had black or dark-colored hair, unless they were older and then it would be gray or white. Jesus is saying that you have no control over the aging process, you have no control over making one of your hairs white or black. You have no control over your life, and that includes changing the color of your hair. (By way of clarification, this verse is not saying that we shouldn't dye our hair; the context is that of making vows and not keeping them.) We have no control over making even one of our hairs white or black, so why do we think we can swear by our life? How foolish is that?

We cannot make divisions between what is God's and what is man's because everything belongs to Him. Paul clearly states this in Colossians 1:16-17, "For by Him all things were created that are in heaven and that are on earth, visible and invisible, whether thrones or dominions or principalities or powers. All things were created through Him and for Him. And He is before all things, and in Him all things consist." The religious leaders were guilty of what Proverbs 20:25 says: "It is a snare for a man to devote rashly something as holy, and afterward to reconsider his vows." Instead of all these creative ways of lying, those who are Kingdom citizens do something else. Instead of lying, we speak the truth. Hopefully, by now, Jesus' audience—along with you and I—are convinced that truth-telling is the only way to live as salt and light. If you're not convinced yet, then perhaps verse 37 will motivate you. Here, Jesus gives a consequence of those who choose to lie.

The Consequence of Lying

Matthew 5:37

But let your "Yes" be "Yes," and your "No," "No." For whatever is more than these is from the evil one. (Matthew 5:37)

The word *but* is a contrast. Instead of making all these foolish vows and swearing by things that will get you out of keeping your vows, Jesus commands us to just be honest. Let your *yes be yes, and your no, no. Yes* is a strong affirmation. *No* is an absolute negative. Both terms are synonyms for communication, but they also include even what is in your thoughts. It means to be honest not just with your mouth but also with your thoughts. This means you don't do what the religious leaders did; you don't say "yes" to someone that you will do something but actually mean "no" in your thoughts.

Jesus follows this command to be truthful in our communication with a consequence for those who choose to not fulfill their oaths or vows, who choose not to keep their word. He says *whatever is more than these is from the evil one*. The correct rendering of this phrase should read *is evil*, not *from the evil one*. Jesus says to speak anything other than truth is evil. It is wicked. James, Jesus' half-brother, says something similar in James 5:12, "But above all, my brethren, do not swear, either by heaven or by earth or with any other oath. But let your 'Yes' be 'Yes,' and your 'No,' 'No,' lest you fall into judgment." "Failure to heed this demand exposes us to the danger of judgment, because making empty oaths and swearing frivolously is in its essence lying, and we will ultimately give an account for it."34 When you put these truths together, it is clear that

34 Susan Heck, *With the Master in the School of Tested Faith* (Mustang: Tate Publishing, 2006), 355.

the consequence of making an oath or vow and not fulfilling it is evil and will cause you to fall into judgment. Solomon knew the gravity of this; he writes in Ecclesiastes 5:4-5, "When you make a vow to God, do not delay to pay it; for He has no pleasure in fools. Pay what you have vowed—better not to vow than to vow and not pay."

Summary

The Command to Not Lie (v 33) is simple—don't lie, but do what you say you will do. The religious leaders of the day exhibited four *Creative Ways of Lying* (vv 34-36); these are certainly not the only four ways of lying they exhibited, but these four are enough. The *Consequence of Lying (v 37)* is that it is evil, it is sinful, and it is wicked!

Maybe you are thinking that these words having nothing to do with us; in reality, nothing could be further from the truth. Jesus is very clear: you either tell the truth or there will be consequences. And those consequences are not good ones, because we know that all liars will have their place in the lake of fire (Revelation 21:8). So, what does this have to do with us?

> Rarely a day or week goes by that we don't make a promise to a friend, or our husband, or our children, but do we keep that promise? For example, we might say to our friend, "I promise I won't tell anyone what you just shared with me," and then you call one of your other friends to tell her the piece of juicy news. Or you promise the kids that you will take them out after school for a special treat, but then you don't fulfill your promise for one reason or another. Or you tell your friend that you will meet her for lunch at noon, but you don't show until 12:15 or, even worse, you don't show at all! Or you tell your husband that you will iron his shirts while he is at work, but you find something better to do with your time. And we

justify these broken promises by saying, "To err is human." But God says to lie is sin.[35]

Or consider this,

> When you tell someone you will pray for him or her, do you? When you sign up for a job or a ministry, are you faithful to be there? When you say you will be there at 9:00, are you there at 9:00? When you say you will pay a bill by the fifteenth of the month, do you? If you have ever taken an oath in court, have you told the truth? Are you keeping your marriage vows—"In sickness and in health, being faithful to you and you alone"—and all other vows you made on your wedding day? If you claim to be a Christian, which, by the way, is a vow and commitment to God, does your life show it? Can your word be trusted? When you say yes, do others know they can count on you? When you say no, do your children know that you mean it? Or does no in your home mean they keep pestering you and you will say yes eventually? I am sure many of us can identify with the following quote by George MacDonald: "I always try—I think I do—to be truthful. All the same I tell a great many petty lies, things that mean one thing to myself though another to other people. But I do not think lightly of it. Where I am more often wrong is in pretending I hear things which I do not, especially jokes and good stories, the point of which I always miss, but seeing everyone laugh, I laugh too, for the sake of not looking a fool. My respect for the world's opinion is my greatest stumbling block, I fear."[36]

---

35 Susan Heck, *With the Master in the School of Tested Faith* (Bemidji: Focus Publishing, 2017), 299.
36 Ibid, 300.

We all know people whose word is a joke. They are undependable, and everything they say goes in one ear and out the other. They are like the boy who cried, "Wolf!"—they cannot be trusted. On the other hand, there are times when we are unable to keep our word due to unexpected circumstances. That is why I believe it is important to say, "If the Lord wills," as James says in James 4:15. When our kids were growing up and we made promises to them—promises like family night, or vacations, or this or that—we communicated this principle to them. As preacher's kids, they were very aware that many times emergencies or crises happened which would force a change in plans; but at such times we were honest with them and made up for it later. I am afraid that with some this is not the case, and it boils down to a lack of being faithful, a lack of integrity, and a lack of being a woman of your word. When you do fail in this area, do you seek forgiveness? Or do you rationalize? The world is looking for honesty, and I am afraid they are seeing very little of it represented by believers. The following are six ways to ensure that your yes remains a yes, and that your no remains a no. They all begin with the word *Be*:

(1) *Be sensitive* to the deception that lying is not sin, especially "little white lies." Not only is it a sin, but a heinous sin. Do not desensitize yourself to the truth. I know people whose habit of lying is to the point they don't even recognize it.

(2) *Be reminded* of Matthew 12:36-37: "But I say to you that for every idle word men may speak, they will give account of it in the Day of Judgment. For by your words you will be justified, and by your words you will be condemned."

(3) *Be filled* with God's spirit and sensitive to His leading in your life in this area. If you are not walking with the Lord, His spirit has been grieved and His voice is dull.

(4) *Be asking* God to make you aware of the way you deceive yourself and others. You might be surprised how deception plays out in your life. Also ask your husband if he sees any form of lying in your life. One year my husband and I held each other accountable for exaggerations, and that exercise was extremely profitable.

(5) *Be feeding* on the Word of God. When you feed your mind on the Word—the *Truth*—and obey it, it will produce what God desires, which is truth in the inner woman or man. A truthful inward spirit is bound to produce truthful outward speech.

(6) *Be careful* what you say—Think before you speak. If you have said something that is not true, go to the person and correct it. Believe me, after you do that several times, hopefully you will be humbled enough to guard your words more carefully.

There is only one person that I know in the whole universe who has kept every promise He has made, and that is our model, our example, the Lord Jesus. One of the promises that He has made to you and me is that He will return. He will keep His Word, and so must we keep our word as well lest we fall into judgment![37]

---

37 Ibid, 300-302.

Questions to Consider

Truth or Consequences
Matthew 5:33-37

1. (a) Read Matthew 5:33-37. What do you think is Jesus' main point in these verses?

2. Memorize Matthew 5:37.

3. (a) According to Numbers 30, what are the requirements for a man making a vow? (b) What are the requirements for a woman making a vow? (c) Why do you think there are different requirements for vow-making for men and women? (d) Do you think we as women should follow this today? (Use Scripture to support your answer, if you are able.)

4. (a) Where does lying come from, according to John 8:44? (b) When does lying begin for each of us, according to Psalm 58:3? (c) What does Ephesians 4:25 say we are to do rather than lie? (d) According to Acts 5:1-9; Colossians 3:9; and James 5:12, what are some reasons we should not lie? (e) According to Proverbs 19:5 and Revelation 21:8, what happens to those who lie? (f) What are some ways that people lie in our culture?

5. (a) What biblical example comes to mind of someone who made a promise and did not keep it? (b) What do you learn from his or her example? (c) What biblical example comes to mind of someone who made a promise and did keep it? (d) What do you learn from their example?

6. (a) Are you a truth teller? (b) How do we rid ourselves of this sin?

7. Lying is a sin that is worthy of eternal punishment if it is not put off. How serious are you about putting to death the sin of lying? Please write a request for yourself asking the Lord to reveal subtle forms of lying in your life as well as helping you to recognize it and put it off.

Chapter 8

Have We No Rights?

Matthew 5:38-42

In January of 1956, the world recoiled in shock with the news. Five American missionaries had been speared to death in the Ecuadorian jungles by the Auca Indians—reportedly the most savage tribe on earth. Years later, it became clear that what had seemed to be the tragic ending of those missionaries' dreams was only the first chapter of one of the most breathtaking missionary stories of the twentieth century. *The Savage, My Kinsman* tells the story, in text and pictures, of Elisabeth Elliot's venture into Auca territory three years after the death of her husband, Jim Elliot. Elisabeth and her daughter Valerie, then three years old, returned to the jungle along with Rachel Saint, the sister of one of the other slain men. The linguistic work of these women brought Christ's message of salvation to the tribe that had killed their loved ones. They became the first to enter Auca territory—and live to tell the story.[38]

We hear this story and think, "Would I return to a savage tribe that had speared my husband to death? Would I love this lost tribe enough to work to learn their language so that the gospel could be shared with them? Would I take my three-year-old daughter and expose her to this savage tribe that murdered her father?" This should be the heart of all God's children, especially as we consider the deeply profound words of Jesus, God's Son, in Matthew 5:38-42 of the Sermon on the Mount.

---

38 Elisabeth Elliot, *The Savage, My Kinsman* (Ann Arbor: Servant Publication, 1981), back cover.

Matthew 5:38-42

> You have heard that it was said, "An eye for an eye and a tooth for a tooth." But I tell you not to resist an evil person. But whoever slaps you on your right cheek, turn the other to him also. If anyone wants to sue you and take away your tunic, let him have your cloak also. And whoever compels you to go one mile, go with him two. Give to him who asks you, and from him who wants to borrow from you do not turn away. (Matthew 5:38-42)

I would love to know what goes through each of your minds when you read these verses. Jesus' words certainly go against our flesh in a most powerful way. And I'm sure they went against the flesh of those listening on the Mount the day Jesus first spoke them, as well. There's nothing new under the sun, and there is no temptation but such is as common to all of us, whether we lived then or now! Is Jesus really saying what we think He is saying? Am I to literally let someone slap me on both sides of my face? Am I to allow myself to be sued and have all my possessions taken from me? What did Jesus really mean by these words?

Before we delve into the text, let's remind ourselves of where we were in our last lesson. We've been looking at several sayings of old that Jesus has been reminding His listeners of. But as He does so, He takes each one and raises the standard of what He expects from those who belong to Him. You will remember that when considering the moral Law of God "the greater stands for the lesser," which, unfortunately, the Jewish leaders had forgotten, limiting the commands to mere outward observances. Jesus was reclaiming the original intent of the Law. In our last lesson, we looked at the importance keeping our vows, and we learned that the religious leaders of the day exhibited four creative ways of lying, four creative ways of getting out of keeping their vows, or their promises, we might say. But we saw that Jesus expects something different from those who follow Him, and we learned that the consequence of lying is that it is evil, sinful, and wicked, and we fall into judgment when we choose to lie!

In our outline for this lesson—*Have We No Rights?*—we will see that Jesus tells us to give up our rights in four areas. (These are not the only ones, of course, but these are the four in our text.) All of these rights start with the letter P.

> *The Right to Our Person* (v 39)
> *The Right to Our Possessions* (v 40)
> *The Right to Our Plans* (v 41)
> *The Right to Our Provisions* (v 42)

But first, let's consider another saying of old that was commonly heard and taught by the religious leaders of Jesus' day.

> You have heard that it was said, "An eye for an eye and a tooth for a tooth." (Matthew 5:38)

This is the fifth time that Jesus mentions something they have heard. This time it is *an eye for an eye and a tooth for a tooth*. Just as with the other four, this one also has reference to the Old Testament. The first reference is found in Exodus 21:23-25: "But if any harm follows, then you shall give life for life, eye for eye, tooth for tooth, hand for hand, foot for foot, burn for burn, wound for wound, stripe for stripe." We also find this mentioned in Leviticus 24:19-21: "If a man causes disfigurement of his neighbor, as he has done, so shall it be done to him—fracture for fracture, eye for eye, tooth for tooth; as he has caused disfigurement of a man, so shall it be done to him." Lastly, there is a hint of this principle in Deuteronomy 19:11-13: "But if anyone hates his neighbor, lies in wait for him, rises against him and strikes him mortally, so that he dies, and he flees to one of these cities, then the elders of his city shall send and bring him from there, and deliver him over to the hand of the avenger of blood, that he may die. Your eye shall not pity him, but you shall put away the guilt of innocent blood from Israel, that it may go well with you."

In order to understand what was written in the Old Testament and how it relates to the shocking standard that Jesus will unfold in the following verses, we must consider biblical times. There was what was called the law of retaliation, or lex talionis, which was given as a protection for justice to be performed. However, even though this was the law, it was not meant to be taken to the ridiculous, so that the one wronged would take personal vengeance. It was intended to be similar to what we have in our day with the laws of our land. The laws we have in place in America are there to protect us and to allow punishment for those who do wrong. We all understand that. If someone murders another person, there is punishment for their crime. In the Old Testament, that punishment was death. In our day, you can kill another person and, unfortunately, it's rare that you receive a death penalty—but that's another topic! What Jesus is condemning here is personal retaliation on those who would harm us. For example, if someone kills one of our loved ones, we don't retaliate by killing the person who did the hideous crime; we allow the laws of the land to deal with it. Or, if my neighbor's dog is an annoyance or my neighbor is mowing their yard too late at night, I don't take a gun and kill them; rather, I report it to the police and let them take care of it. The laws of the land are in place for a reason, and we are to take advantage of them just like those who were living in Christ's day were to take advantage of the laws of the land and allow justice to be done. What Christ will be condemning in the next few verses is personal vengeance or retaliation when we are wronged or when we are asked to do something that might inconvenience us or cost us something. In fact, the things Jesus requires "slaps our Christianity in the face," so to speak (pun intended!) One commentator has said, "The very God who placed that law and its execution where it belongs, into the hands of the government, places another law and its execution, the law of love, into the hearts of Christ's disciples."[39] We must keep in mind the example of our Lord that Peter mentions in 1 Peter, that the Lord did not retaliate when He was reviled or threatened (1 Peter 2:23), along with what Paul says in Romans 12:19 about vengeance being the Lord's and it is He alone who will pay back those who do evil. That's not our job!

---

39 R. C. H. Lenski, *Commentary on the New Testament: Matthew* (CITY: Hendrickson, 2001), 241.

Before we discuss the first right we must give up, I would like to be clear that Jesus is not condemning defending ourselves. If someone were to come against us in some sort of physical threat, we should take action. He even once told the disciples in Luke 22:36, when impending persecution was coming, to sell their clothes and get a sword! He's not saying that we shouldn't be wise in protecting our families from harm. But He is, once again, making it clear that to interpret the law in our own way or to our personal satisfaction is not ours to do. The religious leaders of Jesus' day were using this as a spring board for all kinds of evil and pay-backs against those they resented.

For some of you, these will be shocking words. For others, these words will describe the norm of your life. If you are a mature believer in the faith, then these words will probably describe you because it takes real strength from God to behave in the way His Son is describing. It is the weak, the immature, and the unbeliever who pay back evil with evil. Let's consider the first right we must give up.

The Right to Our Person

Matthew 5:39

> But I tell you not to resist an evil person. But whoever slaps you on your right cheek, turn the other to him also. (Matthew 5:39)

There are a lot of erroneous ideas about what Jesus means here when He says we are *not to resist an evil person*. But first, let me say that to *resist* means to withstand, oppose, or stand against. And, obviously, *an evil person* would be anyone who does evil. Some have believed and taught that Jesus is calling for passivity. In other words, I should just let people hit me, sue me, and the like, and I should remain passive about it. That is not what Jesus is saying. What He is saying is that I shouldn't oppose an evil person by doing evil against them. I don't stand against an evil person by paying back evil for evil. It's what Paul says in Romans 12:17, "Repay no one evil for evil. Have regard for good things in the sight of all men." It's also what Peter says in 1 Peter 3:9, "not returning evil for evil or reviling for reviling, but on the contrary blessing, knowing that you were called to this, that you may inherit a blessing." In fact, even in the Levitical law—which Jesus' audience would have been familiar with—it was written, "You shall not take vengeance, nor bear any grudge against the children of your people, but you shall love your neighbor as yourself: I am the Lord" (Leviticus 19:18). You might be saying to yourself, "Well, if I can't pay them back, then what am I supposed to do?" Jesus gives us four ways that we can resist evil, and these will be as shocking to us today as they were to His audience that day on the Mount.

The first way in which we resist evil, in which we give up our rights, is when it comes to our person, our physical body. Jesus puts it like this, *whoever slaps you on your right cheek, turn the other to him also*. The word *slap* means to smite with the palm of the hand. The rabbis taught that to hit someone with the back of the hand was twice as insulting as hitting them with the palm of the hand. The *cheek* would, of course, be the side of the face. To the Jew, a slap to the face would be the most humiliating and insulting place to be hit. Isaiah prophesies regarding our Lord in Isaiah 50:6, "I gave My back to those who struck Me, and My cheeks to those who plucked out the beard; I did not hide My face from shame and spitting." Christ was an example of someone who allowed Himself to be slapped by those who hated Him. The apostle John records this account in John 18:19-24: "The high priest then asked Jesus about His disciples and His doctrine. Jesus answered him, 'I spoke openly to the world. I always taught in synagogues and in the temple, where the Jews always meet, and in secret I have said nothing. Why do you ask Me? Ask those who have heard Me what I said to them. Indeed they know what I said.' And when He had said these things, one of the officers who stood by struck Jesus with the palm of his hand, saying, 'Do You answer the high priest like that?' Jesus answered him, 'If I have spoken evil, bear witness of the evil; but if well, why do you strike Me?' Then Annas sent Him bound to Caiaphas the high priest."

Personally, I can recall only two occasions of being slapped on my face, and I can attest that both were indeed humiliating. Once, I was slapped by a boyfriend (not my now husband!) whom I immediately broke up with; the other slap came from my mother, for sassing her. I probably deserved the slap from my mother, but I would encourage you moms that slapping on the face is arguably not the best way to discipline a child.

What should I do if someone slaps me? Slap him back? That's certainly what our flesh wants to do. But Jesus says no, if someone slaps you, then you let him slap the other cheek as well. To be fair to the text, it's possible that Jesus may not be talking about a literally slapping—but He might be. For someone to *turn the other [cheek] to him also* would most definitely be a passive attitude and not even in conjunction with what the law allowed at the time. We know this from the account in Acts 23:1-3: "Then Paul, looking earnestly at the council, said, 'Men and brethren, I have lived in all good conscience before God until this day.' And the high priest Ananias commanded those who stood by him to strike him on the mouth. Then Paul said to him, 'God will strike you, you whitewashed wall! For you sit to judge me according to the law, and do you command me to be struck contrary to the law?'" Since slapping someone was insulting, I think it's more likely that Jesus is referring to someone who is insulting you. This is a call to be longsuffering toward others. If someone insults me, I am not to retaliate physically or verbally but allow them to keep on insulting me. If someone wants to be that petty, then we as kingdom citizens should not stoop to their pettiness. It really doesn't matter, in light of eternity, if someone harms our person, our physical well-being, or our feelings, but it does matter if we repay them with evil. Christ is not calling for passive reactions to those who wrong us, but He is calling for profound reactions; He is calling for patience. And in verse 40, Jesus moves on to another right we do not have.

The Right to Our Possessions

Matthew 5:40

> If anyone wants to sue you and take away your tunic, let him have your cloak also. (Matthew 5:40)

In this example, we are presented with someone who wants to sue us. The word *sue* means to condemn, to go to law. We need to think about this in its historical context because when we sue, we sue for money or damages done, but in biblical times you could sue someone for their tunic, which would be their inner garment. Doing so would leave them with only their cloak, or their outer garment. You could also sue for the cloak, but the Law required you to return it each evening so that the one you were suing would have something to sleep in. Exodus 22:26-27 helps us here: "If you ever take your neighbor's garment as a pledge, you shall return it to him before the sun goes down. For that is his only covering, it is his garment for his skin. What will he sleep in? And it will be that when he cries to Me, I will hear, for I am gracious." The law allowed for suing, but you didn't want the guy to have to go completely naked! In our context, we might say, "Don't take them for all they have!"

But Jesus says if they *take away your tunic, let him have your cloak also*! What do I do if someone sues me and takes my stuff? Some of us would fight the lawsuit or file bankruptcy; Jesus says let them have it all. Paul reiterates this in 1 Corinthians 6:6-8, "But brother goes to law against brother, and that before unbelievers! Now therefore, it is already an utter failure for you that you go to law against one another. Why do you not rather accept wrong? Why do you not rather let yourselves be cheated? No, you yourselves do wrong and cheat, and you do these things to your brethren!"

The second right we do not have is a right to our possessions. We saw in our last lesson that God owns everything, right? So, let them have what they want! Who cares?! Better to lose one's possessions than to lose one's soul by retaliating and taking vengeance. There is no profit to gaining the world and losing your soul over material possessions! But Jesus goes even beyond this, with yet a third right we do not have.

The Right to Our Plans

Matthew 5:41

And whoever compels you to go one mile, go with him two. (Matthew 5:41)

Jesus is, more than likely, using a real-life illustration as a reference to something He Himself would experience in the moments before He was crucified. Matthew 27:32 says, "Now as they came out, they found a man of Cyrene, Simon by name. Him they compelled to bear His cross." In New Testament times, a Roman soldier could command anyone under Roman rule to carry anything that soldier might need help with. In this particular instance, the soldiers commanded Simon to carry the cross of Christ, likely because Christ was in such bad physical shape from the scourging He had already received, and the weight of the cross was simply more than He could carry at that moment. Jesus's point is that if you are asked to do something, you do it, and you don't just do what they've asked of you, you do more!

The third thing we have no right to is our plans! This certainly goes against our flesh and our plans for our day, but Jesus is clearly saying that we shouldn't get upset if someone asks us to do something but should do it joyfully and even do extra. We don't like those "divine interruptions" in our day, but Jesus says true kingdom citizens realize that the greatest commands are to love God and love others. We have forgotten that great biblical principle that, "It is more blessed to give than to receive" (Acts 20:35).

We can't go on the next verse without clarifying a few things because I'm confident there are some who will misinterpret this command and go to the other extreme of enabling others. Both James and John are clear in their writings that if we see a brother in need and don't help them, the love of God is not in us. James makes clear that the person he is referring to is naked and destitute of their daily food. John makes clear that you have first investigated the situation and made sure that there is a legitimate need and not a want (see James 2:14-17 and 1 John 3:16-17). We measure what Jesus is saying with the whole of Scripture. We also make sure that we do not enable those who are using the body of Christ to further their laziness. But Jesus is clear: when someone needs help, it is our responsibility to help them and not to bristle when we're asked! And, if this is not enough, Christ ends His shocking words in verse 42 with yet one more right we do not have.

The Right to Our Provisions

Matthew 5:42

> Give to him who asks you, and from him who wants to borrow from you do not turn away. (Matthew 5:42)

There were Old Testament laws for lending and borrowing with which Jesus' audience would have been quite familiar. Exodus 22:25 says, "If you lend money to any of My people who are poor among you, you shall not be like a moneylender to him; you shall not charge him interest." Also, Deuteronomy 15:7-11 says,

> If there is among you a poor man of your brethren, within any of the gates in your land which the Lord your God is giving you, you shall not harden your heart nor shut your hand from your poor brother, but you shall open your hand wide to him and willingly lend him sufficient for his need, whatever he needs. Beware lest there be a wicked thought in your heart, saying, "The seventh year, the year of release, is at hand," and your eye be evil against your poor brother and you give him nothing, and he cry out to the Lord against you, and it become sin among you. You shall surely give to him, and your heart should not be grieved when you give to him, because for this thing the Lord your God will bless you in all your works and in all to which you put your hand. For the poor will never cease from

the land; therefore I command you, saying, "You shall open your hand wide to your brother, to your poor and your needy, in your land."

In biblical times, there were laws that specifically allowed for provisions for the poor and needy, like orphans and widows. If someone I know is in need and asks to borrow something from me, I am not to turn him away; I am to give what he or she needs. And I am to do it with a joyful heart, realizing that everything I have is God's anyway, so it really doesn't even belong to me.

This is the fourth right I do not have—a right to my provisions! Psalm 112:5 states, "A good man deals graciously and lends; He will guide his affairs with discretion" Jesus says in Luke 6:35, "But love your enemies, do good, and lend, hoping for nothing in return; and your reward will be great, and you will be sons of the Most High. For He is kind to the unthankful and evil." Again, we measure this with the whole of Scripture, making sure that it is a legitimate need. But we also measure it with the principle that Paul spells out in 2 Thessalonians 3:10, that if a man will not work, neither should he eat. In addition to this, there is also the principle in 1 Timothy 5 of making sure that you are taking care of those in your family, as that is your biblical responsibility. So, we marry the whole of Scripture's teaching with what Jesus is saying here in Matthew 5. But the bottom line is this: When someone has a genuine need, you meet it. If they need food, you give it to them; if they need to borrow your car, you let them. These are not your things, anyway; everything you have is because God gave it to you. It all belongs to Him!

Summary

Have we no rights? No, we really don't. And specifically, as Jesus articulates here, we don't have rights regarding our person, our possessions, our plans and our provisions. I know this goes against our flesh, especially since we live in a culture where not only is everyone doing what is right in their own eyes, but also where everyone is demanding their rights. The world we live in boldly claims its rights: gay rights, animal rights, children's rights, states' rights, workers' rights, the right to privacy, the right to freedom of expression, the right to protest against anything and the right to remain silent. On and on and on the list goes on all the rights we demand in our postmodern society. But kingdom citizens are more than happy to give up their rights because they are fighting for one right and that is the right to live righteously for the kingdom to come.

Is this your desire, or are you like the religious leaders of Jesus' day, bristling at the words Jesus spoke? Do you think we have *The Right to Our Person* (v 39)? When you are physically slapped, so to speak, when you are insulted, what is your response? Do you want to hit back; do you want to insult the person who has insulted you? Are you in the habit of giving tit-for-tat? When your husband insults you, do you insult him back? When someone embarrasses you, do you fight back by posting nasty things about them on your favorite social media site? Or, when you are insulted by someone, do you let them have the other cheek? Do you repay them with kind words or look for a way to bless them? And, since we are on this topic, I might also be brave enough to ask if you are guilty of being the one who insults others first. Are you the one who slaps others, so to speak?

There is *The Right to Our Possessions* (v 40). I've never been sued, but I am sure it would pose some difficulty for me to lose my possessions. This possibility forces me to ask myself if I am truly willing to lose all for the sake of Christ or for the sake of making sure that my opponent sees Christ in me. Are you making sure that you are obeying the laws of the land so that you won't be sued some day? Are you so money-hungry that you are on the prowl for someone to do you wrong so that you can sue them?

Thirdly, there is *The Right to Our Plans* (v 41). For those of you who are like me, a planner of my days, then this one hits us right between the eyes! What is your attitude when your husband asks you to iron his clothes that he needs for work or church and you are pressed for time? Or your husband asks you to do something that you really don't want to do? Or a lady in your church asks you to help her pack up and move and yet your week is super busy? Or a weary mom asks you to watch her kids so she can get some things done? Or a neighbor asks you to get their mail or water their plants while they're out of town? Do you immediately bristle when you're asked to do something for others, or do you look at these as opportunities for serving? What about interruptions in your perfectly planned day? Do you resent them? Do you become angry or irritated? Remember, Jesus has already said that to be angry without a cause is serious stuff! We should joyfully go the second mile even when we are only asked to go one.

Lastly, there is *The Right to Our Provisions* (v 42). This hits home with our Western Christianity, which thrives on having nice houses, nice cars, and plenty of money in the bank for retirement and living the good life. We think we have to own the latest gadgets and fashions in order to enjoy the abundant life. But Jesus calls us to give to those who ask of us and to those who want to borrow from us. When was the last time someone asked for something from you, and what was your response? At times before I left on a speaking trip, my husband would ask me if I loaned my car to someone to use while I was gone. And on other occasions he has suggested that when we are out of town we should let someone use our home. He is always looking for ways to give, and his doing so puts me to shame. This is what Jesus is saying, along with being willing to give to those who have legitimate needs.

The end of the story at the beginning of this lesson is this: Elisabeth Elliott did indeed return to that savage tribe to work on the linguistics necessary for sharing the gospel with them. This eventually led to the conversion of many, including some of those involved in her husband's killing. Elisabeth Elliot gave up her rights for the sake of the gospel, the right to her person, her possessions, her plans, and her provisions. Paul the apostle also gave up his rights to his person, his possession, his plans, and his provisions, all for the sake of the gospel. Jesus, the very Son of God, gave up His rights for the fulfillment of the gospel—His right to His person, His possessions, His plans and His provisions. Will you give up your rights for the sake of the gospel and for the validation that you indeed are a daughter of your Father who is in heaven?

Questions to Consider

Have We No Rights?
Matthew 5:38-42

1. (a) What is your first reaction when you read Matthew 5:38-42? (b) What do you think is Jesus' main point in these verses?

2. Memorize Matthew 5:38-39.

3. (a) In Romans 12:17-21, what does Paul say that we should do when we are wronged? (b) How do you reconcile Matthew 5:38-42 with Matthew 18:15-20?

4. (a) Read 1 Samuel 24. In what ways do you see David fulfilling what Jesus says in Matthew 5:39? (b) How does this encourage you to do what is right when you are the recipient of evil, even though it might be hard?

5. (a) Give a biblical example of someone who practiced at least one of Jesus' points in Matthew 5:39-42. If you can find one for each of Jesus' points (total of 4), that's great! (b) After citing the biblical example, write what you can learn from their example for your own life.

6. (a) What are some things we can do as kingdom citizens to avoid the attitude or action of repaying evil for evil? (b) How do you or did you help your children, grandchildren, or others with this concept?

7. (a) Are you in the habit of retaliation when someone does you wrong? (You might recall in your mind the last time you were wronged and what your reaction was!) (b) How has this lesson prompted you to act differently? Write your need down in the form of a prayer request.

Chapter 9

Mandates and Motivations
for Loving Our Enemies

Matthew 5:43-48

We have come to the final lesson in chapter five of the Sermon on the Mount. Perhaps some of you are feeling uncomfortable about the lessons taught by our Lord. One man wrote his reaction to this sermon from Jesus: "As to 'caring for' the Sermon on the Mount, if 'caring for' here means 'liking' or enjoying, I suppose no one 'cares for' it. Who can like being knocked flat on his face by a sledge hammer? I can hardly imagine a more deadly condition than that of a man who can read that passage with tranquil pleasure."[40] The Sermon on the Mount is indeed painful, in the same way that getting hit by a sledge hammer is painful! But just as physical pain is an indicator that something is wrong with our bodies, as one surgeon told me years ago, so it is with spiritual pain; it is an indicator that something is wrong with our spiritual life and we need to do something about it. I confess, as your teacher, this has been a painful but much-needed study in my own life, and we aren't even half done! Oh, how quickly we forget some of these basic, fundamental, Christian mandates, and how often we need to be reminded of them! I, for one, am thankful for a loving, heavenly Father and for the help of the Holy Spirit who enables us to get back on the narrow road.

With these things in mind, we have come to a section of the Sermon on the Mount that we all need to shore up on: loving those who are our enemies, loving those who hate us and persecute us. How do we love them? Jesus will share some very important mandates and motivations for loving our enemies. Together, let's read these final verses of chapter five.

---

40 Quote by C. S. Lewis, (R. Kent Hughes, *The Sermon on the Mount: The Message of the Kingdom* (Wheaton: Crossway Books, 2001), 139.)

Matthew 5:43-48

You have heard that it was said, "You shall love your neighbor and hate your enemy." [44]But I say to you, love your enemies, bless those who curse you, do good to those who hate you, and pray for those who spitefully use you and persecute you, [45]that you may be sons of your Father in heaven; for He makes His sun rise on the evil and on the good, and sends rain on the just and on the unjust. [46]For if you love those who love you, what reward have you? Do not even the tax collectors do the same? [47]And if you greet your brethren only, what do you do more than others? Do not even the tax collectors do so? [48]Therefore you shall be perfect, just as your Father in heaven is perfect. (Matthew 5:43-48)

When we studied Matthew 5:38-42 in our last lesson, we saw that citizens of God's kingdom have no rights and actually give up their rights for the sake of others. We saw four areas in which Jesus mentions that we are to give up our rights: Our rights regarding our person: if someone slaps me on my right cheek, I let him slap my left cheek also. Our rights regarding our possessions: if someone wants to sue me and take all I have, I let him. Our rights regarding our plans: if someone asks me to go with them a mile, I go two miles. And our rights regarding our provisions: if someone wants to borrow from me, I don't turn them away. These are indeed hard sayings, but Jesus continues on with more difficult teaching as He deals with our responses to our enemies. In this lesson, *Mandates and Motivations for Loving Our Enemies*, our outline will include:

> *The Misquoted Command Regarding Our Enemies* (v 43)
> *The Mandates Regarding Our Enemies* (v 44)
> *The Motivations for Loving Our Enemies* (vv 45-48)

We now come to the sixth reference to these sayings of old, and this particular saying was not only misrepresented by the religious leaders of the day, it was misquoted!

The Misquoted Command Regarding Our Enemies

Matthew 5:43

You have heard that it was said, "You shall love your neighbor and hate your enemy." (Matthew 5:43)

This is the final time Jesus uses the phrase *you have heard that is was said*. So, we ask again, as we have in the past, "Where is this saying mentioned in the Old Testament?" Leviticus 19:18 is the text Jesus is referring to, and it states, "You shall not take vengeance, nor bear any grudge against the children of your people, but you shall love your neighbor as yourself: I am the Lord." As you can see, there is not a *hate your enemy* part to this verse. That's because there is no such saying in the Old Testament, even though the leaders of the day taught that it was so. They assumed that since the Old Testament taught us to love our neighbor, then the logical conclusion would be to hate our enemy. The false religious leaders of the day were clever at twisting Scripture for their own purposes, just as we see them do in our day. I'm not sure what they taught regarding another command in the Old Testament that would seem to indicate an entirely different response to one's enemies. This one, found in Exodus 23:4-5, has to do with doing good to one's enemy; it says, "If you meet your enemy's ox or his donkey going astray, you shall surely bring it back to him again. If you see the donkey of one who hates you lying under its burden, and you would refrain from helping it, you shall surely help him with it." There is nothing in this text about hating your enemy; instead, it actually calls us to help him by taking care of the ailing or straying animal which belongs to him.

This *love* for my neighbor would be agape love, which is a love that gives what the person needs and not necessarily what they want. And my *neighbor* would be any human being. Jesus makes this clear in Luke 10:25-37:

And behold, a certain lawyer stood up and tested Him, saying, "Teacher, what shall I do to inherit eternal life?" He said to him, "What is written in the law? What is your reading of it?" So he answered and said, "'you shall love the Lord your God with all your heart, with all your soul, with all your strength, and with all your mind,' and 'your neighbor as yourself.'" And He said to him, "You have answered rightly; do this and you will live." But he, wanting to justify himself, said to Jesus, "And who is my neighbor?" Then Jesus answered and said: "A certain man went down from Jerusalem to Jericho, and fell among thieves, who stripped him of his clothing, wounded him, and departed, leaving him half dead. Now by chance a certain priest came down that road. And when he saw him, he passed by on the other side. Likewise a Levite, when he arrived at the place, came and looked, and passed by on the other side. But a certain Samaritan, as he journeyed, came where he was. And when he saw him, he had compassion. So he went to him and bandaged his wounds, pouring on oil and wine; and he set him on his own animal, brought him to an inn, and took care of him. On the next day, when he departed, he took out two denarii, gave them to the innkeeper, and said to him, 'Take care of him; and whatever more you spend, when I come again, I will repay you.' So which of these three do you think was neighbor to him who fell among the thieves?" And he said, "He who showed mercy on him." Then Jesus said to him, "Go and do likewise."

Jesus makes it clear that a neighbor isn't necessarily someone you know. What is so interesting about this story is that the religious leaders avoided the wounded man, just like the religious leaders added "hate your enemy" to the Scriptures in their twisted way of thinking. The Samaritans were despised by the Jews, so the fact that this was the one who reached out to the wounded man would have been an added blow to the lawyer who asked Jesus this question in Luke's Gospel.

Loving one's neighbor was clearly written in the Old Testament, but the Pharisees added "hate your enemy" to it. Jesus says you've heard this too, though the religious leaders would have had a hard time finding it anywhere in the Scriptures! To hate one's enemy would mean to detest anyone who is your adversary. So, we can see that the religious leaders misquoted this command regarding their enemies. Instead of hating their enemies, Jesus sets the record straight by letting them know how they should respond to their enemies, and in doing so, He gives us four mandates regarding our enemies.

The Mandates Regarding Our Enemies

Matthew 5:44

> But I say to you, love your enemies, bless those who curse you, do good to those who hate you, and pray for those who spitefully use you and persecute you, (Matthew 5:44)

Jesus says, *but I say to you*, which is a contrast. Instead of hating your enemies as you have been falsely taught, Jesus says, I'm telling you to *love your enemies*. This is the first mandate regarding our enemies: we are to love them. The Greek word for *love* is, again, agape, which means doing what the person needs and not what they want. It pertains to the direction of our will and of finding our joy in something; it is like the love of God that sent His Son Jesus to die for us because He knew we needed a Savior! The Greek tense here in this verse indicates that this is an ongoing love that we manifest toward our enemies. Jesus is not asking us to love our enemies like we would love close friends and family—that is phileo love, a tender affection—but He is asking us to agape them. So, we might ask, "What does my enemy need in this situation?" That is not always an easy question to answer because sometimes they actually do have needs that we can meet, but also they may need to be confronted about their sin, which is one of the most loving things we can do for anyone, whether foe or friend. The Old Testament is clear in Leviticus 19:17-18, "You shall not hate your brother in your heart. You shall surely rebuke your neighbor, and not bear sin because of him. You shall not take vengeance, nor bear any grudge against the children of your people, but you shall love your neighbor as yourself: I am the Lord."

I have just had this recently illustrated to me, as about a year ago my husband and I moved into a new neighborhood. We have found it to be a good move with the exception of a neighbor's dog that, from time to time, barks incessantly. (Even now as I am typing, it is barking!) I have done the proper thing by graciously asking them to do something about it and explaining that both my husband and I work from out of our home. I've also contacted the local police to find out if barking dogs are considered a public nuisance. So, I wrestle with knowing the proper thing to do. Do I simply ignore my neighbor's dog and allow them to disturb myself and others? Or do I take action by doing something to stop the noise for the sake of my sanity and my other neighbors who have also complained from time to time? What is the proper thing to do? I came to the conclusion that they need to control their dog for the good of others, not just myself, though we haven't had complete success yet! Sometimes the loving thing is to confront.

The second mandate regarding our enemies is to bless them. Jesus says *bless those who curse you*. My neighbor has not yet cursed me that I know of, though she has accused me of poisoning her dog. To *bless* someone means to speak well of them. We are to speak well of those who *curse* us, which indicates that they loathe us and want us to come to doom. This is hard to do, isn't it? My husband has really outshined me in this situation; he is constantly giving our neighbors the benefit of the doubt. That's what love does.

The third way in which Jesus says we are to respond to our enemies is to *do good to those who hate you*. To *do good* means to do well to them. And Jesus describes them as those who *hate* us, which means they detest us. I have had a few people in my life whom I am fairly certain detest me, and there are probably many persons I don't know about who detest me. How we flesh out doing good to those who hate us takes some prayer and creative thinking. And remember what Jesus said in the Upper Room, that we will be hated just because we belong to Him, and that the world hated Him without a cause. They hated Him for no reason at all (see John 15:18-25). My friend, we are seeing an increase in hatred toward believers simply because of the name of Jesus and the fact that we belong to Him. Proverbs 25:21-22 gives us some help in how we can do good to our enemies: "If your enemy is hungry, give him bread to eat; and if he is thirsty, give him water to drink; for so you will heap coals of fire on his head, and the Lord will reward you." Considering these verses, we would do well to look for ways to meet our enemies' legitimate needs.

The fourth and last mandate that Jesus gives regarding our enemies is to *pray for those who spitefully use you and persecute you.* The praying here is to God, and it doesn't mean that we pray the imprecatory Psalms (those that invoke judgment or curses upon one's enemy), though I confess I have done that on occasion in the long ago past! This really isn't the spirit of what our Lord is saying. We can *pray* for them that God will bless them and use them to glorify Himself; we can pray that our relationship with them would be restored in such a way that Christ would be exalted. Jesus describes these enemies here as those who *spitefully use you and persecute you.* This would indicate they slander, insult, and injure you in any way; it could also be a reference to going to court, which is interesting because Jesus has just spoken in verse 40 about those who would sue us. The Greek tense for the words *persecute* and *spitefully use* are ongoing, just like the love we are to have for them is to be ongoing.

We have some wonderful examples in Scripture of those who prayed for the people who spitefully used them and persecuted them. While being crucified on the cross, Christ prayed, "Father, forgive them, for they do not know what they do" (Luke 23:34). Stephen, while being insulted by his persecutors and then being stoned to death, prayed, "Lord, do not charge them with this sin" (Acts 7:60). My friend, that type of praying takes the grace of God! These are interesting words in light of what Jesus has already said in Matthew 5:10-12: "Blessed are those who are persecuted for righteousness' sake, for theirs is the kingdom of heaven. Blessed are you when they revile and persecute you, and say all kinds of evil against you falsely for My sake. Rejoice and be exceedingly glad, for great is your reward in heaven, for so they persecuted the prophets who were before you."

Perhaps you are wondering the same thing as those on the mount with Jesus were probably wondering, that is, "Why in the world would I want to do something as radical as love my enemies, bless those who curse me, and do good to those who hate me and spitefully use me?" Well, Jesus gives us the answer, and just as He has given us four mandates regarding our enemies, so Jesus gives us four motivations for loving our enemies, in verses 45-48.

The Motivations for Loving Our Enemies

Matthew 5:45-48

> that you may be sons of your Father in heaven; for He makes His sun rise on the evil and on the good, and sends rain on the just and on the unjust. (Matthew 5:45)

The first motivation for loving our enemies in the way our Lord describes is this: by doing so, we prove we belong to the Lord. Jesus says *that you may be sons of your Father in heaven*. Jesus is not condoning a "works salvation," as we do not become the children of God by loving our enemies; instead, by loving our enemies we prove that we are genuine children of God. The Greek rendering is this: we are the sons of our Father who is in heaven. We must remember that we were once enemies of God and yet He loved us. Consider Romans 5:8-11, "But God demonstrates His own love toward us, in that while we were still sinners, Christ died for us. Much more then, having now been justified by His blood, we shall be saved from wrath through Him. For if when we were enemies we were reconciled to God through the death of His Son, much more, having been reconciled, we shall be saved by His life. And not only that, but we also rejoice in God through our Lord Jesus Christ, through whom we have now received the reconciliation." The implication of this is that we should follow in His steps in loving our enemies, as 1 John 4:7 states: "Beloved, let us love one another, for love is of God; and everyone who loves is born of God and knows God." I don't know about you, but making sure my faith is genuine, making sure that I am a child of God is strong motivation for loving those who don't love me. Jesus adds that our Father in heaven *makes His sun rise on the evil and on the good*, and He also *sends rain on the just and on the unjust*. Psalm 145:9 says, "The Lord is good to all, and His tender mercies are over all His works." The second motivation for loving our enemies is found in verse 46.

> For if you love those who love you, what reward have you? Do
> not even the tax collectors do the same? (Matthew 5:46)

If you only *love those who love you, what reward have you?* The word *reward* means to pay for services. There is certainly no eternal reward in this kind of love! If you agape only those who agape you, what good is that? That kind of love for others is selfishly motivated by what we can get out of it. Jesus says *even the tax collectors* do that! Now, why does Jesus mention *tax collectors*? Probably because they were the most hated of all men; they were detested and known as intolerant of others. Matthew 9:10-11 gives us a glimpse of this: "Now it happened, as Jesus sat at the table in the house, that behold, many tax collectors and sinners came and sat down with Him and His disciples. And when the Pharisees saw it, they said to His disciples, 'Why does your Teacher eat with tax collectors and sinners?'" Tax collectors were equated with sinners. In fact, we read in Matthew 11:19, "The Son of Man came eating and drinking, and they say, 'Look, a glutton and a winebibber, a friend of tax collectors and sinners!' But wisdom is justified by her children." We are even told that when we discipline a member by putting them out of the church in the final state of church discipline, we are to treat them like a tax collector. Matthew 18:17 says, "And if he refuses to hear them, tell it to the church. But if he refuses even to hear the church, let him be to you like a heathen and a tax collector." In our day, we might equate tax collectors to the IRS or perhaps the government that uses our tax money to spend on their own pleasures. And Jesus says even these rascals love their own. So, the second motivation for loving our enemies is that it proves that our love for others comes from God and not from a human source. Only God's children can love enemies who are pagans in a depraved state. The third motivation is found in verse 47.

> And if you greet your brethren only, what do you do more than others? Do not even the tax collectors do so? (Matthew 5:47)

To *greet* someone would mean to welcome them and to enfold them in your arms. We might liken it to giving someone a handshake and a hug. This would include a hello when you see them and a goodbye when you leave them. Jesus says if you treat *your brethren only* like this, it is not any different than anyone, not even the tax collectors. Why, even they greet their own like that! So, what makes you different; *what do you do more than others*? By loving my enemies, it proves that my love is not hypocritical, is not partial—this is a third motivation for loving others. Jesus' half-brother James is clear about this, in James 2:1-4, "My brethren, do not hold the faith of our Lord Jesus Christ, the Lord of glory, with partiality. For if there should come into your assembly a man with gold rings, in fine apparel, and there should also come in a poor man in filthy clothes, and you pay attention to the one wearing the fine clothes and say to him, 'You sit here in a good place,' and say to the poor man, 'You stand there,' or, 'Sit here at my footstool,' have you not shown partiality among yourselves, and become judges with evil thoughts?" True religion does not love others for what one can receive; true religion loves others because it is motivated by pure love that comes from God. We don't ignore others but embrace them; it is innate within our being as children of God. Jesus ends chapter five with a fourth motivation for loving our enemies—and a phrase that has puzzled theologians for decades!

> Therefore you shall be perfect, just as your Father in heaven is perfect. (Matthew 5:48)

Therefore, because of all that Jesus has said, *you shall be perfect, just as your Father in heaven is perfect.* What does it mean to be *perfect?* It means to be complete in mental and moral character, someone who is without defect. It is a word that was used to describe a piece of machinery that has all its parts in place or a person who has all their parts. Our *Father in heaven* is without blemish and without defect, and we are to strive to be just like Him. The fourth motivation, then, for loving others is to be blameless or complete, just as our Father in heaven is. We don't just prove we are His children by loving our enemies, but we actually love our enemies as He does and thus we resemble Him. [41]

We are to be salt and light in this crooked world, and we are when we love those who are hostile toward us. The world does not love its enemies, but God's children do. The world only loves its own, but God's children love all. The world retaliates against those who do evil, but God's children do not. God's children are more mature than that; their desire is to be perfect just like their Daddy in heaven. Like Father, like children! We are to be pure as He is pure, and we are to be holy as He is holy (see 1 Peter 1:15-16 and 1 John 3:3).

Summary

First, we have seen *The Misquoted Command Regarding Our Enemies* (v 43). The religious leaders added to the Word by making it say what they wanted it to say, which was to hate their enemies. Are you adding to or taking away from the Word of God and, in so doing, leading others astray? Revelation 22:18 warns those who would add to or take away from God's Word. We must make sure that we study to show ourselves approved unto God and that we do

---

41 This command for perfection could refer beyond the issue of loving even enemies to include all six of the moral illustrations beginning in verse 21. In this sense, the concluding issue is that kingdom citizens are to obey the moral Law both outwardly and inwardly, as "the greater stands for the lesser." Hence, we are to be completely obedient in action and thought to the eternal moral Law of God.

not cause anyone to stumble by either embellishing or minimizing God's Word in any way. My friend, we are seeing some of our fellow "Christians" doing this today, not only with their ungodly agenda of homosexual immorality, but also with a myriad of other twisted ways in which they adjust God's Word to their own liking!

Secondly, we have seen *The Mandates Regarding Our Enemies* (v 44). We are to love our enemies, bless those who curse us, do good to those who hate us, and pray for those who spitefully use and persecute us. Who are your enemies? And why are they your enemies? Have you practiced these commands from Christ? How are you loving them, blessing them, doing good to them, and praying for them?

Thirdly, we have learned *The Motivations for Loving Our Enemies* (vv 45-48), of which there are four. We are motivated to love our enemies because it proves that we belong to the Lord. We are motivated to love our enemies because it proves our love comes from God and not a human source. We are motivated to love our enemies because it proves our love is not hypocritical. And, we are motivated to love our enemies because it shows we are striving to be perfect as He is perfect. Are these the things that motivate you to love those who hate you? Or are you motivated to love your enemies by things like looking good before other believers, or being a man-pleaser? Are you motivated by what you can get out of it, by what you might receive? Are you motivated to love your enemies so you can make yourself look good in front of others, or so that you can have a dramatic story to tell?

Indeed, the Sermon on the Mount is painful, like being hit with a sledgehammer. No wonder Jesus' listeners were struck dumb at the end of the sermon! No wonder He reminds them that there are only two roads, one which leads to eternal life and the other which leads to eternal death! No wonder He says not everyone who says, "Lord, Lord," will enter into the kingdom of heaven! I don't know about you, but I'd rather have my "pain" now while there is time to repent, than to have my "pain" in eternal flames when there will be no time for repentance, no time for a second chance. Let's pray that God will change us from the inside out and thus demonstrate that we are indeed the daughters of our Father who is in heaven!

Questions to Consider

Mandates and Motivations for Loving Our Enemies
Matthew 5:43-48

1. (a) As you read Matthew 5:43-48, note all the ways we are to show love to our enemies. (b) Are these the ways *you* show love to *your* enemies? (c) What do *you* think Matthew 5:48 means?

2. Memorize Matthew 5:48.

3. (a) Jesus taught in Matthew 5:13-14 that we are the salt of the earth and the light of the world. Read over Matthew chapter 5 and list all the ways a believer's life should reflect those two things. (b) Does your life reflect these things? (c) What has been the most difficult lesson for you in this chapter and why? (d) Have you made any changes since we started this study?

4. (a) What should be our attitude toward those who are our enemies, according to 2 Samuel 16:5-14; Proverbs 24:17-18; Proverbs 24:28-29; Luke 6:27-36; Romans 12:17-21; and 1 Peter 3:8-12. (b) In what ways do you find these attitudes difficult?

5. How do you reconcile Matthew 5:43-48 with Psalm 139:19-22?

6. (a) How often do you pray for your enemies? (b) How would you use these final words of Jesus in Matthew 5 to help either yourself or someone else who has trouble loving others, especially those who are enemies? (c) How do we practically live out these words?

7. Do you have any enemies? Do you have trouble loving others? Please write your need in a prayer request to share with your group.

Chapter 10

The Contrasted Life of Holiness and Hypocrisy

Matthew 6:1-4

The story is told of a Sunday school teacher who was teaching a class of boys about the Pharisee in Luke 18:9-14. The passage reads like this:

> Also He spoke this parable to some who trusted in themselves that they were righteous, and despised others: "Two men went up to the temple to pray, one a Pharisee and the other a tax collector. The Pharisee stood and prayed thus with himself, 'God, I thank You that I am not like other men—extortioners, unjust, adulterers, or even as this tax collector. I fast twice a week; I give tithes of all that I possess.' And the tax collector, standing afar off, would not so much as raise his eyes to heaven, but beat his breast, saying, 'God, be merciful to me a sinner!' I tell you, this man went down to his house justified rather than the other; for everyone who exalts himself will be humbled, and he who humbles himself will be exalted."

When the teaching time was over, the teacher asked for each of the boys to pray a short prayer. One boy, without any apparent beating on his own chest, prayed: "We thank thee, God, that we are not like that Pharisee!"[42]

As comical as this story is, I'm afraid that some Christians today are inwardly thinking very similar thoughts. Oh, we may not be like that boy who actually voiced his prayer, but in our hearts we very well may be thanking God that we are not like "so and so." We don't realize it, but in essence we are often no different than the "Pharisee" we so loathe. Pharisaism, or hypocrisy, shows itself in numerous

---

42 Paul Lee Tan, *Encyclopedia of 7700 Illustrations: Signs of the Times* (Rockville: Assurance Publishers, 1979), 1266.

ways, and often those ways are subtle. As we begin chapter 6 of the Sermon on the Mount, Jesus will once again bring His audience to evaluate their spiritual lives not on their outward actions but on the inward motives of their hearts. These first four verses of chapter 6 are not short and sweet but short and solemn, especially for those who are willing to do some serious heart evaluation. Let's look at them together.

Matthew 6:1-4

> Take heed that you do not do your charitable deeds before men, to be seen by them. Otherwise you have no reward from your Father in heaven. ²Therefore, when you do a charitable deed, do not sound a trumpet before you as the hypocrites do in the synagogues and in the streets, that they may have glory from men. Assuredly, I say to you, they have their reward. ³But when you do a charitable deed, do not let your left hand know what your right hand is doing, ⁴that your charitable deed may be in secret; and your Father who sees in secret will Himself reward you openly. (Matthew 6:1-4) [43]

As we ended chapter five of Matthew's Gospel, we saw that the religious leaders misquoted and therefore misrepresented the command regarding one's enemies. They got the "love your neighbor" part right, but they conveniently added "hate your enemies" to it, which we learned was not written in the Old Testament. Jesus makes it clear that we are not to hate our enemies, but we are to bless them, do good to them, and pray for them. We are motivated to obey these commands regarding our enemies because it proves that we belong to the Lord, it proves that our love comes from God and not a human source, it proves that our love is not hypocritical, and that we are striving to be perfect as He is perfect.

As we begin chapter six, we'll see that Jesus is still contrasting the true kingdom citizen with the religious hypocrite. Martyn Lloyd-

---

43 In 5:21-48 Jesus illustrated moral righteousness by six illustrations; now, in chapter 6 of Matthew's Gospel, Jesus will illustrate religious righteousness by three particular practices, along with one single focus for kingdom citizens. Again, this is counter to the religious practices of the day, just like the moral illustrations were counter to New Testament times.

Jones says, "We may as well realize at the outset that this chapter 6 is again a very searching one; indeed, we can go further and say that this is a very painful one. I sometimes think that it is one of the most uncomfortable chapters to read in the entire Scriptures. It probes and examines and holds a mirror up before us, and it will not allow us to escape. There is no chapter which is more calculated to promote self-humbling and humiliation than this particular one. But thank God for it." [44]In this first lesson of Matthew 6, *The Contrasted Life of Holiness and Hypocrisy*, we will see:

Hypocritical Living and Its Results (vv 1-2)
Holy Living and Its Results (vv 3-4)

Let's look first at the life of hypocrisy and its results.

The Hypocritical Life and Its Results

Matthew 6:1-2

> Take heed that you do not do your charitable deeds before men, to be seen by them. Otherwise you have no reward from your Father in heaven. (Matthew 6:1)

The words *take heed* are words that we would do well to take heed the meaning of! *Take heed* means pay attention to this; be cautious about this; have your mind hold this matter; ponder it; think about it. What is it that are we to take heed? What is it that we are to be cautious about? *That we do not do our charitable deeds before men.* The term *charitable deeds*, in this particular verse, seems to indicate that these are acts of righteousness. As we come to verse 2, it appears that Jesus will be speaking about a specific deed, that of giving to those in need. And in the following verses He will specify other acts of righteousness by talking about fasting and prayer. There are many things we do that would be considered an act of righteousness or a charitable deed. It might be our giving, our praying, our fasting, our church attendance, our singing, our work, our cooking, and even

44 D. Martyn Lloyd-Jones, *Studies in the Sermon on the Mount* (Grand Rapids: William B. Eerdmans Publishing Company, 1971, 1976), 291.

our play or relaxation time. When you think about it, if we are to do everything to the glory of God, then everything we do can be considered an act of righteousness or an act of unrighteousness depending on our motive for doing it and what kind of act it is! For example, cooking our husband's favorite meal could be an act of righteousness. But if we're cooking and begrudging the time and energy it takes, then what could have been an act of righteousness really becomes an act of unrighteousness.

Jesus says take heed that you do not do your acts of righteousness *before men to be seen by them.* The words *before men* mean in front of them. The words *to be seen by them* actually come from a Greek word which pertains to being theatrical. Obviously, we have no choice but to do many of our deeds before others, but what Jesus is saying here is that we shouldn't do those deeds for the purpose of being seen by others. Being noticed by others should not be our motive. But let's consider a few passages, so that it will be clear that there is nothing wrong with being known as one whose life is characterized by doing good. In Acts 9:36 we read: "At Joppa there was a certain disciple named Tabitha, which is translated Dorcas. This woman was full of good works and charitable deeds which she did." And then in Acts 10:1-2 we read: "There was a certain man in Caesarea called Cornelius, a centurion of what was called the Italian Regiment, a devout man and one who feared God with all his household, who gave alms generously to the people, and prayed to God always." Both Dorcas and Cornelius were known for good works, or giving, but they did not go around boasting about it or doing it to be seen of others. They just did it.

The desire to be seen by men in order to be admired by them was a common problem with the unbelieving Jew. Jesus addresses this in John 5:41-44 when dialoguing with them: "I do not receive honor from men. But I know you, that you do not have the love of God in you. I have come in My Father's name, and you do not receive Me; if another comes in his own name, him you will receive. How can you believe, who receive honor from one another, and do not seek the honor that comes from the only God?" The Jew's desire was to have honor from others, not honor from God. In fact, did you notice the first thing Jesus said, that even He, the very son of God, does not receive honor from men? He did not come to earth to be noticed; He came to serve and to die! In John 12:42-43 we read, "Nevertheless, even among the rulers many believed in Him, but because of the Pharisees they did not confess Him, lest they should be put out of the synagogue; for they loved the praise of men more than the praise of God." This is the sad state of the unbelieving Jew, but not of those who belong to the kingdom. In fact, Paul, who was once an unbelieving Jew but became a believing Jew on the Damascus road, writes in 1 Thessalonians 2:6, "Nor did we seek glory from men, either from you or from others, when we might have made demands as apostles of Christ."

If desiring to be noticed by others is your motive for doing good, then Jesus says *you will have no reward from your Father in heaven.* The Greek word here for reward means, again, pay for services. So, the first result of hypocrisy is that hypocrites receive no reward from God. However, they do receive a reward; it's just not from above. Jesus goes on in verse 2 to mention what kind of reward they have.

> Therefore, when you do a charitable deed, do not sound a trumpet before you as the hypocrites do in the synagogues and in the streets, that they may have glory from men. Assuredly, I say to you, they have their reward. (Matthew 6:2)

Therefore, because of what Jesus has just said, that hypocrites do things to be seen of men, then you as Kingdom citizens should not do as they do! He says *when you do a charitable deed, do not sound a trumpet.* Jesus is now moving from general deeds to a specific deed, that of giving to those who are poor or in need. We have a good example of this in Acts 3:1-3, "Now Peter and John went up together to the temple at the hour of prayer, the ninth hour. And a certain man lame from his mother's womb was carried, whom they laid daily at the gate of the temple which is called Beautiful, to ask alms from those who entered the temple; who, seeing Peter and John about to go into the temple, asked for alms." There were poor people in Jesus day, just as there are in our day, and people were obligated to provide for them, especially the "religious" of the day. And we know from James 1:27 that giving to those in need is the responsibility of all genuine believers. James says there, "Pure and undefiled religion before God and the Father is this: to visit orphans and widows in their trouble, and to keep oneself unspotted from the world."

Perhaps you are wondering, "Did the Pharisees really *sound a trumpet* as they gave their money to the poor?" There is nothing in history that would indicate that the Jews actually blew a trumpet before they performed an act of righteousness, but it is possible that they did. However, this sounding of a trumpet could refer to the noise that was made as money was dropped into the containers used for collecting money for the poor. The openings were wide at one end and then narrow at the other end, much like a trumpet. When one would put their money in, it would make a jingling noise, which could be described as "sounding a trumpet." The more money one put in, the louder the noise would be. In our day we might equate it to letting the person next to you see how big your check is by placing it face up in the offering plate. Or you might let everyone know on Facebook how much you've done for someone in need. We have numerous ways of "sounding the trumpet" in our day.

Jesus tells those who belong to Him not to behave in such a way because such behavior defines those who are hypocrites. A *hypocrite* is an actor under an assumed character, a stage player. They are playing a part, but they are not playing who they really are. And they do this *in the synagogue*—the church, of all places!—*and in the streets*, where everyone can see them. We would say they do it at church, or places where there are any people who are assembled for worship, or a gathering. It might be as simple as a baby or wedding shower, a ladies' retreat, a gathering of people for dinner, anywhere actually, where you are doing things to be seen by others. The religious hypocrites of Jesus' day loved this attention, especially while they were in the house of worship. Matthew 23:6-7 states, "They love the best places at feasts, the best seats in the synagogues, greetings in the marketplaces, and to be called by men,

'Rabbi, Rabbi.'" This is especially appalling because the house of God should be the one place where He is put on display, not us! This should cause us to pause when we are in the house of God to ask ourselves if we are in any way drawing attention to ourselves instead of giving glory to God, whom we have come to worship. In our giving, our singing, our interactions with others, and yes, even in the way we dress, God should be exalted!

These religious hypocrites get exactly what they want; they get *glory from men*, which is *their reward*. They don't glorify God but they glorify themselves, and thus they get glory from men. We've already learned that the term reward means pay for services, and it's interesting that the Greek indicates that this can be either a good reward or a bad reward. When we think of rewards we often think of them as being good, but that is not always the case. The word also has to do with the payment of a receipt in full. In other words, that's all the reward they get, the praise of men; the reward they want is the reward that they get. They desire to be seen of men, to be honored by men, and that satisfies their flesh and that alone is their reward. He is not at all interested in honoring God but in honoring himself; he wants the praise of men. They are like Herod, who took all the glory for himself and was eaten by worms and died. He wanted the praise of men more than the praise of God, and that's what he got. He got the praise of men, and it cost him his life. Charles Spurgeon said, "To stand with a penny in one hand and a trumpet in the other is the posture of hypocrisy."[45]

So, the second result of hypocrisy is that *they have their reward* and that reward is glory or honor from men. Hypocrites receive no reward from God, but they do receive a reward from man, which is praise for their hypocritical living! In contrast to the hypocrites, who do things before men to be seen by them and to receive a selfish reward, we have those who are holy, who do things a tad bit differently, as we'll see in verses 3 and 4.

---

45 John R. W. Stott, *The Message of the Sermon on the Mount* (Downers Grove: Inter-Varsity Press, 1978), 129.

Holy Living and Its Results

Matthew 6:3-4

But when you do a charitable deed, do not let your left hand
know what your right hand is doing, (Matthew 6:3)

But is a word of contrast. Instead of sounding a trumpet when you
do a charitable deed, *you do not let your left hand know what your
right hand is doing*. As we know, the left hand is most commonly our
weakest hand, and the right hand generally has more strength. So,
exactly what is the significance of this? One man helps us here, "The
right hand is normally the active hand. So Jesus assumes we shall use
it when handing over our gift. Then He adds that our left hand must
not be watching. There is no difficulty in grasping His meaning. Not
only are we not to tell other people about our Christian giving; there
is a sense in which we are not even to tell ourselves. We are not to be
self-conscious in our giving, for our self-consciousness will readily
deteriorate into self-righteousness. So subtle is the sinfulness of the
heart that it is possible to take deliberate steps to keep our giving
secret from men while simultaneously dwelling on it in our own
minds in a spirit of self-congratulation."[46] It's the idea Peter speaks
of, when he says about Jesus in Acts 10:38, "how God anointed
Jesus of Nazareth with the Holy Spirit and with power, who went
about doing good and healing all who were oppressed by the devil,
for God was with Him." As Jesus went through life He looked for
ways to be a blessing to others and did not consider His own needs.
He also gave no thought as to what others thought of Him. My
friend, that is what Jesus is saying here. We must go through life
not thinking of what others will think of us or desiring that they will
think of us in a certain way, but we must go through life looking for
ways to give our lives for others. It ought to be so natural that our
left hand doesn't even know what our right hand is doing. This is
our calling, and this is what genuine kingdom citizens do. So, the
first result for those who live in holiness is that they possess genuine
humility and they don't even know it. They think of others as more

---

46 Ibid, 130.

important than themselves (Philippians 2:3). There is a second result for those who live holy lives, and it is found in verse 4.

> that your charitable deed may be in secret; and your Father who
> sees in secret will Himself reward you openly. (Matthew 6:4)

It is interesting that the hypocrite's desire is to be noticed by others, whereas the holy person's desire is to not be noticed at all, but to do their good deeds *in secret*. They are not interested in broadcasting what they do, but they want it to be done quietly, in private. Perhaps this is a struggle for you and deep in your heart you desire some sort of recognition for all that you do. We need to repent of such desires. We need to please only One and that is our Lord Christ!

Jesus has something to say to this. Regarding those who do their good deeds in private, He says *your Father sees in secret*. The fact that God sees what we do should be a sobering thought. Hebrews 4:13 states, "And there is no creature hidden from His sight, but all things are naked and open to the eyes of Him to whom we must give account." Proverbs 15:3 tells us, "The eyes of the Lord are in every place, keeping watch on the evil and the good." We need to keep in mind that not only does God see our acts of righteousness but He also knows our motives for why we do them. He knows our hearts; we do not. As Jeremiah 17:9-10 reminds us, "The heart is deceitful above all things, and desperately wicked; who can know it? I, the Lord, search the heart, I test the mind, even to give every man according to his ways, according to the fruit of his doings."

Our Father who sees in secret, Jesus says, *will Himself reward us openly*. Now, how this is done is really up to our Father, right? However, the word *reward* here is different than the previous word for reward. The Greek word for reward here does not entail the reward being good or bad, but it means to give away a reward that is good, to restore, to reward. And Jesus says He does this *openly*, which means publicly or externally. It might be that this is a temporary reward given here on earth, as in the case of Ruth in the Old Testament. In Ruth 2:11-12, we read, "And Boaz answered and said to her, 'It has been fully reported to me, all that you have done for your mother-in-law since the death of your husband, and how you have left your father and your mother and the land of your birth, and have come to a people whom you did not know before. The Lord repay your work, and a full reward be given you by the Lord God of Israel, under whose wings you have come for refuge.'" Here was a woman who sacrificed much for her mother-in-law. What was her reward? Probably the birth of her son, along with the glorious privilege of being in the lineage of Jesus.

But Jesus could also be referring to heavenly rewards or even to heaven itself. Scripture is clear about rewards in heaven. 1 Corinthians 3:11-15 tells us: "For no other foundation can anyone lay than that which is laid, which is Jesus Christ. Now if anyone builds on this foundation with gold, silver, precious stones, wood, hay, straw, each one's work will become clear; for the Day will declare it, because it will be revealed by fire; and the fire will test each one's work, of what sort it is. If anyone's work which he has built on it endures, he will receive a reward. If anyone's work is burned, he will suffer loss; but he himself will be saved, yet so as through fire." And then in 2 Corinthians 5:10, Paul also writes, "For we must all appear before the judgment seat of Christ, that each one may receive the things done in the body, according to what he has done, whether good or bad." So, there will be some type of rewards in heaven. Now, some might protest this concept and say, "Well, then I'm still doing my good deeds for something and not just doing it because my heart wants to do it." That would be a legitimate concern, because we shouldn't do these things for rewards of any kind, in my opinion. But the fact is that there are rewards and that's the joy! So, the second result of those who live in holiness by doing their acts of righteousness in secret is that they will receive a reward.

Summary

What about you? Are you going through life looking for ways to minister to those in need without fanfare? Or are you going through life looking for ways to call attention to yourself as you perform your acts of righteousness? Do you make sure that all your friends know all the good deeds you are doing, or do you just involve yourself in the needs of others without mentioning it at all? Do you secretly desire to be recognized by others for the things that you do, or are you content with the joy alone of knowing that your Father in heaven is honored by the things you do?

Hypocrisy or holiness, which best describes you? A hypocrite does things in order to be noticed, and they get what they want—praise from men. A holy person does things in secret, exhibiting humility, and they get what they want—praise or reward from God. One individual, the hypocrite, exalts himself, and God will humble him on that day, where there will be weeping and gnashing of teeth. The other individual, the holy person, humbles himself, and God will exalt him on that day, where there will be the Lord God Almighty and the Lamb and there he will reign with Him forever and ever!

Questions to Consider

The Contrasted Life of Holiness and Hypocrisy
Matthew 6:1-4

1. (a) Read Matthew 6:1-4 as well as Matthew 5:13-16. Do you think these passages contradict each other? (b) How do you reconcile them? Use Scripture to back your answer.

2. Memorize Matthew 6:3-4.

3. (a) How would you define a hypocrite? (b) How does Jesus define a hypocrite in Matthew 6:2, 5, 16; Matthew 15:7-8; Matthew 22:15-18; and Matthew 23:13-15, 23-29. (c) What will happen to hypocrites, according to Matthew 24:51? (d) What are some ways that we can be hypocritical? (e) How do you fight hypocrisy in your life?

4. (a) King David was a "man after God's own heart," and yet he wrote Psalm 139, which deals with the glaring reality that God sees our hearts and knows everything about us. We cannot hide any secrets or motives from Him. What accounts in King David's life might have contributed to his writing of this Psalm? (If possible, do some study to find out the background of this Psalm.) (b) Read over Psalm 139 meditatively and prayerfully, asking God to show you any forms of hypocrisy in your life.

5. (a) What are some ways we as Christians "sound the trumpet" or "toot our own horn" to let others know how righteous we are? (b) Do you think praising others for things they have accomplished can aid in causing them to be self-righteous or prideful? (c) How do we balance honoring those we are to honor without causing them to be self-righteous? (Give some thought also to parenting your children and how to balance praising them for a job well done without contributing to their pride.)

6. What do you think Jesus meant in Matthew 6:4 regarding being rewarded for giving in secret?

7. Hypocrisy is a subtle and deadly sin. Please, my friend, prayerfully consider this in your heart, asking God to show you where you are failing. Write your need to share with others.

Chapter 11

The Right and Wrong Way to Pray

Matthew 6:5-8

For the past several years, I have prayed often, sometimes daily, for the sale of a rental home my husband and I own. In my "human reasoning" the sale of this home would be in our best interests for a number of reasons. Perhaps you also have prayed often, sometimes daily or even year after year, for a particular thing. It might be the sale of some property or possession. It might be the salvation of a lost family member or friend. It might be that you are praying for an especially difficult child or grandchild. It might be continual prayers for a husband who doesn't lead your home spiritually as he should. Perhaps your ongoing prayer is for reconciliation with someone. Or maybe your steadfast prayers are for other things I haven't mentioned.

When we consider our ongoing prayers and we consider the text before us in this lesson, a question we might ask ourselves is this: "Am I in violation of what Jesus is saying here in the Sermon on the Mount? Am I using vain repetitions like the heathen do? Do I think I will be heard and answered because of my many words?" These are good questions to ask ourselves and, the Lord willing, we will answer these questions as we study this important passage of Scripture and deal with the right ways and the wrong ways to pray. In our next lesson, we'll continue to deal with the subject of prayer as we examine the model Jesus gives us for praying. And in the lesson after that, we'll consider the third act of righteousness Jesus mentions—our fasting.

Matthew 6:5-8

And when you pray, you shall not be like the hypocrites. For they love to pray standing in the synagogues and on the corners of the streets, that they may be seen by men. Assuredly, I say to you, they have their reward. ⁶But you, when you pray, go into your room, and when you have shut your door, pray to your Father who is in the secret place; and your Father who sees in secret will reward you openly. ⁷And when you pray, do not use vain repetitions as the heathen do. For they think that they will be heard for their many words. ⁸Therefore do not be like them. For your Father knows the things you have need of before you ask Him. (Matthew 6:5-8)

In this lesson, we will consider what Jesus lays out for us in Matthew 6:5-8:

Two Wrong Ways to Pray (vv 5,7)

Two Right Ways to Pray (vv 6,8)

In our last lesson, we saw the stark contrast between the holy life and the hypocritical life. The hypocrites live their lives to be seen by others, and because of that they have no reward from God. They do, however, receive a reward from men—man's admiration or praise—but that is all they get! On the other hand, the holy live their lives serving without any desire to be noticed, resulting in genuine humility, and receive a reward from their Father in heaven.

In our last lesson, we learned that Jesus mentioned acts of righteousness and He specifically mentioned the act of giving to those who are in need. He now turns to address another specific act of righteousness that God's children should be doing—the act of praying. Just like our giving to others in need can be done in a right way and a wrong way, so it is with our work of prayer; it too can be done correctly or incorrectly. Let's consider the first wrong way of praying, in verse 5.

The Wrong Way to Pray

Matthew 6:5, 7

And when you pray, you shall not be like the hypocrites. For they love to pray standing in the synagogues and on the corners

of the streets, that they may be seen by men. Assuredly, I say to
you, they have their reward. (Matthew 6:5)

Notice that Jesus says *and when you pray*. He does not say *if* you
pray. All kingdom citizens, all of God's children, should be praying.
It amazes me that people who claim that they are children of God
will also say, in the very same breath, that they don't pray to God.
I remember a particular visit I had with a woman in which we
were discussing prayer and, specifically, her personal prayer life
and the wonderful fact that the Lord answers our prayers. She said
that was a problem because she didn't pray. I told her that it was a
huge problem because it was an indicator of a much bigger issue—a
possible indication that she was lost. All of God's children should
be praying. How does one get through the day without communion
with the Lord? Prayer should be like breathing for a Christian; as
Paul says, we should be praying without ceasing (1 Thessalonians
5:17). The word *pray* communicates the idea that we direct our
prayers to God. That's who we pray to. In fact, in our next lesson,
Jesus will make this clear when He tells His listeners that when they
pray they are to pray to their Father who is in heaven. We pray to
God in heaven, the real God, not some god of our imagination. That
reality makes it imperative that we know the God of the Bible by
studying His attributes, by studying who He is.

Jesus continues on by saying that when you pray, *you shall not be
like the hypocrites*. What do the hypocrites do? How do they pray?
Jesus says *they love to pray standing in the synagogues and on the
corners of the streets, that they may be seen by men*. We already
learned in our last lesson that the hypocrites loved to be seen when
they did their acts of righteousness, specifically their giving to the
poor. But this time it is in their praying that Jesus says they want to
be seen. He says *they love to pray*. It's interesting that the word for
love that Jesus uses here is phileo, which means they have a fond
affection for this, they have a personal attachment to it. Their love
isn't a love of praying and it is certainly not a love for the God they
pray to, but it is a love; it is a tender affection for the attention they
get out of it. That's what they love!

To understand what Jesus is saying, we need to understand the Jewish custom of the day. The Jews' practice was to pray three times a day. We find this mentioned in Psalm 55:17: "Evening and morning and at noon, I will pray, and cry aloud, and He shall hear my voice." And again in Daniel 6:10, "Now when Daniel knew that the writing was signed, he went home. And in his upper room, with his windows open toward Jerusalem, he knelt down on his knees three times that day, and prayed and gave thanks before his God, as was his custom since early days." There is certainly no sin in praying three times a day, but many religious Jews would pray prayers that were rote—the exact same prayers day after day after day. Their prayers were not like those of Abraham, David, Job, Daniel and others in the Old Testament, who actually talked to God.

Standing was the common posture of prayer for the Jew, so Jesus is clearly not condemning standing to pray. But He is condemning the practice of intentionally praying in places where one loves to stand because they know they'll be noticed. The synagogue was obviously a place where worshippers gathered, so they would most certainly be noticed there. Likewise, corners of busy streets were also places they'd be noticed. The phrase *corners of the streets* actually refers to an open square, so this would be the corner of a wide street. This isn't a narrow street Jesus is referring to, but a wide one, which, of course, would have the most people traveling on it. In this way, the hypocrites could be seen by the biggest crowd. And they would do this for the exact same reason we saw in our last lesson: *that they may be seen by men.* They would do it so that they themselves might shine before men or make a display before men. For this, Jesus says they get the *reward* they seek, the same reward they receive when they do their giving to be seen of men; their reward is being praised by men! They get the reward of being admired by others, of being thought of as really religious and really close to God! But since prayer is, in reality, talking to God, there isn't any real possibility that these hypocrites are genuinely praying because God would have nothing to do with their desire to be noticed. God hates pride; but God loves humility. Those who exalt themselves will be humbled.

This is the first wrong way to pray—to be seen of others. Hypocrites don't pray to God; they pray to men. The hypocrite's prayer life is a ritual, not a relationship, as can be seen in many religions, including Catholicism and Islam, to name a few. But I must also say that many well-meaning Christians do this same thing, and their prayers are nothing more than legalistic rituals. I fear many are just like the Pharisee in Luke 18, praying only to themselves and not to God. Christianity is not a religion; it is a relationship with the living God! God wants fellowship and He desires a relationship with us. The genuine kingdom citizen must pray differently; they must pray the right way. So we turn from the first wrong way to pray to the first right way to pray, in verse 6.

The Right Way to Pray

Matthew 6:6, 8

> But you, when you pray, go into your room, and when you have shut your door, pray to your Father who is in the secret place; and your Father who sees in secret will reward you openly. (Matthew 6:6)

But you, you who are kingdom citizens, you pray differently. This is very similar wording to what we saw in verses two and three about doing alms. But you, you who are my children, you do differently! Instead of desiring to be seen by others when you pray, desire to be seen by your Father in heaven. He is the one who knows the heart of all men. Jesus says *go into your room*, and after *you have shut the door*, then *pray to your Father who is in the secret place*.

The biblical world did not have homes like ours. Some people lived in tents, some lived in homes, but their homes were quite simple. In Jesus' day, it was common for there to be two stories on a home, and the roof was flat and used for living purposes as well. Often, they would add a room on the roof for guests. There was also an outside staircase that went up to the roof. Most Jewish homes would have a private room designated for prayer; it may have been on the roof itself or in the main part of the home. Acts 10:9 says, "The next day, as they went on their journey and drew near the city, Peter went up on the housetop to pray, about the sixth hour."

In our day, we have many parts of our homes that are private where we can go to pray. It may not even be a bedroom, but a closet or a car or our bed or our backyard. It may be like Suzanna Wesley, who had 19 children and yet still found an hour each day to pull her apron up over her head to be alone with God. Dear sister, her prayers must have been powerful because two of her sons were Charles and John Wesley, one who became a beloved hymn writer and the other a theologian. We all must find that "room" where we can go and be alone with God. A literal shutting of the door may not be feasible, but the idea is that you make an effort to shut out all distractions. This should prompt us all to evaluate the time we spend in prayer and in the Word. Do we endeavor to remove all distractions so that we can fully concentrate on the one thing that is needed? Even Jesus drew away to spend time alone with God (see Luke 5:15-16; 6:12; 9:18). I know a woman who puts her cell phone in another room while she is having her sacred time with the Lord. Personally, I am easily distracted by many things, and I think it would be wise for all of us to "shut the door," so to speak, so that the time we spend with our heavenly Father can be undistracted and alone.

Maybe you are asking, "Why should I do that?" Because, Jesus says, *your Father who is in the secret place* also *sees in secret*. Albert Barnes helps us here: "The meaning of the Savior is, that there should be some place where we may be in secret—where we may be alone with God. There should be some 'place' to which we may resort where no ear will hear us but 'His' ear, and no eye can see us but HIS eye. Unless there is such a place, secret prayer will not be long or strictly maintained."[47] Oswald Chambers says, "God is in secret, and He sees us from 'the secret place'—He does not see us as other people do, or as we see ourselves. When we live in a 'secret place,' it becomes impossible for us to doubt God. We

---

47 Albert Barnes, From *Barnes' Notes*, Electronic Database Copyright © 1997, 2003, 2005, 2006 by Biblesoft, Inc. All rights reserved.

become more sure of Him than of anyone or anything else. Enter into 'the secret place,' and you will find God was right in the middle of your everyday circumstances all the time."[48]

If you pray, Jesus says, then your Father who sees in secret *will reward you openly*. We learned about a similar phrase in our last lesson, when we studied verse 4. We saw then that this might be some temporary reward or it could also refer to rewards that we will receive at the judgment seat of Christ. In this particular verse, the reward Jesus is referring to might be as simple as God answering our prayers. We know He doesn't listen to the prayers of the sinner or the one who regards iniquity in their heart, but His ears are open to the prayers of the righteous. He does hear and He does answer and, my friend, that is reward enough (see Psalm 66:18; John 9:31; 1 Peter 3:12; 1 John 5:14-15)!

Before we go on, I want to make sure we understand that Jesus is not condemning public praying. We have numerous examples of public praying in the Word of God. We also know from 1 Timothy that public prayer was expected in the house of worship. What is condemned, however, is praying to be seen by others. And if you're not in the habit of praying in private, then praying in public would seem hypocritical as well. To pray in public in order to be seen and admired by others brings a fleshly satisfaction. To pray in private in order to be heard by God in heaven brings heavenly satisfaction. To pray before men to be seen by them creates an appetite of pride. To pray to God to be heard by Him creates an attitude of humility. Praying like the hypocrites causes us to see ourselves as more important than we are. Praying as a child of God causes us to see ourselves for who we really are, in desperate need of Him! The first right way to pray is to do so in secret. Jesus now warns us against the second wrong way to pray, in verse 7.

---

48 Oswald Chambers, *My Utmost For His Highest* (Grand Rapids: Discovery House, 2012), 236.

The Wrong Way to Pray

Matthew 6:5, 7

And when you pray, do not use vain repetitions as the heathen do. For they think that they will be heard for their many words. (Matthew 6:7)

Notice again, it is not if you pray but *when you pray*. Jesus says *do not use vain repetitions as the heathen do*. The words *vain repetitions* mean to stutter or babble. Martin Luther says it is "to utter a lot of senseless and superfluous words."[49] We have examples of this very thing in God's Word. One example can be found in 1 Kings 18, when Elijah is facing off with the prophets of Baal to see who was the true God, the LORD or Baal. Elijah puts a challenge before them: sacrifice a bull on an altar with wood but no fire, and call on the name of their god to see if he will light the fire. Likewise, Elijah would do the same, calling on the name of his God to see if He would light the fire. The people think this is a great idea. So, we read in 1 Kings 18:26-29: "So they took the bull which was given them, and they prepared it, and called on the name of Baal from morning even till noon, saying, 'O Baal, hear us!' But there was no voice; no one answered. Then they leaped about the altar which they had made." This is the idea of vain repetitions that Jesus is talking about; they cried out day and night "O Baal, hear us!" We know from the rest of the story that this went on for some time and, of course, their god didn't answer. Elijah's God, however, did answer and fire was sent from heaven and devoured not only the sacrifice on the altar but all the water that Elijah had commanded to be poured over it.

In the New Testament, an example of praying with vain repetition can be found in Acts 19, when Paul comes to the town of Ephesus and is distressed because of the worship of the goddess Diana. As is his custom, Paul preaches the gospel to the people there and many are persuaded to turn away from their idolatry. Well, that doesn't set well with a man named Demetrius, a silversmith who was not

---

49 R.C.H. Lenski, *Commentary on the New Testament* (Peabody: Hendrickson Publishers, 2001), 262.

only responsible for crafting idols for the worship of Diana but several other idols as well. Demetrius calls together his workmen and warns them that because of Paul their occupation is in danger. An uproar begins in the city as we have recorded in Acts 19:28-34: "Now when they heard this, they were full of wrath and cried out, saying, 'Great is Diana of the Ephesians!' So the whole city was filled with confusion, and rushed into the theater with one accord, having seized Gaius and Aristarchus, Macedonians, Paul's travel companions. And when Paul wanted to go in to the people, the disciples would not allow him. Then some of the officials of Asia, who were his friends, sent to him pleading that he would not venture into the theater. Some therefore cried one thing and some another, for the assembly was confused, and most of them did not know why they had come together. And they drew Alexander out of the multitude, the Jews putting him forward. And Alexander motioned with his hand, and wanted to make his defense to the people. But when they found out that he was a Jew, all with one voice cried out for about two hours, 'Great is Diana of the Ephesians!'" Just like the worshippers of Baal in the Old Testament crying out for hours to their god, here we have the worshippers of Diana crying out for two hours, "Great is Diana of the Ephesians!" They thought they would be heard for their much speaking, for their many words, just as Jesus says in the Sermon on the Mount. He says the *heathen* do this, which is just another word for Gentile or unbeliever.

Now, this brings to mind an important question: "What is the difference between using many words, as Jesus condemns, and praying often for something?" In addition to the example in the Questions to Consider, we also have the example of the widow and the unjust judge in Luke 18, where we read that God will avenge His own who cry out to Him day and night.

Also, as we will see when we get to Matthew 7:7, Jesus tells us to ask and assures us that when we do ask we will receive, and the Greek rendering there indicates that we are to keep on asking over and over. Even Jesus in His prayer prior to His crucifixion prayed three times that the cup of suffering would pass from Him (Matthew

26). One commentator helps us discern what is meant by using many words; he writes, "'Like the Gentiles' is more than a reference to the custom of the pagans in their praying, for the Jews often prayed in the same way. The heathen tried to tire out their gods with such endless prayers. Mere formulas were repeated over and over again; the Jews had such prayer formulas, Catholics also have them in the form of their rosary." [50] We also see this today with the charismatic movement where they are literally taught to repeat things over and over until they become ecstatic in their speaking. They're taught that this is the biblical form of tongues or some heavenly prayer language (read Acts 2 to see that this is not so).

I had a close friend several years ago who came out of the charismatic movement. Before she did, we would have some pretty serious discussions about her ability to speak in tongues. After leaving the charismatic church, she confessed to me that it was all lies and that she indeed went to a class in her church where they actually taught her how to do this and told her to pick a word and just say it over and over again and eventually she would have the gift of tongues. [51] She knew it was wrong but felt immense pressure to go along with it. In fact, I have since seen for myself this very same thing written on church websites, where they specifically say that in the Christian school they have at their church they will teach your child to speak in tongues. My friend, Jesus is not impressed with your vain words, with your repetitious sounds! Can you pray to Him numerous times regarding the same subject? Of course, you can! But to weary Him with such nonsense as the pagans do is absurd. So the second wrong way of praying is praying with vain repetitions. Jesus now ends this section of the Sermon on the Mount with the second right way to pray, in verse 8.

50 Ibid, 262

51 When Jesus rebuked the practice of praying with "vain repetitions as the heathen do," He cut to the core of much of Charismatic praying today. The Greek word translated "vain repetitions" is battalogeo which is a onomatopoetic term, that is, a mimicking of sounds. The idea refers to countless prayers or saying meaningless-sounding words in our praying. Evidently, the heathen false religions held this kind of praying in high esteem, as they would jabber meaningless-sounding words to their gods, believing that somehow, although they didn't understand what they were praying, their god would understand. Of course, we still have this prayer practice today, as many believe that the spiritual gift of speaking in tongues is a secret prayer language, which only God knows.

The Right Way to Pray

Matthew 6:6, 8

Therefore do not be like them. For your Father knows the things
you have need of before you ask Him. (Matthew 6:8)

Jesus says *do not be like them*, do not be like the heathen. Why?
Because *your Father knows the things you have need of before you
ask Him.* Perhaps this seems confusing to you. When we think about
what Jesus is saying, though, it really isn't confusing. God isn't
impressed with our many words. He is not somehow going to come
to our aid just because we repeat something over and over for hours
on end. He already knows our needs. He want us to come to Him. He
wants our fellowship. He wants to answer our prayers. He desires to
give good things to His children. But He is God and we are not, and
He is not impressed with our vain babblings. "The purpose of prayer
is not to inform or persuade God, but to come before Him sincerely,
purposely, consciously, and devotedly."[52] The second right way to
pray then is not with vain repetitions but with voicing your real
concerns. In our next lesson together, the Lord will continue with
His theme of prayer and teach us how we ought to pray. It is a prayer
most of us can quote but few of us truly understand.

Summary

We have learned *The Wrong Way to Pray* (vv 5, 7) and *The Right
Way to Pray* (v 6, 8). The wrong way is to be seen (v 5); the right
way is to be in secret (v 6). The wrong way is with vain repetitions
(v 7); the right way is to voice real concerns (v 8).

What about your prayer life? Have you examined it lately? Are you
praying correctly or incorrectly? Do you come to prayer meetings
to be seen by others? Do you enjoy praying before others so that
they think of you as more religious than you really are? When you

---

52 John Stott, *The Message of the Sermon on the Mount* (Downers Grove: Intervarsity,
1978), 145.

pray in public, do you actually pray to God, or do you pray to those who are listening? Are you more eager to pray in public than you are to pray in private? Do you love public praying more than private praying? Do you try to impress others with your beautiful prayers or with how much you know? Are you praying to God in your public prayers or are you directing those prayers toward someone who is in your listening audience? When you pray, do you think about what you're praying or do you simply mumble some words you've mumbled before? Do you use the same clichés over and over when you pray? Or are you praying from a sincere heart? Do you tell God what is really on your mind?

Let's get more pointed by asking some questions based specifically on the two right and two wrong ways to pray. Do you pray to be seen by others? Are you wanting to impress people with your knowledge or passion when you pray? If so, Jesus has something to say to you from Matthew 23:14: "Woe to you, Scribes and Pharisees, hypocrites! ... [who] for a pretense make long prayers. Therefore you will receive greater condemnation."

Or do you pray in secret with distractions removed so that you can speak intimately with your Father alone who sees you in secret? If so, Jesus has something to say to you from Matthew 7:11: "If you then, being evil, know how to give good gifts to your children, how much more will your Father who is in heaven give good things to those who ask Him!"

Do you pray like the pagans and think you will be heard for your many words? If so, Jesus has something to say to you from Isaiah 59:2-3: "But your iniquities have separated you from your God; and your sins have hidden His face from you, so that He will not hear ... Your lips have spoken lies, your tongue has muttered perversity."

Or do you pray knowing that your Father in heaven knows you have need of things before you even ask Him? If so, Jesus has something to say to you from Jeremiah 33:3: "Call to Me, and I will answer you, and show you great and mighty things, which you do not know."

I fear many of us, including myself, will have much accounting to do on that day for this "act of righteousness," our praying. By God's grace, let us determine to pray not like the hypocrites; rather, let us endeavor to pray like the holy ones, like God's own children. Would that we all had the attitude of C. S. Lewis, who once said, "I pray because I can't help myself. I pray because I'm helpless. I pray because the need flows out of me all the time, waking and sleeping. It doesn't change God, it changes me."

Questions to Consider

The Right and Wrong Way to Pray
Matthew 6:5-8

1. (a) Read Matthew 6:5-8 and 1 Kings 18:20-46. Who is praying the right way in these passages? (b) Who is praying the wrong way in these passages? (c) What do these passages teach you about the importance of praying correctly?

2. Memorize Matthew 6:6.

3. (a) Jesus says in Matthew 6:5 that the hypocrites love to pray in places where they can be seen. According to Matthew 23:6-7; Mark 12:38-40; and Luke 16:14, what else to do the hypocrites love? (b) What does Jesus say to them regarding these things, in Matthew 23:8-12; Mark 12:40; and Luke 16:15? (c) What other things can one do to be noticed by others? (d) What is the remedy for our self-love? Use Scripture to back your answer.

4. (a) How do you reconcile Matthew 6:7-8 with Luke 18:1-5? (b) What do you think is meant by the words "vain repetitions" in Matthew 6:7? (c) What are some ways believers pray in that way?

5. (a) Since it is true that God knows what we need before we ask Him, as Jesus says in Matthew 6:8, why then do we need to pray? (b) Why do *you* pray?

6. (a) What are some hindrances to praying that one might have? (b) What are some objections some might have to the idea of praying publicly? (c) How do we remedy these?

7. Do you find yourself praying more like the kingdom citizen or the hypocrite? What changes do you think God would have you make after considering what His Son says in the Sermon on the Mount? Please write your need or needs in the form of a prayer request to share with your group. (Remember, God sees your secret heart, so write something that is genuine.)

Chapter 12

The Proper Pattern for Praying

Matthew 6:9-15

Prayer is the soul's sincere desire,
Uttered or unexpressed,
The motion of a hidden fire
That trembles in the breast.

Prayer is the burden of a sigh,
The falling of a tear,
The upward glancing of an eye
When none but God is near.

Prayer is the simplest form of speech
That infant lips can try;
Prayer, the sublimest strains
That reach the Majesty on high.

Prayer is the Christian's vital breath,
The Christian's native air;
His watchword at the gates of death:
He enters heav'n with prayer.

O Thou by whom we come to God,
The Life, the Truth, the Way!
The path of prayer Thyself has trod:
Lord, teach us how to pray![53]

In 1818, these beautiful lyrics were written by James Montgomery, who wrote more than 400 hymns. He terms prayer well: a sincere desire, a fire in the breast, a sigh, an upward glance, simple speech, a strain, the Christian's breath. And yet, with all the words

---

53 *Prayer is the Soul's Sincere Desire*, by James Montgomery, 1771-1854.

Montgomery uses to describe prayer, he ends with, "Lord, teach us how to pray!" And so many of God's children echo the same words: "Lord, teach us how to pray!" Whether we are young in the faith or old, every child of God is in need of more prayer and more instruction in prayer. This is where we find ourselves as we continue in our study of the Sermon on the Mount.

In our last lesson, we learned that Jesus spoke to the multitudes on the Mount regarding two wrong ways to pray and two right ways to pray. It is wrong to pray to be seen by others; it is right to pray in secret before God. It is wrong to pray with vain repetitions; it is right to pray by voicing our real concerns. Perhaps some who were sitting and listening had the same question you might have right now, and that is, "How do I know if I'm praying in the proper way? Is there a model for my praying?" Yes, there is! And Jesus, being the compassionate Savior He is, gives a model prayer for all to hear. He says,

Matthew 6:9-15

In this manner, therefore, pray: Our Father in heaven, hallowed be Your name. [10]Your kingdom come. Your will be done on earth as it is in heaven. [11]Give us this day our daily bread. [12]And forgive us our debts, as we forgive our debtors. [13]And do not lead us into temptation, but deliver us from the evil one. For Yours is the kingdom and the power and the glory forever. Amen. [14]For if you forgive men their trespasses, your heavenly Father will also forgive you. [15]But if you do not forgive men their trespasses, neither will your Father forgive your trespasses.

As Jesus teaches us *The Proper Pattern for Praying*, we will see:

The Proper Person (v 9a)
The Proper Petitions (v 9b-13a)
The Proper Praise (v 13b)
The Proper Posture (v 14-15)

It's interesting to me that over the years people have termed this prayer "The Lord's Prayer," and yet, when you look at its components, it's clear that this is not a prayer Jesus would need to pray. His name *is* hallowed, He *doesn't* sin, and His *is* the kingdom and the power and the glory forever! Perhaps a better title for this prayer would be "The Disciple's Prayer" or—in tune with the message of the Sermon on the Mount—"The Kingdom Citizen's Prayer." With this in mind, let's consider the proper pattern for praying and, as we do, let's look at the proper person we pray to, in verse 9a.

The Proper Person

Matthew 6:9a

> In this manner, therefore, pray: Our Father in heaven, Hallowed be Your name. (Matthew 6:9a)

Jesus begins this section by saying *in this manner, therefore, pray.* The words *in this manner* mean in this way. This is the way or the pattern of praying. The Jewish rabbis had formulas that they would use to teach their disciples to pray. We have a hint of this in Luke 11:1: "Now it came to pass, as He was praying in a certain place, when He ceased, that one of His disciples said to Him, 'Lord, teach us to pray, as John also taught his disciples.'" Evidently, the disciples were aware of John's disciples and the fact that John had taught them some formula for how to pray, and they, therefore, wanted their own Teacher to teach them how to pray.

Jesus continues with the word *therefore*, which always points us back to what has just been said. *Therefore*, or because of what He has just said about the hypocrites praying, because of what He has just said about kingdom citizens guarding themselves from praying in order to be admired by others and from using vain repetitions, because of what He has just said about kingdom citizens praying in secret and speaking what is really on their heart, *in this manner* we ought to *pray*. Even knowing these things, we still need instruction in how to pray. Now, Jesus is not saying this is the prayer we should pray at all times; to do so would be exactly what He has been telling us not to do. There shouldn't be any sign of legalism in our praying. Instead of a legalistic formula, this prayer serves as a model or a pattern for our praying.

Since it is our aim to study this specific prayer, we should begin by defining what the word *pray* means. The word means to supplicate or worship, and it has the idea of prayers that are made to God. This is a great definition because that is what Jesus says next: we are to pray to *our Father in heaven*. This is the proper person we pray to! We don't pray to ourselves like the Pharisees do, and we don't pray to others so that they will be impressed with our praying. We pray to our Father who is in heaven. Notice that it is *our Father*, not your Father or my Father, but ours. This is an indicator that we are a family and that God has many children. It is also, perhaps, a reminder that we are to live and pray for others. It's not just about us; it's about others, which has been much of Jesus' thrust throughout the Sermon on the Mount.

Father is the word Abba. In the Jewish world, when a child was weaned they would learn to say Abba, meaning daddy, and Imma, meaning mother. When Jesus says we are to address God as Abba Father, the Jew listening would think this title for God would be inappropriate and irreverent, even though the Old Testament is replete with examples of this intimate relationship. Hosea is one of example we have. Hosea 11:1-4 states: "When Israel was a child, I loved him, and out of Egypt I called My son. As they called them, so they went from them; they sacrificed to the Baals, and burned incense to carved images. I taught Ephraim to walk, taking them by their arms; but they did not know that I healed them. I drew them with gentle cords, with bands of love, and I was to them as those who take the yoke from their neck. I stooped and fed them." Even in the New Testament we have examples of this. In Galatians 4:6-7, Paul writes, "And because you are sons, God has sent forth the Spirit of His Son into your hearts, crying out, 'Abba, Father!' Therefore you are no longer a slave but a son, and if a son, then an heir of God through Christ." In Romans 8:15-16, Paul writes again,

"For you did not receive the spirit of bondage again to fear, but you received the Spirit of adoption by whom we cry out, 'Abba, Father.' The Spirit Himself bears witness with our spirit that we are children of God." In both of these verses, Paul indicates that without a saving relationship with God we cannot call Him "Father" any more than I can call another man "Father" who is not my legitimate Father. This is imperative in our praying. It is no wonder that Jesus comes to the end of the sermon and tells some that He never knew them. They never had a legitimate, intimate relationship with Him.

In this same way, the term *Father* also indicates a nearness. When we think of an earthly father we know that he is near; he is our protector and our provider. Make sure, my friend, that you can pray "Our Father" knowing that you are "His daughter." Our Father is the proper person we pray to. After we acknowledge that, then we need to know what we are to pray about, right? So, we now turn to the proper petitions. There are six of them; the first three have to do with the Father and the last three have to do with His children.

The Proper Petitions

Matthew 6:9b-13a

Hallowed be Your name. (Matthew 6:9b)

Jesus says *Hallowed be Your name*. This is the first petition, for the Lord's name to be made holy. Now, what exactly is entailed in this request? To *hallow* something means to treat it as holy or pure. This is a prayer that the name of our Father would be made or treated as holy. Dear one, we must make sure we are hallowing His name in an age when His name is constantly being maligned. We hallow or make holy His name by living lives of obedience in our homes, in our churches, in our workplaces, in our thoughts, deeds and actions, and, yes, even in our private lives. There is nothing hidden from this Holy One's eyes.

This first petition is important because it indicates that we need to meditate on just who we're talking to: a holy Father. He is not like an earthly father who is sinful and frail. We have become too casual with God and we need to remember to approach Him with godly reverence and fear. Too often, we mumble a few words and then we're on our way. Instead, we would do well to pause long enough to realize who we are praying to. Our Father in heaven, yes, but He is our holy Father, and it should be our deepest desire to see that His name is hallowed both in our lives and in the whole earth. Martin Lloyd-Jones says, "We tend to be self-centered in our prayers that when we drop on our knees before God, we think only about ourselves and our troubles and perplexities. We start talking about them at once, and of course nothing happens. According to our Lord's teaching here we should not expect anything to happen. That is not the way to approach God. We must pause before we speak in prayer."[54] This would be an affront to the Pharisees, who prayed only with themselves and for themselves. Far from their mind was the holiness of God. It is vain to call our Father holy and yet not live out that holiness! Jesus moves on to the second and third petition in verse 10.

> Your kingdom come. (Matthew 6:10a)

Your kingdom come is the second petition. The word *kingdom* simply means God's reign. When we pray for God's kingdom to come we are praying for God to reign in every place and at all times. This, of course, will culminate when He returns and sets up His everlasting kingdom. Jesus is clear that this petition is for His kingdom, not our kingdom. So often, we tell God how we want the day to go, but rarely do we think of His agenda and His kingdom. The Jew listening to Jesus teach this was hoping that Messiah would usher in a kingdom by political or military force, but that is not the kingdom Christ has in mind here. His kingdom is an everlasting heavenly kingdom. One man helps us think seriously about this petition; he says, "Christians ought not utter this petition lightly or thoughtlessly. Throughout

---

54 D. Martyn Lloyd-Jones, *Studies in the Sermon on the Mount* (Grand Rapids: Wm B. Eerdmans Publishing Co., 1971), 326-327.

the centuries, followers of Jesus suffering savage persecution have prayed this prayer with meaning and fervor. But I suspect that our comfortable pews often mock our sincerity when we repeat the phrase today. We would have no objection to the Lords' return, we think, provided he holds off a bit and lets us finish a degree first, or lets us taste marriage, or gives us time to succeed in a business or profession, or grants us the joy of seeing grandchildren. Do we really hunger for the kingdom to come in all its surpassing righteousness? Or would we rather waddle through a swamp of insincerity and unrighteousness?"[55] This request, along with the one before it and the one after it, are requests that ought to be prayed until the Lord returns.

Your will be done on earth as it is in heaven. (Matthew 6:10b)

The next petition that pertains to our Father is *Your will be done.* This is the third petition—Your will be done. *Your will* would mean your choice, your determination, your decree. God's *will* includes His demands as well as His determination to bring about events. Notice, too, that it is not just Your will be done *on earth* but also *as it is in heaven.* In other words, may Your will be done now on this earth even as Your will is being done now in heaven. This would mean that we are praying not only for God's will to be done in our lives personally but also throughout all the earth.

This isn't a prayer we're to pray with a clenched fist and gritted teeth. We pray, "Your will be done," with a joyful heart, realizing that God's will is truly the best for us, no matter what that may entail. Later in Matthew's Gospel, Jesus Himself will pray this before He goes to the cross: "O My Father, if this cup cannot pass away from Me unless I drink it, Your will be done" (Matthew 26:42). Jesus, being all-knowing, knew what this prayer meant for Him at the time. It meant a horrible death of crucifixion; it meant mocking and scourging; it meant His disciples would forsake Him; it meant drinking the cup of the wrath of almighty God; it meant having His

---

55 D. A. Carson, *The Sermon on the Mount: An Evangelical Exposition of Matthew 5-7* (Grand Rapids: Baker Book House, 1978), 66.

Father forsake Him; it meant bearing the sins of the world. That's what it meant for Him to pray, "Your will be done." And yet the outcome of that prayer was that salvation would be offered to all mankind. My friend, we must not be so comfortable in our praying that we cringe at praying this kind of prayer to Our Father, Our Papa, who knows the beginning from the end and knows that His will is always best. He has our best interest at heart, and even though the answers to our prayers may not be as we want, they will always be as He wants. Oh, that we would echo with the Psalmist in Psalm 40:8: "I delight to do Your will, O my God, and Your law is within my heart."

Before we look at the last three petitions, I want to briefly remind you that the first three petitions have to do with God the Father. Too often, we jump into our prayers with a list of all our needs, but a genuine kingdom citizen is more concerned about the glory of the Father than with having their needs met. As I was writing this lesson, I received a phone call in which I listened to a woman who had chosen to remain silent in the midst of a situation where she knew someone was sinning but refused to confront them about it. She was so fearful of what the outcome might be that she wouldn't do the right thing. I told her that doing the right thing was the one thing in this situation that was guaranteed to glorify God, whereas the alternative would allow that person to remain in their sin, and in so doing affect many others. (Since the writing of this lesson, this dear woman did finally do the right thing, and God has honored it and relieved a huge burden from her heart!) Our praying and our living must be with a view to glorify God. This pattern of praying begins with a desire to honor God before asking for our needs to be met. As we consider the proper pattern Jesus sets for us, we can see that we are certainly in need of getting back to the biblical way of praying. Let's continue on with the last three proper petitions, which have to do with the Father's children's needs.

Give us this day our daily bread. (Matthew 6:11)

Give us this day our daily bread is the fourth petition. To *give* means to deliver or bring forth. And notice that it is not "Give me a new smart phone," "Bring me a new house," "Deliver me a husband," or "Give me a child," but it is give me my daily food. *Daily bread* is that which is needful for the day, and for that day only. This is not a request for tomorrow's food, but for today's food. [56] In the biblical world, most people worked hard each day and at the end of that day were paid their wages. They understood this request far more than we do because most of us are rich and have need of hardly anything—but little do we know we are really blind, miserable, wretched and naked (Revelation 3:17)! Wise Solomon knew the danger of both poverty and riches as he wrote in Proverbs 30:8-9, "Remove falsehood and lies far from me; give me neither poverty nor riches—Feed me with the food allotted to me; lest I be full and deny You and say, 'Who is the Lord?' Or lest I be poor and steal, and profane the name of my God."

Now, this is not a petition that most American people see a need to pray, but there are many people alive today who do regularly need to pray this prayer. As of the writing of this lesson, there are 850 million people who are hungry and malnourished and over half of them are children. 18,000 children die daily because of hunger and malnutrition. And even though this may not be a petition that we think we need to pray, we really should pray it, because we are utterly dependent on God not only for our food but for everything we have and everything we need, even the very breathe we breath. Let's go on to the fifth petition in verse 12.

> And forgive us our debts, as we forgive our debtors. (Matthew 6:12)

---

56 The early church fathers had difficulty with this request, as they couldn't believe that God was concerned about such mundane things as food or physical provision, so they considered this the Lord's Supper. But really, this phrase has nothing in it to refer to a metaphorical or spiritual meaning; Jesus' clear meaning was to pray for our daily physical bread. During New Testament times, the normal practice was to receive a wage following each day's work, usually enough for the next day's provision. Asking for "daily bread" would also refer to the strength and opportunity to work that day or the next. In an agriculturally-based community, the close dependency on God's provision would be a daily reminder that God is the great provider.

The fifth petition is asking our Father to *forgive us our debts*. To *forgive* means to send away and a *debt* is something we owe, something that is due. Oh, my friend, we are debtors to God! We owe so much that we can never repay! And even though our debt has been paid on the cross, even though kingdom citizens repent and bow the knee to Christ's Lordship, we still go on sinning and we still need to be asking God to forgive us. First John 1:9-10 is clear about this; John writes, "If we confess our sins, He is faithful and just to forgive us our sins and to cleanse us from all unrighteousness. If we say that we have not sinned, we make Him a liar, and His word is not in us." Genuine believers confess their sins, and to say that we don't sin is to make God a liar.

Jesus goes on to say that part of the pattern for our praying is not only that we ask our heavenly Father to forgive us but we do so with the intention that we will also *forgive our debtors* in the same way. When we consider the enormous amount of debt we owe to God and the enormous amount of sinning we continually do, how can we not forgive those who sin against us? Jesus illustrates this point in Matthew 18:21-35.

> Then Peter came to Him and said, "Lord, how often shall my brother sin against me, and I forgive him? Up to seven times?" Jesus said to him, "I do not say to you, up to seven times, but up to seventy times seven. Therefore the kingdom of heaven is like a certain king who wanted to settle accounts with his servants. And when he had begun to settle accounts, one was brought to him who owed him ten thousand talents. But as he was not able to pay, his master commanded that he be sold, with his wife and children and all that he had, and that payment be made. The servant therefore fell down before him, saying, 'Master, have patience with me, and I will pay you all.' Then the master of that servant was moved with compassion, released him, and forgave him the debt. But that servant went out and found one of his fellow servants who owed him a hundred denarii; and he laid hands on him and took him by the throat, saying, 'Pay me what you owe!' So his fellow servant fell down at his feet and begged him, saying, 'Have patience with me, and I will pay you all.' And he would not, but went and threw him into prison till he should pay the debt. So when his fellow servants saw what

had been done, they were very grieved, and came and told their master all that had been done. Then his master, after he had called him, said to him, 'You wicked servant! I forgave you all that debt because you begged me. Should you not also have had compassion on your fellow servant, just as I had pity on you?' And his master was angry, and delivered him to the torturers until he should pay all that was due to him. So My heavenly Father also will do to you if each of you, from his heart, does not forgive his brother his trespasses."

What is so shocking about this parable is that the servant who was forgiven his debt by his master owed his master several million dollars in the currency of our day, yet the one who owed this servant money only owed him a few dollars. My friend, we can be just as petty. One man has said of this: "To be a Christian means to forgive the inexcusable because God has forgiven the inexcusable in you."57 And while He is on the subject of sin, Jesus then gives the sixth petition, regarding temptation.

> And do not lead us into temptation, but deliver us from the evil one. (Matthew 6:13a)

This is the sixth petition—*Do not lead us into temptation, but deliver us from the evil one*. What does it mean to *lead into temptation*? The words *lead us* means to carry us into the place, the time, the purpose, the point. *Temptation* is a putting to the proof. What Jesus is saying is that we should pray that we would not be allowed to be led into temptation. Now, perhaps you're wondering about this, since James says in his epistle that we should not say when we are tempted that we are being tempted by God because God can't tempt anyone with evil (James 1:13). The key to understanding what Jesus is saying here may be found in Matthew 4:1-11.

> Then Jesus was led up by the Spirit into the wilderness to be tempted by the devil. And when He had fasted forty days and forty nights, afterward He was hungry. Now when the tempter came to Him, he said, "If You are the Son of God, command that these stones become bread." But He answered and said, "It is written, 'Man shall not live by bread alone, but by every

---

57 Words by C. S. Lewis

word that proceeds from the mouth of God.'" Then the devil
took Him up into the holy city, set Him on the pinnacle of the
temple, and said to Him, "If You are the Son of God, throw
Yourself down. For it is written: 'He shall give His angels
charge over you,' and, 'In their hands they shall bear you up,
Lest you dash your foot against a stone.'" Jesus said to him,
"It is written again, 'You shall not tempt the Lord your God.'"
Again, the devil took Him up on an exceedingly high mountain,
and showed Him all the kingdoms of the world and their glory.
And he said to Him, "All these things I will give You if You
will fall down and worship me." Then Jesus said to him, "Away
with you, Satan! For it is written, 'You shall worship the Lord
your God, and Him only you shall serve.'" Then the devil left
Him, and behold, angels came and ministered to Him.

Some have suggested that this was such a trial for Jesus that He
wanted His children to be spared such an event. That certainly
makes sense because He mentions here that part of this request
is that God would deliver us from the evil one, who is the devil.
We know from the account in Matthew 4 that it was the devil who
tempted Jesus. To *deliver* means to rescue me, to break the bonds or
chains in which one is held. This temptation event was so difficult
for Jesus that angels came and ministered to Him afterward. So, we
might word this request in this way: "Lord, help us not to be drawn
into temptation, but if we are drawn away by our own lusts, deliver
us from evil." What a joy it is to know that these last three petitions,
which pertain to us, we will not need to pray after this life—just like
the first three.

The Proper Praise

Matthew 6:13b

For Yours is the kingdom and the power and the glory forever.
Amen. (Matthew 6:13b)

The prayer ends with a proper praise in verse 13b: *For Yours is the
kingdom and the power and the glory forever. Amen.* Some scholars
argue that these last words are not found in the original manuscripts,

but nonetheless their meaning rings true! His is *the kingdom*, which means the royal rule. His is *the power*, which means the miraculous power. And His is *the glory forever*, which means His kingdom, His power and His glory will not end. We must keep in mind as we pray that all is for the glory of God, for His kingdom. Genuine kingdom citizens pray with the kingdom in mind and with the glory of God in mind. Now, the prayer ends with *Amen*, which means so be it, but then Jesus adds something interesting.

The Proper Posture

Matthew 6:14-15

> For if you forgive men their trespasses, your heavenly Father will also forgive you. (Matthew 6:14)

Why does Jesus add this? Evidently, He believed it was necessary to comment on the fifth petition so that we would realize that we cannot pray with ought in our heart, just as we can't go to worship with ill-will in our heart toward others and think that we have truly worshipped (we saw this in Matthew 5:23-24). Jesus is not saying that God's forgiveness is earned by forgiving others; that would be a works-oriented salvation. But He is saying the same thing He's said throughout the Sermon on the Mount, that is, that genuine Kingdom citizens go through life forgiving others. Why? Because we are the forgiven ones and, as we have already seen, we owe a debt we cannot pay! So, how can we not forgive?! The good news is that if we come to prayer with forgiving hearts toward others, God hears our prayers and He forgives. The bad news, however, is found in verse 15.

> But if you do not forgive men their trespasses, neither will your Father forgive your trespasses. (Matthew 6:15)

Psalm 66:18 states, "If I regard iniquity in my heart, The Lord will not hear." Jesus is clear in Mark 11:25-26: "And whenever you stand praying, if you have anything against anyone, forgive him so that your Father in heaven may also forgive you your trespasses.

But if you do not forgive, neither will your Father in heaven forgive your trespasses." Paul says in Ephesians 4:32, "And be kind to one another, tenderhearted, forgiving one another, even as God in Christ forgave you." We can't pray when we are harboring ill-will in our heart toward someone and think that God will hear us. Genuine believers forgive; hypocrites do not. This has serious implications, I admit, but it flows with the message of the Sermon on the Mount. We either are or we are not God's children (see James 2:13). So, what is the proper posture when we pray? Humility! We come to Him as those who have not only forgiven others, but who have been forgiven by our Father!

Summary

As we close and consider the proper pattern for our praying, have we considered *The Proper Person* (v 9a) we pray to? He is our Father, our Papa, in heaven. Do you stop long enough while praying to consider just who this Person is you are praying to? He is your Father, your Father, and yet with that comes the fact He is like no other. He is holy. Keep this in mind as you pray.

As we pray, we must also pray *The Proper Petitions* (vv 9b-13a). We must not come flippantly to the throne of grace with our list of things we think we need without first acknowledging that we want His will to be done in our lives above anything else, even if there is discomfort involved. We want our lives to reflect His holiness and we want them to be lived for His kingdom. And we really could stop there, but we are also frail and we have needs. We need daily sustenance, we need forgiveness, and we need to be delivered from evil. These petitions are quite a contrast from the typical American Christian's prayer, which might sound somewhat like this: "Lord, bless me, bless my day, and bless this mess. Amen."

We also need *The Proper Praise* (v 13b) in our prayers, acknowledging that God's is the kingdom, the power, and the glory. Our prayers should begin and end with Him, but often, I fear, they begin and end with us and somewhere in the middle we might acknowledge Him.

And of all this praying is to be done with *The Proper Posture* (vv 14-15) of humility. He is the potter; we are the clay. He is the Father; we are the child. He is the forgiver; we are the forgiven ones.

My dear friend, "In this manner, therefore, pray: Our Father in heaven, Hallowed be Your name. Your kingdom come. Your will be done on earth as it is in heaven. Give us this day our daily bread. And forgive us our debts, as we forgive our debtors. And do not lead us into temptation, but deliver us from the evil one. For Yours is the kingdom and the power and the glory forever. Amen."

Questions to Consider
The Proper Pattern for Praying
Matthew 6:9-15

1. (a) Read Matthew 6:9-15 along with Luke 11:1-13. Make notes as to what is similar as well as what is different about these two passages. (b) Why do you think these prayers are not exactly the same? (You might look before and after each prayer for some helpful observations.)

2. Memorize Matthew 6:9-13. Most of it should be familiar to you.

3. (a) What aspects of the prayer mentioned in Matthew 6:9-15 do you see reiterated in David's prayer in 2 Samuel 7:18-29; in Solomon's prayer in 1 Kings 8:22-53; in Jehoshaphat's prayer in 2 Chronicles 20:5-12; and in Daniel's prayer in Daniel 9:3-19? (b) How could these prayers encourage you in your own prayers? (c) How do these prayers along with the prayer in Matthew 6 differ from most modern-day praying? (d) How do you think the religious hypocrites in Jesus' audience received these instructions on praying?

4. (a) In what ways does the story in Luke 7:36-50 illustrate Jesus' words in Matthew 6:12? (b) Are you as quick to forgive others as our Lord is quick to forgive you?

5. (a) Why do you think Jesus mentions the words in Matthew 6:14-15 after His instruction on prayer? (b) What other passage(s) comes to mind that are similar to these words?

6. (a) What does "Our Father" mean to you? (b) How should these words ("Our Father") alone change the way we pray? (c) In what ways do we as His children make His name holy?

7. Does this prayer have new meaning after studying it this week? Please take time to pray this prayer, thinking through each phrase as you do!

Chapter 13

The Forgotten Discipline
of Fasting
Matthew 6:16-18

In his book, *Spiritual Disciplines for the Christian Life*, Donald Whitney outlines twelve disciplines that should be present in the life of every genuine believer. In his chapter on fasting, he says, "Christians in a gluttonous, denial-less, self-indulgent society may struggle to accept and to begin the practice of fasting. Few Disciplines go so radically against the flesh and the mainstream of culture as this one. But we cannot overlook its biblical significance."[58] Whitney pens it correctly when he says that fasting goes against our flesh and our culture. Most of us would agree that many of the other disciplines he mentions in his book are imperative for the genuine believer; disciplines like Bible intake, prayer, worship, evangelism and using our spiritual gifts. But fasting? Are you serious?! Isn't that for super Christians or hum-drum believers? I pray that when we are finished with the text before us, we might be convinced otherwise and begin to implement this forgotten discipline of fasting. Let's read the few short verses we have before us in Matthew 6:16-18.

Matthew 6:16-18

> Moreover, when you fast, do not be like the hypocrites, with a sad countenance. For they disfigure their faces that they may appear to men to be fasting. Assuredly, I say to you, they have their reward. [17]But you, when you fast, anoint your head and wash your face, [18]so that you do not appear to men to be fasting, but to your Father who is in the secret place; and your Father who sees in secret will reward you openly. (Matthew 6:16-18)

---

58 Donald Whitney, *Spiritual Disciplines for the Christian Life* (Colorado Springs: Navpress, 1991), 160.

As we consider *The Forgotten Discipline of Fasting*, we'll see that we need to:

> *Forget Fasting Like the Hypocrites Do* (v 16)
> *Remember to Fast Like Believers Should* (vv 17-18)

The discipline of fasting is important, but it is definitely one we too often neglect. The week I was writing this lesson, I was reminded again of how imperative fasting is. Over the previous year, I had been endeavoring to help a young woman with a very troubled daughter. (I won't go into details about her situation, but suffice to say it is truly the most bizarre situation I have ever encountered.) Despite this mother's efforts to do the right thing, this ongoing situation had only become worse each week instead of better. She called me while I was grocery shopping, hysterically crying over the previous day's events, which were tragic indeed. A few days after her call I just "happened" to be reading in Matthew 17:14-21: "And when they had come to the multitude, a man came to Him, kneeling down to Him and saying, 'Lord, have mercy on my son, for he is an epileptic and suffers severely; for he often falls into the fire and often into the water. So I brought him to Your disciples, but they could not cure him.' Then Jesus answered and said, 'O faithless and perverse generation, how long shall I be with you? How long shall I bear with you? Bring him here to Me.' And Jesus rebuked the demon, and it came out of him; and the child was cured from that very hour. Then the disciples came to Jesus privately and said, 'Why could we not cast it out?' So Jesus said to them, 'Because of your unbelief; for assuredly, I say to you, if you have faith as a mustard seed, you will say to this mountain, 'Move from here to there,' and it will move; and nothing will be impossible for you. However, this kind does not go out except by prayer and fasting." After I read this, I immediately sent an email to this mother encouraging her that she and I both needed to set aside weekly time to fast and pray for this child, something she wholeheartedly agreed to. [59]

---

59 It is true that the phrase, "but this kind never comes out but by prayer and fasting" (Matthew 17:21), is lacking in most of the better manuscripts and was perhaps a scribal insertion from Mark 9:29. Yet, there is still difficulty because most of the better manuscripts on

Fasting: What is it? Do we really need to be doing it? And why don't we do it more often? These are some of the questions that come to my mind when I think of fasting. Hopefully, these questions, and others like them, we can find answers to in the few short verses we have before us.

We began chapter six of Matthew's Gospel with Jesus talking about doing acts of righteousness before others. He began with the righteous act of giving alms, then He addressed the righteous act of praying, and now He will address the righteous act of fasting. We learned in our last lesson that there is a proper pattern for praying, a proper person to pray to, proper petitions to pray for, proper praise to offer up, and a proper posture to take. While fasting is an act of righteousness in and of itself, it is also an extension of prayer. But, as with all the other acts of righteousness, this one also has a right way and a wrong way to be practiced. Let's look at the wrong way of fasting in hopes that we will forget fasting like the hypocrites do!

Forget Fasting Like the Hypocrites Do

Matthew 6:16

> Moreover, when you fast, do not be like the hypocrites, with a sad countenance. For they disfigure their faces that they may appear to men to be fasting. Assuredly, I say to you, they have their reward. (Matthew 6:16)

Notice that Jesus says *when you fast*, not if you fast. This indicates that Jesus assumes we will be fasting. This begs the question: Why, then, don't we fast more often? Why is this a forgotten discipline among genuine believers? It's just like Jesus just said in Matthew 6:5—when you pray, not if you pray. And like He said in Matthew 6:2—when you give, not if you give. Most believers don't go a day without praying, but most believers go a lifetime without fasting.

Mark 9:29 omit the word "fasting" and simply read "prayer." That does not limit the value of fasting, though, as Jesus taught it here in Matthew 6 and elsewhere. e.g., Matthew 9:15.

Since we intend to talk about fasting, it's important that we define it. The word *fast* means to go without food. The Jews would fast often (Zechariah 8:19), but the only biblically commanded fast was the Day of Atonement. They fasted to commemorate the beginning of the attack on Jerusalem (Jeremiah 39:2-14); the burning of the temple (Jeremiah 52:12; Zechariah 7:3); the death of Gedaliah (Jeremiah 41); and the capture of Jerusalem (Jeremiah 39:1; 52:7). The Pharisees fasted twice a week, on Monday and Thursday of each week. In Luke 18:12, we read, "The Pharisee stood and prayed thus with himself, 'God, I thank You that I am not like other men— extortioners, unjust, adulterers, or even as this tax collector. I fast twice a week; I give tithes of all that I possess.'" Jesus Himself fasted for 40 days and 40 nights, according to Matthew 4. This particular fast occurred right before His temptation by the devil in the wilderness.

Clearly, Jesus is not against fasting, but He is against fasting in the wrong way. He says *do not be like the hypocrites*, as they fast *with a sad countenance*. Hypocrites, we know, are actors under an assumed character; they're not genuine. And they fast with a *sad countenance*, which means they put on a face that looks sullen and gloomy; they appear to be mournful. Perhaps you're wondering why this is so bad, especially since so many of the fasts recorded in Scripture were performed because of mourning over sin. The mourning itself is not what Jesus is condemning here; He is condemning looking mournful so that others will think you are more spiritual than you really are. Jesus says *they disfigure their faces*. One man helps us here:

> That is, they do not anoint and wash themselves as usual: they are uncombed, filthy, squalid, and haggard. It is said that they were often in the habit of throwing ashes on their heads and faces; and this, mixing with their tears, served still further to disfigure their faces. So much pains will people take, and so much suffering will they undergo, and so much that is ridiculous will they assume, to impose on God and people. But they deceive neither. God sees through

the flimsy veil. Human eyes can pierce a disguise so thin. Hypocrites overact their part. Not having the genuine principles of piety at heart, they know not what is its proper expression, and hence they appear supremely contemptible and abominable. Never should people exhibit outwardly more than they feel; and never should they attempt to exhibit anything for the mere sake of ostentation.[60]

Why do they do all this? The answer is the same as with the other acts of righteousness that these hypocrites do: so *that they may appear to men to be fasting*. They do it for show. And what do they get? Jesus says *they have their reward*; they get the reward they're desiring more than anything. Their reward is to be noticed by others. [61]

While we're considering this verse, I think it would behoove us to also consider two passages, in Isaiah and in Zechariah, which further illustrate the danger of hypocritical fasting. Consider Isaiah 58.

> Cry aloud, spare not; Lift up your voice like a trumpet; Tell My people their transgression, and the house of Jacob their sins. Yet they seek Me daily, and delight to know My ways, as a nation that did righteousness, and did not forsake the ordinance of their God. They ask of Me the ordinances of justice; They take delight in approaching God. "Why have we fasted," they say, "and You have not seen? Why have we afflicted our souls, and You take no notice?" In fact, in the day of your fast you find pleasure, and exploit all your laborers. Indeed you fast for strife and debate, and to strike with the fist of wickedness. You will not fast as you do this day, to make your voice heard on

60 From Barnes' Notes, Electronic Database Copyright © 1997, 2003, 2005, 2006 by Biblesoft, Inc. All rights reserved.

61 During New Testament times, the Pharisees fasted on Mondays and Thursdays each week. In Luke 18, a Pharisee is praying in the temple and reminds God that he "fasts twice a week." According to the book of Exodus, Moses received the tablets of the law on Mount Sinai on two different occasions; and according to Jewish tradition, Moses went up on the mountain to get the law on a Monday and on a Thursday. So, the Pharisees fasted out of respect for reception of the Law of Moses. It's also interesting that these two days were the two major Jewish market days, where cities and towns would be crowded with merchants and shoppers—and the Scribes and Pharisees no doubt knew that the biggest audiences would be publicly reminded of their religious parade of fasting.

high. Is it a fast that I have chosen, a day for a man to afflict his soul? Is it to bow down his head like a bulrush, and to spread out sackcloth and ashes? Would you call this a fast, and an acceptable day to the Lord? Is this not the fast that I have chosen: to loose the bonds of wickedness, to undo the heavy burdens, to let the oppressed go free, and that you break every yoke? Is it not to share your bread with the hungry, and that you bring to your house the poor who are cast out; when you see the naked, that you cover him, and not hide yourself from your own flesh? Then your light shall break forth like the morning, your healing shall spring forth speedily, and your righteousness shall go before you; the glory of the Lord shall be your rear guard. Then you shall call, and the Lord will answer; you shall cry, and He will say, "Here I am." If you take away the yoke from your midst, the pointing of the finger, and speaking wickedness, if you extend your soul to the hungry and satisfy the afflicted soul, then your light shall dawn in the darkness, and your darkness shall be as the noonday. The Lord will guide you continually, and satisfy your soul in drought, and strengthen your bones; you shall be like a watered garden, and like a spring of water, whose waters do not fail. Those from among you shall build the old waste places; you shall raise up the foundations of many generations; and you shall be called the Repairer of the Breach, The Restorer of Streets to Dwell In. If you turn away your foot from the Sabbath, from doing your pleasure on My holy day, and call the Sabbath a delight, the holy day of the Lord honorable, and shall honor Him, not doing your own ways, nor finding your own pleasure, nor speaking your own words, then you shall delight yourself in the Lord; and I will cause you to ride on the high hills of the earth, and feed you with the heritage of Jacob your father. The mouth of the Lord has spoken.

God says, essentially, "Don't come to Me fasting and praying when you're oppressing others or have something against others; don't fast when you're doing it for your own pleasure or for the praise of others; don't fast when you aren't honoring me on the Sabbath day or the Lord's Day. Get your heart right first; then, I will hear your prayers when you fast." This is much like what we've already been learning in our study on the Sermon on the Mount. Consider Zechariah 7.

Now in the fourth year of King Darius it came to pass that the word of the Lord came to Zechariah, on the fourth day of the ninth month, Chislev, when the people sent Sherezer, with Regem-Melech and his men, to the house of God, to pray before the Lord, and to ask the priests who were in the house of the Lord of hosts, and the prophets, saying, "Should I weep in the fifth month and fast as I have done for so many years?" Then the word of the Lord of hosts came to me, saying, "Say to all the people of the land, and to the priests: 'When you fasted and mourned in the fifth and seventh months during those seventy years, did you really fast for Me—for Me? When you eat and when you drink, do you not eat and drink for yourselves? Should you not have obeyed the words which the Lord proclaimed through the former prophets when Jerusalem and the cities around it were inhabited and prosperous, and the South and the Lowland were inhabited?'" Then the word of the Lord came to Zechariah, saying, "Thus says the Lord of hosts: 'Execute true justice, Show mercy and compassion everyone to his brother. Do not oppress the widow or the fatherless, the alien or the poor. Let none of you plan evil in his heart against his brother.' But they refused to heed, shrugged their shoulders, and stopped their ears so that they could not hear. Yes, they made their hearts like flint, refusing to hear the law and the words which the Lord of hosts had sent by His Spirit through the former prophets. Thus great wrath came from the Lord of hosts. Therefore it happened, that just as He proclaimed and they would not hear, so they called out and I would not listen," says the Lord of hosts. "But I scattered them with a whirlwind among all the nations which they had not known. Thus the land became desolate after them, so that no one passed through or returned; for they made the pleasant land desolate."

God says much the same thing in Zechariah as He said in Isaiah: "Don't pretend you're fasting for Me when you're not obeying me, when you fail to show mercy and compassion, and when you oppress others. I will not hear you." We know from our study in the Sermon on the Mount that this was a great transgression of the Scribes and Pharisees. They obeyed the letter of the law but omitted justice, mercy, and faith. They devoured widows' houses and oppressed others less fortunate than themselves. These are serious issues to remember when we consider that we must not fast as they did.

We must forget fasting like the hypocrites do. They pretend to be fasting by altering their outward appearance so that others will think they are religious. They get what they want, which is not answers to their vain prayers but admiration from others. However, kingdom citizens do need to fast, and they need to remember to fast as believers should. Let's consider this in verses 17 and 18.

Remember to Fast Like Believers Should

Matthew 6:17-18

> But you, when you fast, anoint your head and wash your face, (Matthew 6:17)

But you, Jesus says, in contrast to them, you be different. He says *when you fast*. Once again, Jesus assumes His children will fast. They may not need to fast as often as they will when He is gone, according to Matthew 9:14-17. While the bridegroom Jesus is with them, they don't need to fast as often, but when the bridegroom is gone, then they will need to fast more often. Jesus says, instead of having a sad countenance like the hypocrites, you *anoint your head*. This means do as you would normally do; put oil on your head. Instead of disfiguring your face, wash your face. "The Jews and all neighboring nations were much in the habit of washing and anointing their bodies. This washing was performed at every meal; and where it could be effected, the head, or other parts of the body, was daily anointed with sweet or olive oil. In a warm climate, exposed to the great heat of the sun, this practice conduced much to health, preserved the skin smooth and tender, and afforded a most grateful sensation and odor."[62] Today, we would say, "Just do your normal routine." Take a shower, wash your hair, and put on your makeup. Don't look any different than you would on any other day. Don't appear as if anything is different. And what is the reason that kingdom citizens do this? It's certainly not to be seen of men, that's for sure, but quite the contrary, as we see in verse 18.

---

62 From Barnes' Notes, Electronic Database Copyright © 1997, 2003, 2005, 2006 by Biblesoft, Inc. All rights reserved.

> so that you do not appear to men to be fasting, but to your Father
> who is in the secret place; and your Father who sees in secret
> will reward you openly. (Matthew 6:18)

Instead of fasting to be seen and noticed by men like the hypocrites, a child of God desires not to call attention to themselves at all. They do not want to appear to men to be fasting. The only person they're concerned about knowing is their *Father* in heaven. Does that mean others can't know that I'm fasting or that I can't fast with others? No. We have numerous examples in Scripture of kings calling a nation to fast, which would indicate that whole groups of people were fasting together. We also have examples like King David, Cornelius, and Esther, who fasted, and the Scriptures indicate that others were aware of it. What Jesus is condemning here is a motive of the heart, that of wanting to be noticed by others. The kingdom citizen is concerned about only One Person knowing about their fasting, and that is their *Father who is in the secret place.* If others know they are fasting, that's fine, but it is not their mission to see that others find out.

Jesus then gives encouragement as He says that same *Father who sees in secret will reward you openly.* How this reward is openly done, I do not know. But I do know this: In every single example of fasting and praying that is recorded in God's Word, God intervenes, except in the case of David fasting and praying for seven days for his sick child. But remember, in that case, God had already spoken through Nathan the prophet and declared that the child would die. This was the punishment for David's adultery with Bathsheba. David did not die, but the child did (see 2 Samuel 12-13). God is a God who cannot lie and we must remember this even in our fasting and praying.

The Pharisees planned their fasts twice a week. A genuine kingdom citizen's fast is not necessarily planned, but most often it is spontaneous, due to genuine mourning over sin or troublesome circumstances. Many times, a genuine fast is not difficult because you're so overcome with sorrow that you can't even think of eating.

The mother I mentioned earlier in this lesson called me not many days later, and before I hung up I prayed with her and told her that I would fast with her for this child as much as I was able to. Being so distraught from the night's events, she said, "I'm fasting today as I just can't eat," to which I replied, "That's a genuine fast." One man has said of this,

> The grief of the "soul" is so absorbing as to destroy the natural appetites of the "body." People in deep affliction eat little, and often pine away and fall into sickness, because the body refuses, on account of the deep sorrow of the mind, to discharge the functions of health. "Fasting, then, is the natural expression of grief." It is not arbitrary; it is what every person in sorrow naturally does. This is the foundation of its being applied to religion as a sacred rite. It is because the soul, when oppressed and burdened by a sense of sin, is so filled with grief that the body refuses food. It is, therefore, appropriate to scenes of penitence, of godly sorrow, of suffering, and to those facts connected with religion which are suited to produce grief, as the prevalence of iniquity, or some dark impending calamity, or storm, or tempest, pestilence, plague, or famine. It is also useful to humble us, to bring us to reflection, to direct the thoughts away from the allurements of this world to the bliss of a better one. It is not acceptable except it be the "real expression," of sorrow; the natural effect of the feeling that we are burdened with crime."[63]

Does this mean we can only fast over sin? Of course not. We have examples in Scripture of believers fasting for a sick child, a journey, ministry, elders and so on. I've encouraged others to fast for their marriage, for the salvation of others, for a wayward child, their own personal walk, and other things. I think we must ask ourselves the

63 From Barnes' Notes, Electronic Database Copyright © 1997, 2003, 2005, 2006 by Biblesoft, Inc. All rights reserved.

hard question, that is, "Am I hungrier for food than I am for God? Am I willing to give up a meal or two to lay hold of God and to petition Him for my needs? Am I desperate enough?"

When Abraham Lincoln served as the President of the United States, he did something that perhaps would be foreign to our day and age. He proclaimed the day of April 30th as a day of fasting and prayer. He told the nation that this day would be set aside as a day of national humiliation—a time when men should confess their sins and seek genuine repentance, seeking the truth in the Holy Scriptures. President Lincoln said we have "become intoxicated with unbroken success, we have become too self-sufficient to feel the necessity, too proud to pray to the God who made us. Let us humble ourselves before the offended Power, and confess our national sins and pray for mercy and forgiveness."[64] These words sound strange to us living in the 21st century, but oh, how we would long for our current president to do the same! Even in our churches, when is the last time your church leadership called your church to fast and pray?

Summary

So, *Forget Fasting like the Hypocrites Do* (v 16). They pretend to be fasting by altering their outward appearance so that others will think they are religious. They get what they want, which is not answers to their vain prayers but the admiration of others. Instead, we must *remember to Fast Like Believers Should* (vv 17-18). Kingdom citizens don't alter their outward appearance and they aren't concerned about being admired by others. They pray real prayers and they also get a real reward, a reward which their Father gives them, which is far better than the admiration of others.

Is fasting a forgotten discipline for you? My friend, the bridegroom is gone, and yes, He will return someday soon, but in the meantime we cannot forget this forgotten discipline. Remember to fast like a genuine kingdom citizen while you are waiting for your Bridegroom to return and take us to our eternal home and to the marriage supper

---

64 http://www.abrahamlincolnonline.org/lincoln/speeches/fast.htm

of the lamb, where there will never be a need for fasting again!

We have now considered the third and final act of righteousness mentioned by Jesus in Matthew 6: alms giving, praying and fasting. There are some questions we would do well to ask ourselves as we consider our own acts of righteousness and our motives for doing them. Do we do these things for our glory or for God's glory? Do we do these things for our financial gain or for eternal gain? Do we do these things for the praise of men or for the praise of God? Do we do these things to please others or to please God? One man has said, "So we must choose God for our audience. As Jesus watched the people putting their gifts into the temple treasure, so God watches us as we give. As we pray and fast secretly, He is there in the secret place. God hates hypocrisy but loves reality. That is why it is only when we are aware of His presence that our giving, praying and fasting will be real."[65]

65 John R.W. Stott, *The Message of the Sermon on the Mount* (Downers Grove: Inter-Varsity Press, 1978), 140-141.

Questions to Consider
The Forgotten Discipline of Fasting
Matthew 6:16-18

1. Read Matthew 6:16-18 along with Matthew 9:14-17. Why do you think Jesus mentions fasting in the Matthew 6 passage, but then tells the disciples in Matthew 9 that they won't need to fast until He is gone?

2. Memorize Matthew 6:16-18.

3. Consider the following passages and answer the following questions. You might want to make a chart with columns so that it will be easier to keep track of your answers. (a) Who is fasting? (b) What are they fasting for? (c) Where are they fasting? (d) How long did they fast? (e)What attitudes accompanied their fasting? (f) What were the results of their fasting? Exodus 34:28-35; Judges 20:26; 1 Samuel 1:9-20; 1 Samuel 7:4-14; 31:1-13; 2 Samuel 1:1-12; 12:1-23; 1 Kings 21:1-27; 2 Chronicles 20:1-30; Ezra 8:21-23; Nehemiah 1:1-11; 9:1-3; Esther 4:1-17; 9:31; Psalms 35:13; 69:10; 109:21-24; Daniel 6:16-23; 9:1-3; Joel 1:14-16, 2:12-15; Jonah 3:5-9; Matthew 4:1-11; Matthew 6:16-18; Matthew 17:14-21; Luke 2:36-38; Acts 10; 13:1-3; 14:21-23; 27; 1 Corinthians 7:1-7.

4. (a) What do you learn about the importance of fasting from the previous question? (b) Why do you think we do not fast more often? (c) What is most difficult about fasting and praying for you?

5. (a) Are you mourning over your own sin or the sin of another? (b) Are you facing a difficult trial? (c) Is your heart burdened over any matter? (d) In light of this lesson, why not consider fasting and praying to seek the face of God?

6. What is your prayer after considering this lesson? Please write it down to share with others.

Chapter 14

Do You Know Where *Your* Treasure Is?

Matthew 6:19-24

"Worldly ambition has a strong fascination for us. The spell of materialism is very hard to break."[66] Such words are alarming, yet true. The fact that Americans alone spend more than 1.5 trillion dollars each year on unnecessary stuff is evidence enough to demonstrate this truth—stuff like pleasure boats, jewelry, alcohol, candy, entertainment, and tobacco. Consider these shocking facts: Each year Americans spend 60 billion dollars a year on pets; 10 billion a year on make-up; 2 billion on Halloween costumes; 7.4 billon on decorations and candy; 478 billion on home furnishings; 469 billion on holiday shopping; 500 million on gum; 13 billion on chocolate; 65 billion on soft drinks; 60 billion dollars on weight loss programs; and one in five Americans spends more money paying for their cell phones than they do on food. "Worldly ambition has a strong fascination for us. The spell of materialism is very hard to break."[67] And it was this spell that the Jewish leadership in Jesus' day had fallen prey to.[68]

---

66 John Stott, *Christian Counter-Culture* (Downers Grove: Intervarsity, 1978), 154.

67 Ibid.

68 During the times when Jesus walked the earth, the religious leadership of the Jews were almost obsessed with money and wealth. The High Priest and priestly families, for example, controlled enormous wealth, which they received from extortion prices on the sale of sheep, doves, wine, and oil for sacrifices at the temple in Jerusalem. The famous "booths of the sons of Annas" on the Mount of Olives brought in the equivalent of multi-millions of dollars each feast day, and called for Jesus to cleanse the temple on at least two and probably three occasions. The Sadducees, for example, were from wealthy aristocratic families, who controlled power by land ownership and befriended the Roman empire to protect their wealth. However, like the wealthy of any society, they were not popular with the common people. The Scribes' and Pharisees' philosophy of life contrasted with the priestly families and the Sadducees, for they basically held to a simplified standard of living without luxury. They sought to separate themselves from the world and from anything common, but even this did not exempt them from coveting wealth! On one occasion, Jesus taught: "No servant can serve two masters; for either he will hate the one and love the other; or else he will be loyal to the one, and despise the other. You cannot serve God and

But for the kingdom citizen, worldly ambition should not hold any fascination for us. The spell of materialism should be an oxymoron to us. Jesus puts it like this:

Matthew 6:19-24

> Do not lay up for yourselves treasures on earth, where moth and rust destroy and where thieves break in and steal; [20]but lay up for yourselves treasures in heaven, where neither moth nor rust destroys and where thieves do not break in and steal. [21]For where your treasure is, there your heart will be also. [22]The lamp of the body is the eye. If therefore your eye is good, your whole body will be full of light. [23]But if your eye is bad, your whole body will be full of darkness. If therefore the light that is in you is darkness, how great is that darkness! [24]No one can serve two masters; for either he will hate the one and love the other, or else he will be loyal to the one and despise the other. You cannot serve God and mammon.

As we consider the question, *Do You Know Where Your Treasure Is?*, we will examine eight essential facts we should keep in mind when considering your answer. These facts will also aid in helping you to determine where your treasure is. They will be spelled out with the acronym TREASURE, in hopes that we can remember them more easily (though they will not be presented in this order):

Thieves Steal It (v 19)

Resources Reveal It (v 21)

Eyes Reveal It (v 23)

Avoid Accumulating It (v 19)

Sacrifices Reveal It (v 24)

Unwelcome Pests Destroy It (v 19)

Rust Corrupts It (v 19)

Eternity Reveals It (v 20)

---

mammon. (cf. Luke 16:13) And then the historian Luke records, "Now the Pharisees, who were lovers of money, also heard all these things; and they derided Him" (cf. Luke 16:14). The Pharisees had renounced wealth, but that didn't stop their wicked hearts from coveting wealth.

In our last lesson, we considered what Jesus taught regarding fasting. We learned that we should not fast like the hypocrites do. They pretend to be fasting by altering their outward appearance so that others will think they're religious. They get the very thing their hearts truly desire, which is not answers to their vain prayers but, rather, the admiration of others. In contrast, we learned that we should fast like kingdom citizens by not altering our outward appearance and by not being concerned about the admiration of others. We should pray real prayers, voicing real concerns, which results in a real reward given by our Father, which is far better than the admiration of men.

In the passage before us now, Jesus is still teaching on the fact that our righteousness must exceed that of the Scribes and Pharisees. The Scribes and Pharisees were hoping for an earthly kingdom. Along with that was their belief that wealth was a sign of God's favor. (There's certainly nothing new under the sun, as that is what many false teachers believe even today.) But, once again, Jesus will teach something that will rock their world and challenge their thinking, because a genuine child of God has an entirely different attitude about his or her possessions. Let's consider our first verse and the first four facts that will aide us in determining where our treasure lies.

> Do not lay up for yourselves treasures on earth, where moth and rust destroy and where thieves break in and steal; (Matthew 6:19)

Jesus begins with a command: *do not lay up for yourselves treasures on earth*. This command is an absolute denial. In other words, God forbid that we should ever lay up treasures on earth! The phrase *lay up* means to store up, so it has the idea of accumulating treasure of some sort. And notice that Jesus says these treasures are *for yourself*. He is not condemning laying up treasures for others or for God, but He is condemning the obsession with storing up wealth for oneself. We should at this point define what *treasure* is. The word actually means wealth or some deposit. In biblical times, treasures consisted of clothes, monies, land, and other commodities.

Jesus is not condemning the owning of wealth in and of itself, but He is condemning a particular motive behind acquiring wealth. Some live for wealth; some are just blessed with it. Jesus is also not condemning saving for your future, as there's sufficient biblical precedent for that. Proverbs 13:22 states, "A good man leaves an inheritance to his children's children, but the wealth of the sinner is stored up for the righteous." Jesus is not condemning owning a house or any other material possession, but He is condemning laying up for treasures for oneself. There is nothing wrong with owning things as long as they don't own you!

So, the first fact about treasures is this: **Avoid accumulating it**! Why would we want to accumulate stuff or invest in material things when 1 John 2:15-17 tells us that everything that is in the world is either the lust of the flesh, the lust of the eyes, or the pride of life? Why would we want to accumulate stuff or invest in material things when Peter tells us that everything on the earth is eventually going to burn up (2 Peter 3:10-13)?

Perhaps this prompts the question in your mind, "Why shouldn't I lay up treasures on earth?" Jesus gives us several reasons why we shouldn't. He says because *moth and rust destroy* it. This is the second fact about treasures: **Unwelcomed pests destroy it.** Jesus mentions a specific pest, a moth, but I would also add that welcomed household pets like dogs and cats can also destroy wealth. (I know this for a fact because when we had these kinds of pets, they destroyed quite a bit of our stuff!) Also, pests like mice and squirrels can do a fair bit of damage to our stuff. But Jesus uses a *moth*. A moth is an insect that likes to deposit its eggs in garments, especially wool. I'm sure many of us have had the experience of reaching for a woolen garment in our closet, only to discover that something has been gnawing away at it since the last time we wore it—and that something was a moth. The biblical world was no different than ours in that they took great pride in their clothes, and the finest ones were made of wool. But even way back then, moths would eat them! Consider Job 13:28, "Man decays like a rotten thing, like a garment that is moth-eaten." Or Isaiah 51:8; while speaking about the righteous person's enemies, God says through Isaiah, "For the moth will eat them up like a garment, and the worm will eat them like wool; but My righteousness will be forever, and My salvation from generation to generation."

The third fact about those things we treasure so much is this: **Rust corrupts it.** The word *rust* does not refer to rust as we would think of it; it refers to anything that can *destroy*, or corrupt, things like metal. The moth destroys our garments; the rust destroys our monies and any other material possessions which are susceptible to physical corrosion. It might be mold, mildew, or even just time that destroys our precious possessions.

The fourth fact about treasure is this: **Thieves steal it.** Jesus says *thieves break in and steal*. In biblical times, when someone would steal from another person's home they could literally dig through a wall to gain access into a house. This would not have been a difficult task because homes were made of mud and other weak substances. Homes weren't built with the materials we have available to us in most modernized countries. They also did not have security alarms and security cameras. More than likely, you've been the victim of thievery at some point or another. When I had been married about 5 years, our home was robbed and my wedding ring was stolen, along with some other items. When we consider that thieves may very well steal our stuff, why do we store up so much of it for them to carry off?

All these things we hold so dear can be taken away by a pesky bug, a corroding element, or a simple thief. Nothing we have is secure, except the Word of God, our souls, and their eternal destination. Jesus' half-brother James says something that should give us all pause; he says in James 5:1-3, "Come now, you rich, weep and howl for your miseries that are coming upon you! Your riches are corrupted, and your garments are moth-eaten. Your gold and silver are corroded, and their corrosion will be a witness against you and will eat your flesh like fire. You have heaped up treasure in the last days." Instead of laying up treasures here on earth, we are to lay them up somewhere else. Let's consider where that is, in verse 20.

> but lay up for yourselves treasures in heaven, where neither moth nor rust destroys and where thieves do not break in and steal. (Matthew 6:20)

But is a word of contrast. Instead of laying up treasures on earth, I am to lay them up *in heaven*. How do I *lay up treasures in heaven*? By investing my time, my energies, and my monies in things that last for eternity. We work for the kingdom to come, which is forever, and not the kingdom that is here and now and gone tomorrow. Jesus is clear that *neither moth nor rust destroys* there and *thieves do not break in and steal*. In Luke 12:32-34, Jesus says, "Do not fear, little flock, for it is your Father's good pleasure to give you the kingdom. Sell what you have and give alms; provide yourselves money bags which do not grow old, a treasure in the heavens that does not fail, where no thief approaches nor moth destroys. For where your treasure is, there your heart will be also." Peter is also clear that heavenly treasure is the best! Listen to 1 Peter 1:3-5: "Blessed be the God and Father of our Lord Jesus Christ, who according to His abundant mercy has begotten us again to a living hope through the resurrection of Jesus Christ from the dead, to an inheritance incorruptible and undefiled and that does not fade away, reserved in heaven for you, who are kept by the power of God through faith for salvation ready to be revealed in the last time." Eternity and its rewards are forever!

So, the fifth fact about our treasure is this: **Eternity reveals it.** Paul is clear about this in 2 Corinthians 5:10: "For we must all appear before the judgment seat of Christ, that each one may receive the things done in the body, according to what he has done, whether good or bad." At that time all will be revealed, not only our deeds done in our flesh but also our motives behind them. Eternity will indeed reveal where our treasure really is. Some will barely make it into heaven, saved by fire; others will have much eternal reward and treasure, as Paul writes of in 1 Corinthians 3:9-15. Maybe you're wishing that you could find out before eternity where your treasure is. Well, you can, and Jesus tells us how in verse 21.

For where your treasure is, there your heart will be also.
(Matthew 6:21)

Where your treasure is, Jesus says, *your heart will be also*. Where your deposit is, your heart is. Have you ever wondered what your heart is really devoted to? You can find it when you honestly evaluate where you spend or deposit the majority of your time, your money, and your energy. Here, then, is another fact about where your treasure is: **Resources reveal it.**

When Jesus speaks of the *heart*, He is referring to one's thoughts or feelings, our inner person, the whole of our being, who we really are. We know that out of the abundance of the heart the mouth speaks (Matthew 12:34), but have we also considered that out of the abundance of the heart our actions speak as well? In fact, I think our actions speak louder than our words. People can say all the religious stuff they want to, but their actions do indeed speak louder than their words. You cannot be doubled-minded; you cannot have a divided heart. Either your heart is set on your earthly home or your heart is set on your heavenly home. "Nowhere did Jesus magnify poverty or criticize the legitimate getting of wealth. God made all things, including food, clothing, and precious metals. God has declared that all things He has made are good (Genesis1:31). God knows that we need certain things in order to live (Matthew 6:32). In fact, He has given us 'richly all things to enjoy' (1 Timothy 6:17). It is not wrong to possess things, but it is wrong for things to possess us. The sin of idolatry is as dangerous as the sin of hypocrisy!"[69]

Whatever you love more than God is your god. Whatever you spend your time and money on is your god. For example, it might be your home. There's certainly nothing wrong with having one, but if all your monies and all your time are spent remodeling it and getting all the latest stuff for it, then you have succumbed to the temptation to make your home your treasure. It might be a child or a grandchild for whom you spend lavish amounts of money and invest all your

---

69 Warren Wiersbe, *Be Loyal: Following the King of Kings* (Colorado Springs: David C. Cook, 2010), 60.

energies; that child or grandchild has become your treasure. We should cherish them and love them, and they are certainly gifts from God, but we shouldn't enable them, coddle them, or love them above our loyalty to Christ. Perhaps it is spending money on all the latest stuff you think you need, like a new car, a new phone, a new whatever, while you forsake helping out a neighbor, family member, or church member in need; your heart has revealed where your treasure is, no matter what you say.

It has been disheartening to me as I've met scores of women over the years who know a great deal about the latest fashions, recipes, jewelry, and home décor, but little if anything about the Bible. We can search the Scriptures and we will not find that the holy women of old focused on such earthly pursuits. These things can become idolatrous and go against the grain of genuine Christianity. Perhaps, we would do well to remind ourselves of Paul's words in 1 Timothy 6:6-8: "Now godliness with contentment is great gain. For we brought nothing into this world, and it is certain we can carry nothing out. And having food and clothing, with these we shall be content." Our treasure reveals where our heart is, and it may very well indicate that we have a heart problem. But we may also have an eye problem, as Jesus explains in the next few verses.

> The lamp of the body is the eye. If therefore your eye is good,
> your whole body will be full of light. (Matthew 6:22)

Jesus is using *the eye* as a picture of our heart. In the physical realm, light enters into the eye and helps us to see. If your eyesight is not good, it's because the light doesn't enter in the way that it should, causing your vision to become distorted; sometimes this can even result in complete blindness. Jesus is the light that enters into our heart and helps us to see spiritually. *If therefore your eye is good* and single-focused on Him, *your whole body* or life is good, is *full of light*. This means that the whole direction of your life is single-focused; you're not divided between earthly treasures and heavenly treasures.

It's interesting that Jesus also refers to our eye in Matthew 7:1-5, where He also seems to refer to our eye as imagery representative of our heart: "Judge not, that you be not judged. For with what judgment you judge, you will be judged; and with the measure you use, it will be measured back to you. And why do you look at the speck in your brother's eye, but do not consider the plank in your own eye? Or how can you say to your brother, 'Let me remove the speck from your eye'; and look, a plank is in your own eye? Hypocrite! First remove the plank from your own eye, and then you will see clearly to remove the speck from your brother's eye."

We need to fix our eyes on Jesus the Author and Finisher of our faith, as Paul says in Hebrews 12:2, and not on the treasures the world as to offer. But if your eye sees something—clothing or a new house or a new car or jewelry—and you know that you really don't need it but your heart is coveting it, if you choose to feed that lust, before long you'll want more and more and more. You will never be content and you will never be satisfied because you have a bigger problem—your whole life is full of darkness, as we see in verse 23.

> But if your eye is bad, your whole body will be full of darkness.
> If therefore the light that is in you is darkness, how great is that
> darkness! (Matthew 6:23)

But is a contrast. In contrast to your eye being good, here we have the eye which is bad. *If your eye is bad, your whole body* is *full of darkness*. The religious leaders of the day had an eye disease, in the spiritual sense. Remember, Jesus has already told them, when He was addressing lust, that if their eye caused them to sin, then they should pluck it out (Matthew 5:28-29). That same eye has another lust, that of materialism. So, Jesus says if your eye is bad, your heart and your whole body *is bad*, it is *full of darkness*. If there is no light coming in, then you cannot see. And if your eye is bad, then there is only darkness in your life, then your *whole body*, your whole life, is dark. And Jesus says *how great is that darkness*; which means how large is that darkness. "Jesus explained why by pointing out that a concentration on material success would lead to the darkened eye and the divided heart. The eye is the organ of perception through which our whole personality is guided (vv. 22-23). If we focus our vision on what the world calls success, our perception will be distorted and the light of God's revelation of reality will be blocked out. Our whole personality will be darkened."[70] In Mark 7:17-23, Jesus illustrates this truth: "When He had entered a house away from the crowd, His disciples asked Him concerning the parable. So He said to them, 'Are you thus without understanding also? Do you not perceive that whatever enters a man from outside cannot defile him, because it does not enter his heart but his stomach, and is eliminated, thus purifying all foods?' And He said, 'What comes out of a man, that defiles a man. For from within, out of the heart of men, proceed evil thoughts, adulteries, fornications, murders, thefts, covetousness, wickedness, deceit, lewdness, an evil eye, blasphemy, pride, foolishness. All these evil things come from within and defile a man.'"

So, ladies, do you want to know where your treasure is? Your **Eyes reveal it.** Proverbs 28:22 states, "A man with an evil eye hastens after riches, and does not consider that poverty will come upon him." Jesus ends this portion on a somber note. Just in case His audience hasn't heard what He's said in the previous statements, He makes it perfectly clear in verse 24.

> No one can serve two masters; for either he will hate the one and love the other, or else he will be loyal to the one and despise the other. You cannot serve God and mammon. (Matthew 6:24)

No man, no pastor, no pastor's wife, no Sunday school teacher, no church member, no professing believer can serve two masters. It is an impossibility. The word *master* means authority and indicates that it has your loyalty. You cannot at the same time serve or be a slave to God and serve or be a slave to something else. Perhaps, you are wondering why you can't serve two different masters. Jesus says it's because you *will hate the one and love the other,* or *be loyal to*

---

70 Lawrence O. Richards, *The Bible Teacher's Commentary* (Colorado Springs: Victor, 2004), 548.

one and despise the other. To *hate the one* which means to detest it, and to *love the other* is to <u>agape</u> it. To *be loyal to the one* means to be devoted to it, and to *despise the other* means to think against it.

The final indication, then, of where your treasure is, is this: **Sacrifices reveal it**. You absolutely *cannot serve God and mammon*. *Mammon* refers to an idol who was known as the god of riches. It could refer to possessions like monies, land, houses, cars, boats, technical devices, sports, collections, shopping, kids, grandkids, and even oneself. It is impossible to serve both God and mammon.

Summary

So, what are the eight facts we learn from Jesus about our treasure?

1. *Thieves steal it* (v 19). Have you ever been robbed? What was your attitude about the things that were taken from you? How you responded is a revealer of your true heart.

2. *Resources reveal it* (v 21). Have you kept a tally of where your money goes each month? What about a journal of your time and even your physical energy? These things reveal where our treasure is.

3. *Eyes reveal it* (v 23). What occupies your thoughts, your lusts? What things do your eyes look at more than anything else? Social media, internet, TV, the Word of God, creation? Where your eyes go is a revealer of your heart.

4. *Avoid accumulating it* (v 19). What things do you have an excess of in your home right now? Why are you accumulating them? Your possessions say a lot about where your heart is.

5. *Sacrifices reveal it* (v 24). What is the one thing or individual you think you can't live without? What do you spend the bulk of your day doing? With whom do you spend the bulk of your time? These things are a revealer of your heart's treasure.

6. *Unwelcomed pests destroy it* (v 19). When was the last time you had some item destroyed by an unwelcomed pest and what was your attitude? Your response is an indicator of what you treasure. (To be practical, I certainly would do what I could do to rid my belongings of unwelcomed pests, because material things are a gift from God and we should be good stewards of them.)

7. *Rust corrupts it* (v 19). When was the last time you had something you own ruined by some sort of corrosion? What was your attitude when you realized this thing was destroyed? This, too, is a revealer of your heart's desire.

8. *Eternity reveals it* (v 20). It is appointed for us once to die and after that to face the judgment. Each one of us will give an account for what we have done in our bodies, whether good or bad. What will your account look like as you stand before God and give account of your time, your energies, and your monies? What will eternity reveal about your treasure?

In Joshua 24:15, Joshua said to the nation of Israel, "And if it seems evil to you to serve the Lord, choose for yourselves this day whom you will serve, whether the gods which your fathers served that were on the other side of the River, or the gods of the Amorites, in whose land you dwell. But as for me and my house, we will serve the Lord." In 1 Kings 18:21, "Elijah came to all the people, and said, 'How long will you falter between two opinions? If the Lord is God, follow Him; but if Baal, follow him'. But the people answered him not a word." In Matthew 4:10, we read, "Then Jesus said to him, 'Away with you, Satan! For it is written, 'You shall worship the Lord your God, and Him only you shall serve.'" In Romans 6:16, Paul said to the church at Rome, "Do you not know that to whom you present yourselves slaves to obey, you are that one's slaves whom you obey, whether of sin leading to death, or of obedience leading to righteousness?" James warned his audience in James 4:4, "Adulterers and adulteresses! Do you not know that friendship with the world is enmity with God? Whoever therefore wants to be a friend of the world makes himself an enemy of God." The apostle

John warned the church at Ephesus in 1 John 2:15-16, "Do not love the world or the things in the world. If anyone loves the world, the love of the Father is not in him. For all that is in the world—the lust of the flesh, the lust of the eyes, and the pride of life—is not of the Father but is of the world." We have been fully warned, but what will we do about it?

Where is *your* treasure? Take some time this week to go on a "treasure hunt" to discover whether your treasure is here on earth or up in heaven.

Questions to Consider

Do You Know Where Your Treasure Is?
Matthew 6:19-24

1. (a) What do you think is the main idea of Matthew 6:19-24? (b) How does Luke 12:16-34 help you to further understand Matthew 6:19-24?

2. Memorize Matthew 6:24.

3. (a) What are the dangers of laying up treasures here on earth, according to Psalm 39:6; Proverbs 23:5; Ecclesiastes 5:10-17; Luke 12:16-21; and 1 Timothy 6:8-10? (b) What are the delights of laying up treasures in heaven, according to 2 Corinthians 4:18, Colossians 3:1-4 and 1 Peter 1:3-5? (c) Do you think it is wrong to save for the future? To save for a rainy day? To save for your children or grandchildren? Prove your answers from the Scriptures.

4. (a) Jesus says that what we treasure is a revealer of our heart. With that truth in mind, what can you discern about the hearts of the individuals written about in the following Scriptures? 2 Kings 5:20-27; Luke 16:19-31; Luke 18:18-23; Acts 5:1-11. (b) What do your daily activities reveal about your heart? (You might consider what you spend your time on, your money on, and your energies on.) (c) Considering what we learn in Proverbs 4:23 and Jeremiah 17:9-10, why is the heart so important?

5. (a) What are some possible "treasures" one might store up? (b) Are there any treasures that you think you can't live without? (This doesn't have to be just things; it can be people, ambitions, desires, etc.) (c) What does this indicate about your heart?

6. (a) How can we discern where our treasure is? (b) How can we discern if we are serving God or serving something else? (c) Why is it impossible to serve God and something else at the same time?

7. Matthew 6:19-24 is a lesson that is much needed in our society, a society that is obsessed with having things and having comfort. Please do some serious heart examination and then, in response to that heart examination, write a prayer request to share with others.

Chapter 15

Needless Worry, Needful Worship!

Matthew 6:25-34

The morning that I was writing this lesson, one of the day's top news stories revealed that Brussels, Belgium, had been put on maximum security alert due to serious and imminent threat of attack by terrorists. This followed closely after the sobering attacks which took place in Paris, France, on November 13, 2015, leaving 130 dead. And just a week after the Paris attacks, November 20, there were yet more terrorist attacks in Mali, which killed 19 people. Closer to home, there had been threats on our own soil in New York, Washington D.C., and Atlanta.

Increased threats on our nation and other nations leave most of us a little bit on edge and possibly even prone to worry about our lives and the lives of those we love. For some of us, terrorist threats pose no concern at all, but we are prone to worry about things that pertain to our daily lives, like our health or the health of a family member; financial stress; the purity of our children and grandchildren; who we're going to marry; what we will do if our spouse dies before we do; how we're going to get everything done that we need to do; paying our taxes; the aging process. These are just a sampling of the things that might be worry factors for us. But for the life of the kingdom citizen, there should be absolutely no cause for worry whatsoever! Perhaps that comes across to you as an extreme statement, but Jesus would disagree with you, because He commands His children to never worry! Let's listen in.

Matthew 6:25-34

> Therefore I say to you, do not worry about your life, what you
> will eat or what you will drink; nor about your body, what

you will put on. Is not life more than food and the body more than clothing? [26]Look at the birds of the air, for they neither sow nor reap nor gather into barns; yet your heavenly Father feeds them. Are you not of more value than they? [27]Which of you by worrying can add one cubit to his stature? [28]So why do you worry about clothing? Consider the lilies of the field, how they grow: they neither toil nor spin; [29]and yet I say to you that even Solomon in all his glory was not arrayed like one of these. [30]Now if God so clothes the grass of the field, which today is, and tomorrow is thrown into the oven, will He not much more clothe you, O you of little faith? [31]Therefore do not worry, saying, "What shall we eat?" or "What shall we drink?" or "What shall we wear?" [32]For after all these things the Gentiles seek. For your heavenly Father knows that you need all these things. [33]But seek first the kingdom of God and His righteousness, and all these things shall be added to you. [34]Therefore do not worry about tomorrow, for tomorrow will worry about its own things. Sufficient for the day is its own trouble.

In our last lesson, we learned eight facts about treasures, which help us in determining where our treasure is. Our current lesson flows naturally from the last one, because if we are laying up treasure on earth, then the natural tendency regarding this stuff is to be anxious about it. Kingdom citizens—those who are laying up treasure in heaven—put off worry and anxiety because they know that everything is secure in heaven in the arms of a loving Father. Those who put their trust in their earthly treasures, however, are filled with anxiety and worry because their thoughts are consumed with earthly stuff.

Having said all that, I am not so naive as to think that some genuine believers do not have temptations to worry, but my prayer is that after we study this text we will do as Jesus commands and stop worrying! In this lesson, *Needless Worry, Needful Worship*, we will consider:

The Reasons Why We Should Not Worry (vv 25-34)
The Reasons Why We Should Worship Instead
   (also vv 25-34)

We will see that there are eight of each. Let's look at the first reason why we should not worry and the first reason why we should worship instead.

1. Why We Should Not Worry
and
Why We Should Worship Instead

Matthew 6:25

> Therefore I say to you, do not worry about your life, what you will eat or what you will drink; nor about your body, what you will put on. Is not life more than food and the body more than clothing? (Matthew 6:25)

Therefore, because of what He's just said, because all this earthly stuff is not eternal, stop worrying about it. Be concerned for greater things, eternal things. Stop worrying about and living for earthly stuff, and start trusting in and living for eternal stuff. Because of this, Jesus says *do not worry about your life*. The word *life* pertains to the basic necessities, the things Jesus mentions in this passage: food, water, and clothes. These are the essentials for our lives. *Do not* is a present imperative in the Greek, which indicates that they were at that moment worrying about these things. We who live in affluent societies need to remember that Jesus' words here were delivered in a hot and dry climate where water was scarce. Food was typically gathered and eaten in one day. They didn't have abundant amounts of food in storage, water wasn't flowing out of the kitchen sink, nor were there water bottles available for purchase at the store. Clothes were obviously available, but few possessed an abundance of them, which is probably why Jesus mentions them last.

So, Jesus says *do not worry*, which means stop it! Do not do this! Stop this and don't start it ever again! Take no thought about these things! This doesn't mean that I shouldn't put some thought into what I'm going to cook for dinner or buy at the grocery store, or what clothes I need to put on for the day, but I'm not to worry about this stuff. In my humble opinion, we women spend far too much time browsing recipes, clothes catalogues, and the internet for this stuff. We have an obsession with earthly things that the biblical world would deem ridiculous. Wouldn't it be great if we would have this type of obsession for God and for serving others? One man says, "Yet taking care of the body has always been a common obsession with men. Even when we are not starving or thirsty or naked, we still give an inordinate amount of attention to our bodies. We pamper the body, decorate it, exercise it, protect it from disease and pain, build it up, slender it down, drape it with jewelry, keep it warm or keep it cool, train it to work and to play, help it get to sleep, and a hundred other things to serve and satisfy our bodies."[71]

Since Jesus is going to condemn worry, then we would do well to define it. *Worry* means to be pulled apart in different directions. We get our English word *strangle* from this word, which is a great parallel to worry because worry does indeed strangle us. "Have you ever noticed what happens when you become anxious about something? It begins to dominate your thinking, and you see everything in the light of your anxiety."[72] When we worry about anything, it takes our thoughts off of God and onto whatever we are worrying about.

So, the first reason we should not worry is because life is more than earthly concerns, and we should worship instead because life involves heavenly concerns. "One day when he was away from home someone came running up to John Wesley saying, 'Your house has burned down! Your house has burned down!' To which Wesley replied, 'No it hasn't, because I don't own a house. The one I have been living in belongs to the Lord, and if it has burned down, that is one less responsibility for me to worry about.'"[73] In verse 26, Jesus gives His audience a live illustration as to why they should not worry.

---

71 John MacArthur, *The MacArthur New Testament Commentary: Matthew 1-7* (Chicago: Moody Press, 1985), 421.

72 Sinclair Ferguson, *The Sermon on the Mount* (East Peoria: The Banner of Truth Trust, 1987), 142.

73 MacArthur, *The MacArthur New Testament Commentary*, 420

2. Why We Should Not Worry
and
Why We Should Worship Instead

Matthew 6:26

> Look at the birds of the air, for they neither sow nor reap nor
> gather into barns; yet your heavenly Father feeds them. Are you
> not of more value than they? (Matthew 6:26)

Remember, Jesus is teaching outside on the side of a mountain of
some sort. More than likely, birds are flying around, and He points
them out as He's speaking. There were about 20 different types
of birds in the land of Palestine at the time. Jesus says *look at the
birds in the air*, or behold the birds. *They neither sow nor reap nor
gather* their food *into barns*. They don't plant seeds and harvest
them. Jesus isn't condoning laziness here, because birds certainly
do work as they build nests and watch over their young and look for
food for themselves and their babies. They don't just fly around the
sky opening their mouths waiting for food to fall in. They do work,
but they don't worry. We, too, should work, but we also should not
worry. God is not far away.

The Psalmist reminds us of this in Psalm 145:15-16; he writes, "The
eyes of all look expectantly to You, and You give them their food
in due season. You open Your hand, and satisfy the desire of every
living thing." Again, in Psalm 147:9, we read, "He gives to the beast
its food, and to the young ravens that cry." It's funny that Jesus
mentions that the birds don't store up their food in *barns*, because
He just mentioned in Matthew 6:19 that all our earthly treasures are
prone to decay and rot, and that would certainly include the food
we try to store up for some potential catastrophe. It will eventually
expire.

Since it is true that God feeds the birds, which have no eternal soul,
then the logical conclusion is: *Are you not of more value than they?*
You are a human soul; they are animals. You are more important
than the birds, and yet God feeds them, so why would you worry

that you might not have adequate food? How ridiculous is that?!
A cute poem I found is a good reminder for us all:

> Said the robin to the sparrow,
> "I should really like to know
> Why these anxious human beings
> Rush about and worry so."
> Said the sparrow to the robin:
> "Friend, I think that is must be
> That they have no heavenly Father,
> Such as cares for you and me."[74]

The second reason why we should not worry is because God cares for the animal life, and we should worship instead because God cares for you more than the animal life. Jesus presents a second question in verse 27.

3. Why We Should Not Worry
and
Why We Should Worship Instead

Matthew 6:27

Which of you by worrying can add one cubit to his stature?
(Matthew 6:27)

You might have read this question and wondered what Jesus is saying. First, we need to define *one cubit*. It was a measurement in biblical times that was roughly the length of a person's forearm, from the tip of the middle finger to the tip of the elbow, about 22 inches. However, the Greek here means length or duration of life. Obviously, Jesus isn't talking about getting taller; He is, however, talking about adding years to one's life. When we worry, we don't add any more days or years to our lives. And, while Jesus doesn't say this in the text, it is more likely, in fact, that worry will take away years from your life. It has been proven that worry affects

---

74 Words by Elizabeth Cheney.

your whole body. It affects your heart; your nervous system; your appetite; your sleep; it weakens your immune system; it causes acid reflux, bowel issues, digestive problems, backaches, headaches, and even skin problems. As I was writing this lesson, one of my brothers had recently been in the hospital because of heart issues. On one of my visits to see him, the cardiologist came in and my brother mentioned that he was probably doing too much hard labor and that had probably caused his heart to act up. The cardiologist replied that physical work wasn't the culprit, that hard work wouldn't kill him, but that stress would. My brother quickly indicated that he had indeed been under a lot of stress at work.

According to Psalm 139:16, our days were written before we were even born, so why do we think that we can add anything to our lives, especially by worrying about them? We all have an expiration date given to us from our Father and we cannot add to or take away from it by worry. **The third reason why we should not worry is because you can't add any years to your life, and we should worship instead because God has numbered your days.** Jesus now gives another illustration regarding the sin of worry in verse 28.

4. Why We Should Not Worry
and
Why We Should Worship Instead

Matthew 6:28-30

> So why do you worry about clothing? Consider the lilies of the field, how they grow: they neither toil nor spin; (Matthew 6:28)

Jesus further illustrates the folly of worry by challenging His listeners regarding their worry over their clothing. He says that they should *consider the lilies of the field* and *how they grow*, how *they neither toil nor spin*. Again, it's likely that there were lilies within view as Jesus was teaching. The word *consider* means to learn thoroughly, to note carefully, to diligently consider this. The *lilies of the field* would have been familiar flowers to Jesus' listeners and probably were either white or purple in color. Solomon mentions them in Song of Solomon 2:1-2, "I am the rose of Sharon, and the lily of the valleys. Like a lily among thorns, so is my love among the daughters." Lilies *grow*, Jesus says, which means they enlarge, but they don't *toil* or *spin*. Not toiling would indicate that they don't feel fatigued. And spinning would be a reference to something women did in the biblical world. Proverbs 31:19 states, "She stretches out her hands to the distaff, and her hand holds the spindle." The spindle and distaff were instruments used for spinning, or making thread. And that thread was used for making clothes. The lilies grow without fatigue or effort. Jesus goes on to say,

> and yet I say to you that even Solomon in all his glory was not arrayed like one of these. (Matthew 6:29)

Even Solomon in all his glory was not arrayed, or as beautiful, as *one of these* lilies. As we mentioned, lilies were likely white or purple, but even Solomon's robe, which was also more than likely white or purple, wasn't as brilliant as these lilies. So, the conclusion of this is in verse 30.

> Now if God so clothes the grass of the field, which today is, and tomorrow is thrown into the oven, will He not much more clothe you, O you of little faith? (Matthew 6:30)

If God so clothes the grass of the field, if He makes the lilies more brilliant than Solomon's robe, and yet that amazing lily is here *today* and *tomorrow is thrown into the oven, will He not clothe you?* In biblical times, they would use stubble, herbs, and other stuff to heat their ovens. Once the flowers of the field were faded and no longer useful for beauty, the women would gather them and use them as kindle in the oven for their baking. If God cares about the lilies who have no soul, that are here today and thrown into the oven tomorrow for fuel, does He not care more for you, you who have an eternal soul? **The fourth reason why we should not worry is because God clothes and cares for the plant life and we should worship instead because God clothes and cares for you more than the plant life.**

5. Why We Should Not Worry
and
Why We Should Worship Instead

Matthew 6:30

> Now if God so clothes the grass of the field, which today is, and tomorrow is thrown into the oven, will He not much more clothe you, O you of little faith? (Matthew 6:30)

Jesus rebukes their worry by saying *O you of little faith*, or you who are lacking confidence. "Little-faithed ones" is the more literal translation of the Greek. Worry is contrary to faith, to what we say we believe. The just, the righteous, live by faith. **The fifth reason why we should not worry is because worry indicates you have little faith, and we should worship instead because worship shows you have great faith.** After giving two wonderful illustrations of how futile worry is, from the plant life and the animal life, Jesus reminds His audience again in verse 31 to stop worrying.

6. Why We Should Not Worry
and
Why We Should Worship Instead

Matthew 6:31-32

> Therefore do not worry, saying, 'What shall we eat?' or 'What shall we drink?' or 'What shall we wear?' (Matthew 6:31)

Therefore, because of what I just said, because of my care for the birds and the flowers, neither of which have a soul, because my care for you is far greater, then *do not worry*. What a loving Lord to repeatedly remind us to stop worrying! Don't worry about the necessities of life, about food, water, and clothing! He's already instructed His listeners in Matthew 6:11 that they are to ask for their daily bread, which is a necessity of life. Instead of worrying about their needs, they are to pray about those needs. Obviously, we need to eat and drink and put on clothes, and there is nothing in the text that indicates Jesus is prohibiting that. But we are not to *worry* about these things.

The biblical world would find our world to be obsessive, and we are, with so much variety of food and clothing and even water. We have so much and yet we complain about what we don't have. We would do well do remind ourselves of what our brother Paul says, that we are to be content with food and clothing (1 Timothy 6:8). But Jesus gives us another reason in verse 32 for why we should not worry, and this one should disturb us just as it did Jesus' audience.

> For after all these things the Gentiles seek. For your heavenly Father knows that you need all these things. (Matthew 6:32)

Jesus says don't worry about these things because this is what *the Gentiles seek*. In the biblical world, *gentile* was a reference to a pagan, or an unbeliever. In 1 Thessalonians 4:5, we read, "not in passion of lust, like the Gentiles who do not know God." *Seek* means to search, to intensively crave something. It behooves us, dear friends, to examine ourselves in light of what Jesus is saying here. If worry is your mantra, then your belief in a sovereign God is in question. If worry describes you, then Jesus would be suspect about your conversion. Worry is a "respectable" sin among believers, but it is not respectable to God. The Gentiles do this, but kingdom citizens do not.

We must keep in mind that throughout the Sermon on the Mount Jesus is contrasting hypocrisy with genuine kingdom citizenship. His children don't worry, but hypocrites do worry. Again, this leaves us to examine ourselves in light of this respectable sin. Unbelievers are watching us, and if we are going through life worrying, then it makes the gospel unattractive because it demonstrates that we are no different than they are. We need to show the world that Jesus gives peace. In fact, it is a promise He makes in John 14:27.

Jesus says don't worry about these things because *your heavenly Father knows that you need all these things*. We must not forget that God is all-knowing and that He knows we need certain things before we even ask them of Him. Dear one, you do not want to be a worrier! **The sixth reason why we should not worry is because unbelievers are characterized by worry, and we should worship instead because God knows you have needs.**[75] Instead of seeking these earthly worries as the Gentiles do, kingdom citizens seek something else, as verse 33 shows us.

7. Why We Should Not Worry
and
Why We Should Worship Instead

Matthew 6:33

> But seek first the kingdom of God and His righteousness, and all these things shall be added to you. (Matthew 6:33)

But, in contrast to seeking that stuff, *seek first the kingdom of God*. It's interesting that to *seek* here means to worship. That's why in the title of this lesson I have contrasted worry with worship. Instead of worry, I am to worship. A very interesting passage of Scripture related to this is found in Matthew 14:22-33:

> Immediately Jesus made His disciples get into the boat and go before Him to the other side, while He sent the multitudes away. And when He had sent the multitudes away, He went up on the mountain by Himself to pray. Now when evening came, He was alone there. But the boat was now in the middle of the sea, tossed by the waves, for the wind was contrary. Now in the fourth watch of the night Jesus went to them, walking on the

---

75 The opposite of worry or anxiety is contentment. Remember the Apostle Paul's reminder to his disciple Timothy: "and having food and clothing, with these we shall be content." (cf. 1 Timothy 6:8) The idea is one of tranquility and satisfaction with God's providential dealings in our lives. And this is something we grow into; we cultivate; we learn. The Apostle was able to say: "I have learned in whatever state I am, to be content. I know both how to be abased, and I know how to abound. Everywhere and in all things I have learned both to be full and to be hungry, both to abound and to suffer need." (cf. Philippians 4:11-12) And the opposite of this content, tranquil trust and satisfaction with God's providential dealings in our lives, is worry and anxiety. This is why worry is such a terrible and destructive sin, because it denies the goodness and sovereignty of God!

sea. And when the disciples saw Him walking on the sea, they were troubled, saying, "It is a ghost!" And they cried out for fear. But immediately Jesus spoke to them, saying, "Be of good cheer! It is I; do not be afraid." And Peter answered Him and said, "Lord, if it is You, command me to come to You on the water." He said, "Come." And when Peter had come down out of the boat, he walked on the water to go to Jesus. But when he saw that the wind was boisterous, he was afraid; and beginning to sink he cried out, saying, "Lord, save me!" And immediately Jesus stretched out His hand and caught him, and said to him, "O you of little faith, why did you doubt?" And when they got into the boat, the wind ceased. Then those who were in the boat came and worshipped Him, saying, "Truly You are the Son of God."

The disciples were afraid, they were worried about the wind and then about Jesus walking on the water. Impetuous Peter challenged the Lord by saying, "If you're really Him, then I'll walk to you on the water!" Of course, Peter began to doubt, and then he began to sink. Jesus says he is of little faith. He and Peter got into the boat and they all worshipped Him. How much worry they would have saved themselves by worshiping Him first! Acknowledging who He is and that He is the Son of God would have saved them a lot of worry. Acknowledging that there is nothing too hard for Him would have kept them from a lot of worry. If our minds are stayed on Him instead of on our troubles, we have peace. (In the Questions to Consider, you will probably notice that the antidote to worry is worship almost every time!)

When Jesus says seek first the kingdom of God, *first* indicates that this is the most important thing I do. If I am doing this, then I don't have time for worry. To seek *the kingdom of God* means to seek the expanding of His kingdom, not ours. We share the gospel truth and we live out the gospel truth, and if we spend our time doing these things, then the other lesser things like food, water, and clothing seem rather unimportant. When we seek His kingdom, we are more concerned about the souls of others and where they will spend eternity than we are with what we'll eat or drink or wear. I know where I'm going, so who cares if I don't have enough food or clothes?! What does it matter if my life is going exactly the way I want it to, or if the relationships I have are perfect? Why are we so obsessed with material things when others are lost and dying and going to a Christless eternity? In fact, we saw in a previous prayer that we are to pray for His kingdom to come (Matthew 6:10)!

The second thing we seek after is *His righteousness*. To *seek* would indicate a serious strenuous effort, a pursuit, and in this case it's a pursuit of His righteousness, His holiness, and purity of life. The whole Sermon on the Mount has been a sermon on righteous living. We've even learned that genuine kingdom citizens seek for all the righteousness there is. So, we should be seeking these things. When we start living right and seeking His righteousness, then these other things seem insignificant. In fact, Jesus wasn't concerned about clothing and food. He didn't even have a place to lay His head. He was born in a stable and buried in a borrowed tomb. When He was hungry and tempted by the devil, He was clear about what was essential; listen to His words in Matthew 4:1-4, "Then Jesus was led up by the Spirit into the wilderness to be tempted by the devil. And when He had fasted forty days and forty nights, afterward He was hungry. Now when the tempter came to Him, he said, 'If You are the Son of God, command that these stones become bread.' But He answered and said, 'It is written, "Man shall not live by bread alone, but by every word that proceeds from the mouth of God."'" Even the Psalmist didn't worry about food, but sought after being righteous instead; in Psalm 37:25 he says, "I have been young, and now am old; yet I have not seen the righteous forsaken, nor his descendants begging bread." **The seventh reason we should not worry is because there are greater things to be concerned about, and we should worship instead because as you seek heavenly things all this other stuff will be taken care of.** In fact, Jesus says they *will be added unto you*, which means they will be placed additionally unto you. Jesus brings His thoughts about sinful worry to a close in verse 34 and gives us yet another reason why we should not worry.

8. Why We Should Not Worry
and
Why We Should Worship Instead

Matthew 6:34

> Therefore do not worry about tomorrow, for tomorrow will worry about its own things. Sufficient for the day is its own trouble." (Matthew 6:34)

Therefore, because of everything He has already said, *do not worry*. Jesus has now mentioned this sin of worry five times! This time He says do not worry *about tomorrow*. Why shouldn't I worry about tomorrow? Because *tomorrow will worry about its own things*. These are interesting words that Jesus says here, because if tomorrow will worry about its own things, then when tomorrow gets here it will really be today, and we still shouldn't worry because tomorrow will always be the next day! There's no need to worry—period! When we consider Lamentations 3:22-23, we should be encouraged about all our tomorrows: "Through the Lord's mercies we are not consumed, because His compassions fail not. They are new every morning; great is Your faithfulness."

Jesus goes on to say that *sufficient for the day is its own trouble*. Today has enough trouble of its own. Today has enough concerns, and even the concerns we have we should rid ourselves of because they are in the hands of a loving Father. **The eighth reason why we should not worry is because He holds all the tomorrows in His hands, and we should worship instead because He holds all the tomorrows in His hands.** "Worry is not a trivial sin, because it strikes a blow both at God's love and at God's integrity. Worry declares our heavenly Father to be untrustworthy in His Word and His promises. To avow belief in the inerrancy of Scripture and in the next moment to express worry is to speak out of both sides of our mouths. Worry shows that we are mastered by our circumstances and by our own finite perspectives and understanding rather than by God's Word. Worry is therefore not only debilitating and destructive but maligns and impugns God."[76]

76   MacArthur,   *The   MacArthur   New   Testament   Commentary*,   425.

Summary

We need to seriously evaluate our lives in light of what Jesus is saying in this lesson. Worry is a serious sin and one we should not take lightly. Years ago, when I really struggled with certain fears, I did a word study on fear and discovered that the whole of Scripture teaches that we are forbidden to be fearful of anything except the Lord (with the exception of one verse which commanded us to fear, or revere, one's parents, in Leviticus 19:3).

What's got you worried this day? Is it possible terrorist attacks by our enemies? Is it a situation or person that is causing you to be worried? When Peter wrote 1 Peter, he told his readers to cast all their care upon God because He cares for them (1 Peter 5:7). These Christians were going through intense persecution; in fact, Peter refers to it as a fiery trail. Many were being sewn up in the skins of wild animals and then put in an arena so that wild animals could tear them apart limb by limb. Many were being rolled in pitch and set on fire as torches for Nero's garden. Many were forced to flee their homes. Yet Peter tells them not to worry but to worship by casting all their care upon God. Instead of worrying, we need to worship God.

Paul says something very similar in Philippians 4:6, where he writes, "Be anxious for nothing, but in everything by prayer and supplication, with thanksgiving let your requests be made known unto God." He gives us four words for prayer in this verse: *prayer* means to worship; *supplication* means to pray from an acute sense of need; *thanksgiving* indicates that we are thankful for the opportunity to trust God; and *requests* are petitions for definite and specific needs. Jesus, Peter, and Paul are all three saying the same thing—stop needless worry and start needful worship! Will you do this? Let's determine, with the help of the Lord, to stop needless worry and start needful worship!

Question to Consider
Needless Worry, Needful Worship
Matthew 6:25-34

1. (a) What things are repeated in Matthew 6:25-34? (b) What would be some possible reasons that Jesus would repeat these things?

2. Memorize Matthew 6:33-34.

3. From the following passages, answer the following questions. (a) Who was worried? (b) What were they worried about? (c) What was either the answer to their worry or the result of their worry (if it is mentioned)? (d) What do you learn regarding worry from these examples? Matthew 1:18-24; 8:23-27; 10:27-31; 14:22-33; Luke 1:26-38; 10:38-42; John 14:1-4, 27-31; Philippians 4:6-7.

4. (a) Jesus rebukes His audience for their worry by telling them they are of little faith (Matthew 6:30). What were the reasons He uses that same phrase in Matthew 8:23-27; Matthew 14:22-33; and Matthew 16:5-12? (b) What things can we do to increase our faith during times of trouble? (c) What situations in your own life cause you to have little faith?

5. (a) Jesus gives several illustrations from Matthew 6:25-34 as to why we should not worry. What are some other possible illustrations that you can think of that might illustrate how futile it is to worry? (b) Is there ever a time when Christians should worry? Why or why not? Prove your answer with Scripture.

6. (a) What things are you tempted to worry about? (b) What do you do when you are tempted to worry? (c) What are the biblical cures for worry? Use Scripture to support your answers.

7. After considering question six more carefully, please write a corresponding prayer request to share with your group.

Chapter 16

An Often Quoted (but Misquoted) Passage: Judge Not!

Matthew 7:1-5

Many years ago, the Lord in His kindness taught me a lesson that, Lord willing, I shall never forget. The lesson He taught me pertains specifically to the truths taught in the Scripture we are going to study in this lesson. In the church my husband was pastoring, there was a young couple who were somewhat involved. But, as time went on, I noticed that there were many seasons in which their attendance was haphazard. Instead of seeking to find out why, I became very critical in my heart toward them and wondered why they were "forsaking the assembling" of believers. As time went on, I became more and more critical in my thoughts, and they seemed to attend less and less. One particular Sunday, they asked if my husband and I could meet with them after church, as there was something they wanted to tell us, and, of course, we agreed. They began to unfold their story, of a surgery one of them had had years before. They knew that surgery was a mistake now, but in their carnality at the time, they did it. As a result of the surgery, this individual had developed numerous complications and had become quite ill, to the point that they developed a disease which rendered them terribly fatigued and battling a host of other symptoms. I remember so vividly the shame and remorse I felt that day because I had judged them in my heart without ever seeking to find out why their church attendance was slim.

Judging others is something that we all are guilty of, and more than likely, we all have been recipients of someone falsely judging us. As we turn our study toward chapter seven of the Sermon on the Mount, Jesus has some profound things to say regarding this topic

---

of judging others. This passage contains what may very well be one of the most misquoted passages in all the Word of God. Read along with me, if you will, Matthew 7:1-5.

Matthew 7:1-5

Judge not, that you be not judged. ²For with what judgment you judge, you will be judged; and with the measure you use, it will be measured back to you. ³And why do you look at the speck in your brother's eye, but do not consider the plank in your own eye? ⁴Or how can you say to your brother, "Let me remove the speck from your eye"; and look, a plank is in your own eye? ⁵Hypocrite! First remove the plank from your own eye, and then you will see clearly to remove the speck from your brother's eye.

In our last lesson, we considered the sin of worry and how needless it is. We learned that we are not to worry, and to replace our worry with worship.

As Jesus continues contrasting kingdom citizens and the Pharisees of His day, He deals with the very important topic of judging. The Pharisees were known for their self-righteous attitude, which led them to judging others. Those who belong to the kingdom should not behave in such a deplorable way, because they are hungering and thirsting for all the real righteousness there is, not self-righteousness.

As we consider this often-misunderstood passage, we will consider three questions:

> *What Does It Mean to Not Judge?* (v 1a)
> *What are the Reasons I am Not to Wrongly Judge Others?* (vv 1b-2)
> *What Must I Do to Judge Others Correctly?* (vv 3-5)

Let's consider this often-quoted-but-misquoted verse in Matthew 7:1 and discover what Jesus really meant when He gave us this command to judge not.

What Does It Mean to Not Judge?

Matthew 7:1a

Judge not, that you be not judged. (Matthew 7:1)

Jesus says *judge not*. The words indicate an absolute denial. In other words: God forbid that we should ever judge others. Some people stop right there and think this means that we should not judge anyone. The homosexual movement chants this verse to Christians; US citizens who see suspicious activity of a Muslim neighbor are afraid to report it for fear that they'll be accused of profiling or judging; Christians who point out the error of a false teacher are told that they're not to judge; believers use this verse as an excuse for not confronting another believer's sin because they do not want to "judge." On and on the list goes of ways this verse is taken out of context.

There are a couple of things we must consider when we are trying to understand what Jesus meant when He said we are not to judge. First, what does the word *judge* actually mean? It means to condemn, to punish, to judge harshly or rashly. We could also say that it means to be judgmental. This meaning of the Greek alone should be enough to counter those who would advocate for no judging whatsoever. But, second, we also have to consider that in this very chapter alone Jesus advocates judging in the proper way. In verse 5, and later on in Matthew 7:15-20, He will encourage this; in that passage, He says, "Beware of false prophets, who come to you in sheep's clothing, but inwardly they are ravenous wolves. You will know them by their fruits. Do men gather grapes from thornbushes or figs from thistles? Even so, every good tree bears good fruit, but a bad tree bears bad fruit. A good tree cannot bear bad fruit, nor can a bad tree bear good fruit. Every tree that does not bear good fruit is cut down and thrown into the fire. Therefore by their fruits you will know them." Jesus gives us license to judge men by their fruits.

So, we know from these two reasons that Jesus is not saying that we are never to judge. Unfortunately, many people will stop at verse one and say that we should never judge anyone about anything. They say we should be tolerant and silent when it comes to the faults and sins of others. But that is reading into the text something that isn't there. Those who claim this fail to read and interpret the whole section on judging. There are numerous other passages in Scripture that command us to judge others, as you will see in the Questions to Consider.

As we study this important topic of judging, we must remember that the whole Sermon on the Mount is contrasting the false religious leaders of Jesus' day with genuine kingdom citizens. The Scribes and the Pharisees took great pride in their self-righteousness; they looked down on others and were very judgmental. This is simply another sin of which they were guilty. But, we, too, must be careful about this, because we often become judgmental by being self-righteous and unmerciful like the Pharisees.

So, what does it mean to not judge? It means that I am forbidden to be judgmental of others by judging their motives. I am forbidden to have an attitude of self-righteousness, thinking that I am above anyone else. And Jesus gives two reasons why I must not wrongly judge others. The first reason alone should be enough for each of us to stop judging others.

What are the Reasons I am Not to Wrongly Judge?

Matthew 7:1b-2

Judge not, that you be not judged. (Matthew 7:1)

The first reason I should not wrongly judge others is because I will be judged. Jesus says judge not, *that you be not judged.* The Greek tense here indicates that this is a once for all judgment, the final judgment. People who are self-righteous forget that there is a day coming when the Judge of all the earth will be the final judge. There is a God, and it is not you or me.

The apostle Paul also warns us of the danger of judging in areas which are forbidden. Consider Romans 14.

> Receive one who is weak in the faith, but not to disputes over doubtful things. For one believes he may eat all things, but he who is weak eats only vegetables. Let not him who eats despise him who does not eat, and let not him who does not eat judge him who eats; for God has received him. Who are you to judge another's servant? To his own master he stands or falls. Indeed, he will be made to stand, for God is able to make him stand. One person esteems one day above another; another esteems every day alike. Let each be fully convinced in his own mind. He who observes the day, observes it to the Lord; and he who does not observe the day, to the Lord he does not observe it. He who eats, eats to the Lord, for he gives God thanks; and he who does not eat, to the Lord he does not eat, and gives God thanks. For none of us lives to himself, and no one dies to himself. For if we live, we live to the Lord; and if we die, we die to the Lord. Therefore, whether we live or die, we are the Lord's. For to this end Christ died and rose and lived again, that He might be Lord of both the dead and the living. But why do you judge your brother? Or why do you show contempt for your brother? For we shall all stand before the judgment seat of Christ. For it is written: "As I live, says the Lord, Every knee shall bow to Me, and every tongue shall confess to God." So then each of us shall give account of himself to God.

> Therefore let us not judge one another anymore, but rather resolve this, not to put a stumbling block or a cause to fall in our brother's way. I know and am convinced by the Lord Jesus that there is nothing unclean of itself; but to him who considers anything to be unclean, to him it is unclean. Yet if your brother is grieved because of your food, you are no longer walking in love. Do not destroy with your food the one for whom Christ died. Therefore do not let your good be spoken of as evil; for the kingdom of God is not eating and drinking, but righteousness and peace and joy in the Holy Spirit. For he who serves Christ in these things is acceptable to God and approved by men. Therefore let us pursue the things which make for peace and the things by which one may edify another. Do not destroy the work of God for the sake of food. All things indeed are pure, but

it is evil for the man who eats with offense. It is good neither to eat meat nor drink wine nor do anything by which your brother stumbles or is offended or is made weak. Do you have faith? Have it to yourself before God. Happy is he who does not condemn himself in what he approves. But he who doubts is condemned if he eats, because he does not eat from faith; for whatever is not from faith is sin.

There isn't room in this lesson to fully unpack the whole of Romans 14, but suffice it to say that Paul is very clear that we are forbidden to judge others regarding what they eat. (This is a common issue with many a believer in our day!) He reminds the Roman believers that there is one Judge and it is not them—it is God—and each one will stand before Him and give an account. Paul is very clear in verses 10-11 to remind them, and us, that we *all* will stand before God and we *all* will bow to Him. There is one God and it is not us!

Jesus' half-brother James reminds his readers, some of whom who were looking down on the poor, that they will be judged in the same manner as they judge others. In James 2:13, he writes, "For judgment is without mercy to the one who has shown no mercy. Mercy triumphs over judgment." And later on in his epistle he rebukes those who were looking down on others by using their tongue for evil. He says in James 4:11-12, "Do not speak evil of one another, brethren. He who speaks evil of a brother and judges his brother, speaks evil of the law and judges the law. But if you judge the law, you are not a doer of the law but a judge. There is one Lawgiver, who is able to save and to destroy. Who are you to judge another?" James is reminding them of the same thing that Paul reminded his readers of in Romans 14, that there is one Lawgiver, one Judge, and it is not you or me. But Jesus gives yet another reason why we should not wrongly judge others, in verse 2.

> For with what judgment you judge, you will be judged; and with the measure you use, it will be measured back to you. (Matthew 7:2)

For means this is the reason you should not judge. If you do, *you will be judged*, and it will be *with what judgment you judge*. Jesus is saying that when I make a decision to judge, then I will be judged or condemned. I am judged with the same judgment I have judged others. This means how I choose to judge others will be how I will be judged. Let me pause and ask you a couple questions: "When was the last time you falsely judged another person?" and "Would you like to be falsely judged in the same way?" That is what Jesus is saying. And He says *with the measure you use, it will be measured back to you*. The word *measure* means degree. In whatever measure, or to whatever degree, I judge, it will be returned back to me. In other words, we will be judged by the same degree or rule that we judge others. It could be that others will judge us in the same way we judge them or that God will judge us in the same way we have judged others. It's the principle mentioned in Obadiah 1:15, "For the day of the Lord upon all the nations is near; as you have done, it shall be done to you; your reprisal shall return upon your own head." So, the second reason I do not want to judge others wrongly is because I will be judged by others. How this gets fleshed out I do not know, but I imagine if we took a poll we all could recount a time that it did indeed happen to us. We must not forget the principle set forth in Galatians 6:7: "Do not be deceived, God is not mocked; for whatever a man sows, that he will also reap."

So, the two reasons we should not wrongly judge others are because we will be judged by God and because we will be judged by others in the same manner we have judged. Perhaps, at this point, those listening to Jesus had the same question you might have, and that is: "Am I never to judge anyone for anything? Is there not a time to judge?" Yes, there is, and we have plenty of scriptural precedent for righteous judging, but before we can judge correctly, we must do some correcting of ourselves. How do we judge others correctly? Jesus gives the answer in verses 3-5.

What Must I Do to Judge Others Correctly?

Matthew 7:3-5

And why do you look at the speck in your brother's eye, but do not consider the plank in your own eye? (Matthew 7:3)

Jesus helps us to correct our false way of judging others by asking a couple of questions. The first one is *why do you look at the speck in your brother's eye, but do not consider the plank in your own eye?* A *speck*, or mote as your translation might say, is a twig or a piece of straw or chaff. A *plank* would be a stick of timber or a large beam; we might liken it to a 2-by-4. The idea is that we forget the enormity of our own sin but quickly see the sin in others.

Jesus' speaking of the eye is interesting for two reasons. First, the eye is the part of our physical bodies with which we see, and the Pharisees were always comparing themselves with others and looking (with the eye) to find fault in others. Second, Jesus has just said in Matthew 6:22-23 that the lamp of the body is the eye and that if your eye is good your body is good, but if your eye is evil your body is evil. There, Jesus was using the eye as imagery to represent the heart. In the physical realm, light enters into the eye, enabling us to see. If the light doesn't enter in as it should, your vision will be distorted; such a condition may ultimately result in total and complete blindness. In the spiritual realm, Jesus is the light which enters into the eye of our heart and helps us to see spiritually. If, therefore, our eye is good and focused singly on Him, our whole body or life will be good. Jesus is using the eye as a picture of the heart.

The context of Matthew 6 flows naturally into the context of Matthew 7. That is, if our focus is on Christ and not on the sins of others, then we will not be so quick to see their imperfections. Instead, we'll be focusing—as we should—on our own sin, the 2-by-4's in our own lives, and not the twigs in our brothers' lives. One commentator has said of this, "The image of the eye teaches us another truth:

We must exercise love and tenderness when we seek to help others (Ephesians 4:15). I have had extensive eye examinations, and once had surgery to remove an imbedded speck of steel; and I appreciated the tenderness of the physicians. Like eye doctors, we should minister to people we want to help with tender loving care. We can do more damage than a speck of dirt in the eye if we approach others with impatience and insensitivity."[77] God speaks to Ezekiel in Ezekiel 16:51-52 and says, "Samaria did not commit half of your sins; but you have multiplied your abominations more than they, and have justified your sisters by all the abominations which you have done. You who judged your sisters, bear your own shame also, because the sins which you committed were more abominable than theirs; they are more righteous than you. Yes, be disgraced also, and bear your own shame, because you justified your sisters." It has been said that "We find it so easy to turn a microscope on another person's sin while we look at ours through the wrong end of a telescope!"[78] In this same line of thinking, Jesus poses a second question in verse 4 that is somewhat similar to the question He has just posed.

> Or how can you say to your brother, 'Let me remove the speck from your eye'; and look, a plank is in your own eye? (Matthew 7:4)

Do you see how ridiculous this is? We're walking around with a 2-by-4 in our eye while approaching our brother about a twig in his eye! We can't see clearly to help him! We first have to get the beam out of our own eye if we're ever to see clearly, which is Jesus' point in verse 5.

> Hypocrite! First remove the plank from your own eye, and then you will see clearly to remove the speck from your brother's eye. (Matthew 7:5)

---

77 (From *The Bible Exposition Commentary*. Copyright © 1989 by Chariot Victor Publishing, and imprint of Cook Communication Ministries. All rights reserved. Used by permission.)

78 R. Kent Hughes, *The Sermon on the Mount: The Message of the Kingdom* (Wheaton: Crossway, 2001), 231.

Hypocrite! Jesus speaks very strongly here; He's saying, "You hypocrite; you play-actor; you who say you have no sin ... get the sin out of your life before you try to help someone else!" The Pharisees' gross sin is so clearly illustrated in the parable Jesus gives in Luke 18:9-14, "Also He spoke this parable to some who trusted in themselves that they were righteous, and despised others: 'Two men went up to the temple to pray, one a Pharisee and the other a tax collector. The Pharisee stood and prayed thus with himself, 'God, I thank You that I am not like other men—extortioners, unjust, adulterers, or even as this tax collector. I fast twice a week; I give tithes of all that I possess.' And the tax collector, standing afar off, would not so much as raise his eyes to heaven, but beat his breast, saying, 'God, be merciful to me a sinner!' I tell you, this man went down to his house justified rather than the other; for everyone who exalts himself will be humbled, and he who humbles himself will be exalted."

It's interesting that in many places in the Gospels Jesus refers to the Scribes and Pharisees as blind. In Matthew 23 alone, He repeatedly refers to them as "blind guides," "fools and blind," and "blind Pharisee." In fact, in Luke 6, where we find verses that are similar to those ones we're studying in Matthew 7, Jesus begins the section by saying, "Can the blind lead the blind? Will they not both fall into the ditch?" (Luke 6:39). The Scribes and Pharisees were known for judging others without first looking to see the sin in their own lives. They needed to get the planks out of their own eyes and then they would see clearly to remove the specks out of their brothers' eyes. Think of it, in the physical sense, if I have a 2-by-4 in my eye, there is no way I can help anyone get a twig out of their eye. I need to remove the lumber first so that I can see clearly. In other words, first, before you help your brother, clean up your own act! The word *remove* means to cast it out. Once you do this, Jesus says, *then you will see clearly*, which means you will recover full vision. Before, you could not see clearly because of your own sin, but after removing the plank you will be able to see clearly again.

So, what must I do in order to judge others correctly? I must get the 2-by-4 of sin out of my own eye, so that I can see clearly to help my brother with his sin! Those who are kingdom citizens, who are mourning over their own sin, will with all humility try to help another one with their sin. That was the heart of King David in Psalm 51, after he repented of his adultery with Bathsheba and the murder of her husband Uriah. He begged God to give him a clean heart so that then he could teach sinners the right way (Psalm 51:18).

Summary

What Does It Mean to Not Judge? (v 1a) It means that I am not self-righteous or judgmental when it comes to the sins of others. How does it fare with you, dear one? Do you find yourself being critical and judgmental of others? Do you look down upon others for things like how they school their children? Do you judge those who don't homeschool, or public school, or private school? Do you judge others who don't discipline their children in the same manner you do? Do you judge those who don't use your preferred translation of the Bible? Do you judge others who drink coffee or eat certain foods which you think are big no-no's? Do you judge others for driving a nicer car than yours? Do you judge those who choose to wear make-up, jewelry, or dye their hair? You see, the list can go on and on of all the petty things for which we can choose to judge others. But Jesus says we are not be judgmental.

What are the Reasons I am Not to Wrongly Judge? (v 1b-2) Jesus gives two reasons why I am not to wrongly judge others: I will be judged by God, and I will be judged by others. We must remember, when we are tempted to judge others so harshly, that we are not God; there is only one God, and neither you nor I are Him. One day, we will all stand before God and give an account for all that we have done in our body, whether good or bad. Likewise, we must also remember the law of reaping and sowing. If we want to be falsely and harshly judged by others, then we should continue on in our sinful judging of them. How we have judged others will come back upon us! May we all keep this in mind the next time we're tempted to judge others harshly.

What Must I Do to Judge Others Correctly? (vv 3-5) I must first get the 2-by-4 out of my own eye so that I will be able to help someone else. What are the 2-by-4's you're lugging around? Have you examined yourself lately to see what blind spots you have that are hindering your effectiveness for the kingdom? Consider asking your husband or your close friend to help you see what those blind spots might be. Are you actively mortifying the deeds of the flesh, as Jesus reminded us? Are you cutting off your arm and gouging out your eye (figuratively) in an effort to put off your sin?

I know that some of you will take this lesson and misquote it. That is, you will avoid all confrontation and all judging of others. Yet, that is still a misquoted and misused application of this passage. There are many passages in the Word of God that speak to our need to help others who are in sin. (Consider Leviticus 19:17-18; Matthew 18:15-18; Galatians 2:11-14; 6:1; 2 Thessalonians 3:14-15; 2 Timothy 3:16-17; James 5:19-20; and Romans 15:14.) As we do this, however, we must make sure that we ourselves are pure in heart and not judgmental of others; we must help them in genuine love. I know in my own life I am indebted to those who have lovingly confronted me when I needed it, who have lovingly pointed out my blind spots, those sins that need to be rooted out. But I also know that I have been grieved when others have falsely judged me for things that are not biblical, or have judged my motives when I had nothing but good intentions. Remember, as one person has said, that "Judging a person doesn't define who they are, it defines who you are."[79] Or as another has said, "By judging others we blind ourselves to our own evil and to the grace which others are just as entitled to as we are."[80]

---

79 Author unknown
80 Dietrich Bonhoeffer, *The Cost of Discipleship* (New York: Touchstone, 1995), 185.

Questions to Consider

An Often Quoted (but Misquoted) Passage! Judge Not!
Matthew 7:1-5

1. (a) What do you think is the main point of Matthew 7:1-5? (b) Why do you think Jesus uses the human eye as He teaches on the importance of not judging others?

2. Memorize Matthew 7:5.

3. (a) In what ways is judging condemned in Romans 2? (b) How does Romans 2 correlate with what Jesus says in Matthew 7:1-5?

4. (a) How do you reconcile Matthew 7:1-5, which forbids judging others, with the following passages that give us freedom to judge others? Leviticus 19:17-18; Matthew 18:15-18; John 7:21-24; Romans 16:17-18; 1 Corinthians 5:9-12; Titus 3:9-11; and 1 John 4:1-3.

5. (a) Read 2 Samuel 11-12:15. In that passage, who needed to "get the beam out of their own eye so that they could see clearly"? (b) Psalm 51 was written after the account in 2 Samuel 11-12. What verses in Psalm 51 indicate that David could then see clearly to help others? (c) How do these passages encourage you to obey what Jesus says in Matthew 7:3-5?

6. (a) Who else needed to "get the beam out of their eye" before judging others, in Genesis 38:12-26 and John 8:1-11? (b) What are some common ways we judge others while we ourselves are guilty of the same sin? (c) Why is it imperative as parents that we make sure we are not practicing this form of hypocrisy before our children?

7. (a) In what ways should we as God's children avoid judging others? (b) In what things should we judge others? Support your answers with Scripture. (c) What are some common ways that Matthew 7:1-5 has been misused as it pertains to judging others?

8. In what ways do you wrongly judge others? Please put your need in the form of a prayer request.

Chapter 17

Stop Giving Out Truth!

Matthew 7:6

The apostle Paul once wrote a very pointed statement to the church at Galatia that I have pondered off and on in my pilgrimage with the Lord. In Galatians 4:16, Paul wrote, "Have I therefore become your enemy because I tell you the truth?" The fact is, many times we do become people's enemies because we speak the truth of God's Word to them. My husband and I have made many enemies over the years, some I'm sure due to our own failures, but many because of this fact alone: we have lovingly told them the truth of what God says in His Word. We have lovingly warned others of the danger they're in as they choose to remain in their disobedience. We've both had people scream at us, curse at us, hang up the phone on us, and even threaten our lives. My husband even had one man show up at the door with a gun ready to shoot him! Admittedly, these are not our most "fun" times in ministry, but they are expected! There's nothing new under the sun, as these types of things were going on way back in Genesis! But the question we have to face in this lesson is this: Does there ever come a time in the life of a kingdom citizen when we stop giving out the truth to certain people? The answer to that question is: yes, there is. This is where we find ourselves as we arrive at Matthew 7:6 in our study of the Sermon on the Mount. Jesus tells the audience on the mount that there comes a time when we stop giving out truth. He says:

Matthew 7:6

> Do not give what is holy to the dogs; nor cast your pearls before swine, lest they trample them under their feet, and turn and tear you in pieces.

In our last lesson, we looked at an often-quoted-but-misquoted passage and discovered what it really means when Jesus says we are not to judge. We learned that what Jesus condemns is a harsh, condemning, self-righteous judgment.

After that lesson, some of us may be terrified to do any judging or exhorting out of fear of being judged by God or others, or out of fear of judging wrongly, or out of fear of not getting all the "2-by-4's" out of our own eyes. But that is not God's will for us. We learned that there is ample evidence in Scripture of our responsibility to judge righteously and lovingly admonish when needed. We must be willing to give out truth and we must be willing to be persecuted and hated for doing so. But, there does come a time when we do not continue to try to help others by giving them the truth of God's Word, or the truth of the gospel, and that is Jesus' point as He continues teaching.

As we consider this next verse, we will consider:

> *The Command to Stop Giving Out the Truth* (v 6a)
> *To Whom Do We Stop Giving the Truth?* (v 6a)
> *Why and When Do We Stop Giving Them the Truth?* (v 6b)
> *What is Truth?*

Let's look first at the command to stop giving out truth.

The Command to Stop Giving Out the Truth

Matthew 7:6a

Do not give what is holy to the dogs; nor cast your pearls before swine, (Matthew 7:6a)

Jesus says *do not give what is holy to the dogs*. The words *do not* express an absolute denial: do not do this! This is similar to what Solomon wrote in Proverbs 23:9: "Do not speak in the hearing of a fool, for he will despise the wisdom of your words." Some will stop right here and use these words to justify their disobedience in sharing truth with others. Some will even come up with their own definitions of dogs and pigs. But Jesus is clear: yes, there is a time when we don't share truth, but it is only to certain people whom He calls dogs and pigs. Jesus certainly doesn't seem very "religiously-correct" in His terms, but let's look more closely at what He means. We turn now from the command to stop giving out the truth to the second part of this verse, where we consider who we are stop giving this truth to.

To Whom Do We Stop Giving the Truth?

Matthew 7:6a

> Do not give what is holy to the dogs; nor cast your pearls before swine, (Matthew 7:6a)

Jesus specifically says that we stop giving out truth to *dogs* and *pigs*. In order to grasp what Jesus is saying here, we need to understand the nature of these two terms. Neither of these animals was domesticated in the biblical world and they certainly were not used as pets, as is common in the 21st century. Statistics tell us that 37-47 percent of all Americans own a dog. Statistics regarding pig ownership are a little more difficult to find, but I know of people who have pot-bellied pigs for pets, though it is not nearly as common as owning a dog. (My daughter's family has Guinea pigs, but that's not the type of pig Jesus is speaking of.) Unlike our culture, in the biblical world these animals were not domesticated and were mostly viewed as detestable. Dogs wouldn't be put on a leash, taken to the vet for their shots and to the groomer for their bath or to get their nails done, dressed up in sweaters and bows, or buried in a pet cemetery. The world of the Bible would actually think that we are ridiculous for doing these things!

Most dogs in Jesus' day were savage, mangy creatures. They were scavengers, eating just about anything, even human blood. They'd growl at almost anyone, whether food was given to them or not. This is perfect imagery for what Jesus is saying, that is, there are individuals who are like savage dogs who hate the truth of God's Word. They will growl at anything you try to give them; therefore, don't give holy things to them!

What does it mean that we do not *give holy things* to them? The word *holy* means that which is morally blameless. Since Jesus is speaking of dogs, His audience would clearly understand that He is referring to giving these dogs meat, and by referring to it as holy, they would have in mind the holy meat that was to be sacrificed on the altar in the Temple. They would never give such meat to dogs! Are you kidding?! It would be unthinkable to give meat that was to be sacrificed to God to a mean and mangy dog.

Jesus' use of these terms is not derogatory; Paul uses them also in Philippians 3:1-2, where he says, "Finally, my brethren, rejoice in the Lord. For me to write the same things to you is not tedious, but for you it is safe. Beware of dogs, beware of evil workers, beware of the mutilation!" *Dogs* was simply a reference to the unbelievers. Jesus illustrates this also in Matthew 15:21-28:

> Then Jesus went out from there and departed to the region of Tyre and Sidon. And behold, a woman of Canaan came from that region and cried out to Him, saying, "Have mercy on me, O Lord, Son of David! My daughter is severely demon-possessed." But He answered her not a word. And His disciples came and urged Him, saying, "Send her away, for she cries out after us." But He answered and said, "I was not sent except to the lost sheep of the house of Israel." Then she came and worshipped Him, saying, "Lord, help me!" But He answered and said, "It is not good to take the children's bread and throw it to the little dogs." And she said, "Yes, Lord, yet even the little dogs eat the crumbs which fall from their masters' table." Then Jesus answered and said to her, "O woman, great is your faith! Let it be to you as you desire." And her daughter was healed from that very hour.

Jesus was not being demeaning toward this woman in the least; as Gentiles, the unbelieving world was commonly known as dogs. The fact that she was a Gentile—and a woman, at that—makes it all the more astounding that Christ spoke to her at all. (The disciples could take a lesson from Him on compassion!) The point is that the woman herself even knew that her race made her a dog. Why would Jesus give her anything if she was a dog? Because Jesus is not saying that we don't give truth to dogs, but to the kinds of dogs that will eat us up when we do! We must always remember context.

Jesus will describe in the next phrase how we can know when we're to stop giving truth to people. But, first, we need to describe pigs, or *swine*. Pigs, as we mentioned, would not be domesticated animals; they were detestable to the Jews. We also know that they didn't even consider pigs fit to eat because they were classified as unclean. They eat almost anything and they wallow around in the mud.

Jesus says don't *cast your pearls before swine. Pearls* were very precious in biblical times and were highly valued. In Matthew 13:45-46, Jesus says, "Again, the kingdom of heaven is like a merchant seeking beautiful pearls, who, when he had found one pearl of great price, went and sold all that he had and bought it." Even in heaven, pearls are considered of great value; consider Revelation 21:21: "The twelve gates were twelve pearls: each individual gate was of one pearl. And the street of the city was pure gold, like transparent glass." Pearls, then, because they were precious and valuable, became an emblem of truth. Jesus is saying: "Don't give precious truth or doctrine to pigs! Don't throw those pearls before pigs!" God's Word is precious and of great value; don't waste it on dogs and pigs. [81]

---

81 Peter helps define these people's character, as he says they had for a time escaped the pollutions of the world but now were entangled again in it, with the end result being worse than the beginning (cf. 2 Peter 3:19-22). These, evidently, were people who sincerely considered the claims of Jesus Christ on their life and for a time even separated themselves from ungodliness but then abandoned themselves to their old way of life. They made a determined decision to reject Christ, the gospel, holy living, and remain in their sin! These people had the gospel preached to them at one time and considered it for a time but then turned away. And Jesus would add, essentially, "Don't waste your time and effort trying to win such apostate dogs and swine." John Calvin helps summarize them, saying: "It ought

Why and When Do We Stop Giving Them the Truth?

Matthew 7:6b

lest they trample them under their feet, and turn and tear you in pieces. (Matthew 7:6b)

You might be wondering why we should refrain from giving the pearls of God's truth to these dogs and pigs. Jesus gives us the answer; He says *lest they trample them under their feet, and turn and tear you in pieces. They* refers to the dogs and pigs, and *trample them under the feet* means to reject or disdain it and completely trample it down. Not only that, but Jesus says *they will turn and tear you in pieces*, which means they turn around, reverse their position, and tear you up! We don't give doctrine to those who are intent on tearing us to pieces. One man helps us here: "In verse 6 Jesus warns against feeding holy meat to scavengers (dogs). Being the garbage collectors of the time, dogs were considered unclean. To feed meat from the altar to dogs was a sin. This meat was to be eaten by the priests or burned. The dog who ate such meat would give no thought to the fact that it came from the altar. He would make no distinction between it and any other meat. Likewise, a pig would care nothing about the value of pearls. He would simply trample them underfoot, turn on you and attack you because what you gave him was not edible. Neither the dog nor the pig will appreciate what you have done."[82] We can try to help unbelievers and we should certainly share the gospel with them, but we must remember that they will not necessarily receive our correction and it could turn out that we will be hated and persecuted for our efforts. Thankfully, Jesus has

---

to be understood that dogs and swine are names given not to every kind of debauched men, or to those who are destitute of the fear of God and of true godliness, but to those who, by clear evidences, have manifested a hardened contempt of God, so that their disease appears to be incurable." (John Calvin, *Commentary on a Harmony of the Evangelists* (Edinburgh: Calvin Translation Society, 1845). These are people who have had the gospel clearly explained to them but have made a definite decision to reject Christ with scorn and contempt and live in sin.

82 Jay E, Adams, *The Christian Counselor's Commentary: The Gospels of Matthew and Mark* (Woodruff: Timeless Texts; 1999), 67.

already addressed that and how we are to respond to it, here in the Sermon on the Mount, in Matthew 5:11-12 and 43-47.

What *Is* Truth?

We could end our lesson right here, but I fear that some will be tempted to do spiritual gymnastics with this verse just as they've done with the verses we studied in our last lesson. Many respond to the warning of Matthew 7:6 by intentionally neglecting the responsibly of sharing truth altogether because they fear rejection or persecution. Being lacerated and trampled on doesn't sound like a picnic, does it? And yet, we are commanded in the Great Commission to go into all the world and preach the gospel (Matthew 28:19-20). Some of us are fearful because we don't even know what this gospel message is that we're to be sharing. Some of us are fearful because we don't know enough of the Bible to talk intelligibly with those who are unbelievers. With these things in mind, and since we've been talking about truth and the fact that there is a time that we stop sharing the truth with some people, I thought this would be a good place to pause and give what I believe are four essential truths that we must share when presenting the whole gospel to the whole person. (This is also a good time for each of us to stop and examine ourselves in light of what we've learned in the Sermon on the Mount and to make sure that we, ourselves, have embraced the truths of the gospel.)

I have called this section *What Is Truth?* These are truths, they are the holy things—the pearls—that we must share regardless of the response we receive. Some will believe these truths; some will not; still others will turn on us. Their response is not up to us; it is up to God. But it is our responsibility to share the truth, the truth of the liberating gospel.[83] Perhaps you're wondering what I mean when I say, "the liberating gospel." Simply put, to be liberated means to be set free from a situation, especially imprisonment or slavery. You see, before salvation, we were enslaved to sin and we were enslaved to an enormous amount of it. Romans 6:17-18 puts it well: "But God be thanked that though you were slaves of sin, yet you obeyed from

---

83 As a point of clarification, I am not talking about Liberation Theology.

the heart that form of doctrine to which you were delivered. And having been set free from sin, you became slaves of righteousness." I remember in my own life that after I embraced this liberating gospel, I was no longer a slave to sin, but I was a slave to doing what is right, which is what righteousness is. I had been set free by the gospel, by the good news.

These four points all begin with the letter L, in hopes that it will make it easy for you to remember them as you endeavor to share with those who are lost.

1. *Lone God.* The first thing we must come to grips with before we can be liberated by the gospel is that God is a lone God. There is one God and He is the only God; there are no other gods but Him. The very first four words of the Bible are: "In the beginning God ..." (Genesis 1:1). Before I was set free by the gospel, I had many gods, many idols, in my life: the god of pleasure, the god of self, the god of self-righteousness, and several others. You see, I made up what God was like in my own mind, but it wasn't the God of the Bible. Paul talks about this in 1 Corinthians 8:5-6; "For even if there are so-called gods, whether in heaven or on earth (as there are many gods and many lords), yet for us there is one God, the Father, of whom are all things, and we for Him; and one Lord Jesus Christ, through whom are all things, and through whom we live." Just because a person is enslaved to sin, just because that person has made up gods in his or her mind, doesn't make the fact there is one God any less true. Malachi 2:10 is clear: "Have we not all one Father? Has not one God created us?" In Mark 12:32, one of the religious leaders of Jesus' day said, "You have spoken the truth, for there is one God, and there is no other but He." Even the religious leaders of Jesus' day knew that there was one God, but they did not believe in His Son for salvation. James indicates that many believe in one God but are not saved. Listen to James 2:19, "You believe that there is one God. You do well. Even the demons believe—and tremble!" The demon-world has enough sense to tremble at the thought of the true God, which is more than most people living today. There is no fear of God before most people's eyes; God isn't even in their thoughts!

But God's Word is clear: there is only one God.

This truth poses a problem, and the problem is this: how does one have a relationship with this awesome God? Paul gives us a hint in 1 Timothy 2:5-6: "For there is one God and one Mediator between God and men, the Man Christ Jesus, who gave Himself a ransom for all, to be testified in due time." This brings me to my second point regarding the liberating gospel.

2. *Loving God.* The second thing we must understand is that this Lone God, this One God, is also loving. He loves us. He wants to be in loving relationship with those whom He has created. A familiar passage that illustrates this truth is John 3:16-17, which says, "For God so loved the world that He gave His only begotten Son, that whoever believes in Him should not perish but have everlasting life. For God did not send His Son into the world to condemn the world, but that the world through Him might be saved." As you are sharing with those who are outside, you can say something like: "My friend, God loves you and He loves you so much that He sent His only Son into the world as a baby to grow up and die on the cross for your sins. This is utterly amazing!" Romans 5:6-10 tells us, "For when we were still without strength, in due time Christ died for the ungodly. For scarcely for a righteous man will one die; yet perhaps for a good man someone would even dare to die. But God demonstrates His own love toward us, in that while we were still sinners, Christ died for us. Much more then, having now been justified by His blood, we shall be saved from wrath through Him. For if when we were enemies we were reconciled to God through the death of His Son, much more, having been reconciled, we shall be saved by His life." Imagine this, that God so loved us while we were still enslaved to our sin that His Son Jesus died in our place so that we might be set free from our sin. But even though God loved us and sent His Son to die for us, it is imperative that we must realize that there is absolutely nothing we can do to merit this wonderful gift of salvation. We cannot earn our way to heaven. Many are taught that if they do enough good works then they will have entrance into eternal glory, but nothing could be further from the truth. Titus

3:3-7 says, "For we ourselves were also once foolish, disobedient, deceived, serving various lusts and pleasures, living in malice and envy, hateful and hating one another. But when the kindness and the love of God our Savior toward man appeared, not by works of righteousness which we have done, but according to His mercy He saved us, through the washing of regeneration and renewing of the Holy Spirit, whom He poured out on us abundantly through Jesus Christ our Savior, that having been justified by His grace we should become heirs according to the hope of eternal life." Not only can we not do anything to deserve or earn this great gift but we have to realize that it is God who loves and chooses us, not we who love and choose God. John is clear in 1 John 4:9-11, "In this the love of God was manifested toward us, that God has sent His only begotten Son into the world, that we might live through Him. In this is love, not that we loved God, but that He loved us and sent His Son to be the propitiation for our sins." Also, we know from John 15:16 that we did not choose God, but He chose us!

Perhaps, you're wondering why anyone would want to believe in a dead person. What makes this Jesus different from any other god that is worshipped in our world today? The answer brings us to my third point.

3. *Living God.* This man who died on the cross for our sins is alive. He is not dead. Paul makes this clear in 1 Corinthians 15:3-4: "For I delivered to you first of all that which I also received: that Christ died for our sins according to the Scriptures, and that He was buried, and that He rose again the third day according to the Scriptures." We have the accounting of the resurrection in all of the gospel accounts, but listen to the one in Matthew 28:1-7: "Now after the Sabbath, as the first day of the week began to dawn, Mary Magdalene and the other Mary came to see the tomb. And behold, there was a great earthquake; for an angel of the Lord descended from heaven, and came and rolled back the stone from the door, and sat on it. His countenance was like lightning, and his clothing as white as snow. And the guards shook for fear of him, and became like dead men. But the angel answered and said to the women, 'Do not be afraid,

for I know that you seek Jesus who was crucified. He is not here; for He is risen, as He said. Come, see the place where the Lord lay. And go quickly and tell His disciples that He is risen from the dead, and indeed He is going before you into Galilee; there you will see Him. Behold, I have told you.'" This is an essential fact of the liberating gospel because without a living Savior we are doomed indeed. Paul puts it this way in 1 Corinthians 15:17-19: "And if Christ is not risen, your faith is futile; you are still in your sins! Then also those who have fallen asleep in Christ have perished. If in this life only we have hope in Christ, we are of all men the most pitiable."

These three are all amazing truths: this God is the lone God; He is a loving God; and He is a living God. There is no other religion that can say that: not Buddha, Allah, Muhammad, or any of the other 2870 gods that have been worshipped since the beginning of time (and those 2870 doesn't even include the gods of our own making!). None of those gods are the only God, none of them love their worshippers, and none of them are living. Only the true God, this awesome God, loves His children, gives them eternal life, and is still living. This is a humbling fact, that the awesome God of all the Earth would choose any of us. This brings me to my fourth and final point, which is what makes this gospel even more liberating.

4. *Lord God.* He is Lord! Lord is a word which means Master, Owner. Many in our day love the fact that Jesus is their Savior, but to think of Him as their Lord is not such a wonderful fact to some. Yet, in the New Testament, Jesus is referred to as Savior only 24 times, but there are more than 600 references to Him as Lord. Acts 16:31 is clear: "Believe on the Lord Jesus Christ, and you will be saved." This means when an individual becomes a believer, a Christian, that individual takes on a new Lord. He or she is no longer the master of their own life, but their life is now yielded to a new Master, that being the Lord Jesus Christ. This, my friend, is liberating! It means that I am no longer a slave to my own fleshly desires, but I am a slave to His desires and I delight to do His will. It means that I have been made dead to my old life and have been risen to a new life, a life in Christ Jesus, my Lord. It means that I choose to repent of

my sins, to turn away from them. It means that I choose to walk in obedience to His Lordship. To some, this idea of Christ being our Lord is offensive, but we would do well to remind them of a sobering passage in Philippians 2:5-11: "Let this mind be in you which was also in Christ Jesus, who, being in the form of God, did not consider it robbery to be equal with God, but made Himself of no reputation, taking the form of a bondservant, and coming in the likeness of men. And being found in appearance as a man, He humbled Himself and became obedient to the point of death, even the death of the cross. Therefore God also has highly exalted Him and given Him the name which is above every name, that at the name of Jesus every knee should bow, of those in heaven, and of those on earth, and of those under the earth, and that every tongue should confess that Jesus Christ is Lord, to the glory of God the Father."

One day, every knee will bow to His Lordship. I would rather bow in this life than in the life to come, because those who choose to wait till then will be cast into everlasting punishment in hell. Now, some will respond to this by saying, "Well, I like the idea of taking Him as Savior, but taking Him as Lord—I'm not ready for that." Well, Jesus would warn of such thinking, because it is foreign to what the Bible says concerning His Lordship. In Luke 6:46-49, Jesus says, "But why do you call Me 'Lord, Lord,' and not do the things which I say? Whoever comes to Me, and hears My sayings and does them, I will show you whom he is like: He is like a man building a house, who dug deep and laid the foundation on the rock. And when the flood arose, the stream beat vehemently against that house, and could not shake it, for it was founded on the rock. But he who heard and did nothing is like a man who built a house on the earth without a foundation, against which the stream beat vehemently; and immediately it fell. And the ruin of that house was great."

This liberating gospel has four important elements that we would do well to consider. They are: God is the Lone God; He is the Loving God; He is the Living God; and He is the Lord God. You can ask the following questions to those with whom you're sharing the gospel.

First, "Do you believe that there is one God?" This is an important question. I remember asking a relative once if they believed in God, and they responded by saying that they believed in a god. That answer had a lot of implications. There is only One God.

Second, "Do you believe that He loves you?" If they don't believe He loves them, they will have a hard time obeying Him. It's like in marriage: a wife whose husband who loves her has an easier time submitting to his headship. However, if her husband doesn't love her, especially the way Christ loved the church, as husbands are commanded to do, that wife will find it difficult to submit to his leadership.

Third, ask them, "Do you believe that He sent His Son to die for your sins and that He is now alive?" 1 Corinthians 15:3-4 states, "For I delivered to you first of all that which I also received: that Christ died for our sins according to the Scriptures, and that He was buried, and that He rose again the third day according to the Scriptures."

The fourth question is essential. Ask them, "Will you submit to Him as Lord? Will you bow your knee to His Lordship?" Without making Him Lord, there is no liberating gospel. Without submitting to Him as Lord, they will still be dead in their trespasses and sins because they will still be living as lord of their own life. I would encourage them that this is the most important decision of one's life, and it is a matter of eternal life or eternal death. Paul said that, knowing the terror of the Lord, he persuaded men (2 Corinthians 5:11). Remind them to not harden their hearts and that today is the day of salvation. Encourage them not to put it off, because they might someday find themselves looking back in regret, and then it will be too late!

Obviously, the gospel is not the only truth we give to people, but without the truth of the gospel, which has the power to save, it is difficult to give any other truth or doctrine from God's Word. We must be faithful to give out the truth, no matter what, whether it is the truth of the gospel or any truths of God's Word.

Summary

The Command to Stop Giving Out the Truth (v 6a). Jesus commands this, but it's only with a certain type of people and for certain reasons. My question to you is this: have you stopped giving out all truth to all people? Are you ashamed of the gospel? Are you ashamed of the fact you are a Christian? We must only stop giving out the truth when doing so lines up with the reasons Christ has given.

To Whom Do We Stop Giving the Truth? (v 6a). Dogs and pigs, or, we might say, those who are lost. Again, there is a qualifier that Jesus gives, but I ask you: Who are the people in your circle of friends and family who are lost? Have you exhausted all efforts in sharing the gospel with them? If not, why not?

Why and When Do We Stop Giving Them the Truth? (v 6b). We stop giving out the truth when the people we're sharing with become angry and attempt to trample on us and tear us into pieces. (There are numerous examples of this in the Scriptures, but Matthew 10:14-15; John 8:59; and Acts 18:1-6 are a few that are helpful to consider.) It might be that they ask you to stop shoving religion down their throat. It might be that they threaten your life. I will stop and say this: just because this happens does not mean all hope is lost! When you look at Christ in the New Testament, He had seasons where He withdrew from trying to impact His family and others, and then He had seasons where He would try again, and we would do well to follow His example. There is no harm in waiting a reasonable amount of time, praying and asking God for another window of opportunity, and trying again. Ask God for creative ways to share or for events to happen in the lives of others that might give them pause to think about some seed of the gospel that has been planted in their minds.

What Is Truth? The truth is that the Christ died for our sins, that He was buried, and that He rose again. The truth is that we must submit ourselves to His Lordship. The truth is the whole of Scripture. Are you giving out the whole truth and nothing but the truth? Are you willing to suffer for telling the truth?

I want to leave you on an encouraging note, since this one verse we've considered is pretty heavy. While the truth of this verse might be a reality in many of our lives, with our family and our friends, all hope is not lost. As a pastor's wife, my husband and I have numerous opportunities to give out the gospel, along with many other truths from God's Word. Not all receive that truth, and many reject it, some literally fulfilling this verse. But many years ago, my husband and I counseled a young woman who, though she did not turn on us or try to kill us, did not receive what we were saying. Several years passed and our paths crossed again. She started a discipling relationship with me and she mentioned the meeting that my husband and I had with her years before. She said, "What you said that day haunted me and rang in my ears for the past several years. I have never forgotten it." I share that to encourage you, to remind you that even though you think all hope is lost with a certain individual, only God knows what seeds have been planted there, and only God knows what future fruit might be born from those seeds of truth.

My friend, give out the truth, and leave the results to God. If it's rejected, wait, pray, and hope for another opportunity. As Paul said to his son in the faith, Timothy, I now close by saying to you: "I charge you therefore before God and the Lord Jesus Christ, who will judge the living and the dead at His appearing and His kingdom: Preach the word! Be ready in season and out of season. Convince, rebuke, exhort, with all longsuffering and teaching. For the time will come when they will not endure sound doctrine, but according to their own desires, because they have itching ears, they will heap up for themselves teachers; and they will turn their ears away from the truth, and be turned aside to fables. But you be watchful in all things, endure afflictions, do the work of an evangelist, fulfill your ministry" (2 Timothy 4:1-5).

Questions to Consider
Stop Giving Out Truth!
Matthew 7:6

1. (a) Do you think there is a connection between Matthew 7:6
    and Matthew 7:1-5? (b) If so, what is that connection? (c) Do
    you think there is any connection between Matthew 7:6 and
    Matthew 7:7? (d) If so, what is that connection?

2. Memorize Matthew 7:6.

3. (a) What do you learn about dogs from the following passages?
    1 Kings 14:11; Psalm 22:16; Psalm 59:6; Proverbs 26:11;
    Isaiah 56:11; 2 Peter 2:18-22; Revelation 22:14-15. (b) What
    do you learn about pigs from the following passages? Leviticus
    11:7; Matthew 8:28-34; Luke 15:11-16; 2 Peter 2:18-22. (c)
    How does this better help you to understand what Jesus says in
    Matthew 7:6?

4. (a) Read Acts 7. Who is giving holy things to "dogs"? (b)
    What was the result of this? (c) Jesus calls unbelievers dogs
    and swine in Matthew 7:6. What words does Stephen use to
    describe unbelievers in Acts 7:51-53? (d) How is Acts 7:54-
    60 a great illustration of what Jesus is saying in Matthew 7:6?
    (e) What happened after the stoning of Stephen, according to
    Acts 8:1-4? (f) How does this encourage you when you are
    persecuted for giving out the truth?

5. (a) What attitudes should we have as we share truth with those
    who are not redeemed, according to Matthew 10:16; Colossians
    4:5-6; 1 Peter 3:1-6? (b) What were the responses of those who
    were given truth, according to Matthew 15:12-14; Acts 13:44-
    46; 18:5-8; 28:23-31? (c) In Matthew 10:11-15, what does
    Jesus say we should do when someone refuses the truth? (d)
    How do you respond when the gospel message is rejected?

6. (a) Do you think there comes a time that we stop sharing the gospel with an individual? (b) How would one discern that? Use Scripture to support your answer.

7. Is there someone you know who needs the gospel? Have you exhausted all efforts in sharing with them? Please write a prayer request regarding this, so that others might pray for you.

Chapter 18

The Promise of Answered Prayer

Matthew 7:7-11

Someone once said, "God answers all prayers. Sometimes He says, 'Yes.' Sometimes He says, 'No.' Sometimes He says, 'Wait.' And sometimes He says, 'You've got to be kidding me!'"[84] In a way, that quip is true and we've all probably experienced God saying "yes" to our prayers, saying "no" to our prayers, and even saying "wait" to our prayers. I'm quite sure as well that, even though God hasn't said, "You've got to be kidding Me!" to any of our prayers, many of us have probably looked back and said something like that to ourselves: "I can't believe you really asked God for that! You've to be kidding me!" As we come to Matthew 7:7-11, we have to deal with what appears to be a passage indicating that God answers everyone who asks and gives to everyone who seeks and knocks. Is this what Jesus meant when He spoke these words on the mount? Let's begin our study and find out.

Matthew 7:7-11

> Ask, and it will be given to you; seek, and you will find; knock, and it will be opened to you. ⁸For everyone who asks receives, and he who seeks finds, and to him who knocks it will be opened. ⁹Or what man is there among you who, if his son asks for bread, will give him a stone? ¹⁰Or if he asks for a fish, will he give him a serpent? ¹¹If you then, being evil, know how to give good gifts to your children, how much more will your Father who is in heaven give good things to those who ask Him!

---

84 Author unknown.

It might seem odd to you that Jesus starts speaking again about prayer, since He already addressed prayer back in chapter 6. But when we consider that He has given some sobering words concerning our need to be careful about wrongfully judging others, our need to correctly judge others, and the fact that as we do some will turn on us like wild dogs, then you can understand why Jesus reminds us again to pray. We need to pray before judging anyone, to seek His help in determining whether it is a righteous judgment, and to make sure that we are not being judgmental. We also need to pray for wisdom concerning what to say, when to say it, and how to say it. We need to pray when those we confront turn on us and devour us. In reality, we are to pray about everything, as Paul says in 1 Thessalonians 5:17, and the task of confronting others certainly demands our praying!

As we consider *The Promise of Answered Prayer*, we will see:

> *The Points of Prayer* (v 7)
> *The Promise of Prayer* (v 8)
> *The Principles of Prayer* (vv 9-10)
> *The Provision of Prayer* (v 11)

We will find that Jesus mentions three of them in verse 7.

The Points of Prayer

Matthew 7:7

> Ask, and it will be given to you; seek, and you will find; knock, and it will be opened to you. (Matthew 7:7)

The first point of prayer that Jesus mentions is to ask. The word *ask* means to request or beg, and it has the idea of an inferior asking from a superior. We depraved people are begging or asking from a divine, sovereign, holy God. This implies that there must be humility from us when we pray. God hates pride and the Pharisees certainly exhibited it. Remember the Pharisee who prayed with himself, thanking God that he wasn't like others, and reminding

God of all his accomplishments? God is under no obligation to hear such prideful praying. We must remember the humility of the tax collector, who beat his breast and did not even feel worthy to look up into heaven (Luke 18:9-14). This is what Jesus is saying when He urges us to ask.

The Greek tense here also indicates that we are to keep on asking. We don't stop praying, and there are many things we don't stop praying about. I just received an email from a lady who said she'd been praying 28 years for something. Does that mean she should stop praying because God hasn't yet answered her request? No! We keep on asking, knowing that God is in heaven and we are on earth, and He alone knows the beginning from the end. As a biblical counselor, when women come to me for counseling, one of the things I often do is ask them how much they've prayed about their situation, and I find it interesting that they usually tell me they haven't prayed about it at all or very little. They could save themselves a lot of heartache, as well as the need to seek out a counselor, if only they would ask the Wonderful Counselor! So many of us do not have because we do not ask, as James explains in James 4:2. And in James 1:6, he admonishes us that we must ask in faith, without doubting. This is a problem for most Christians, because they lack the faith to believe that God will indeed answer their prayers. Not long ago, a dear lady, whom I have the joy of partnering with in discipleship, agreed to pray with me that we would grow in our faith, because we are both keenly aware of our being weak in faith when it comes to God answering our petitions.

Jesus says we are to ask and *it will be given* to us! You might be thinking, "Well, I have asked and it has not been given to me!" There are two things we must consider in this matter of unanswered prayer. First, we must take into account all of Scripture—all 66 books, the whole counsel of God—when considering why God may not be answering our prayers. There are hindrances to prayer, as you saw in the Questions to Consider, and we would do well to ponder those hindrances when it appears God is not answering our prayers. Second, we have to consider the context of the verses we're studying here in Matthew 7, as it seems to be asking about when to judge righteously, about when to stop casting pearls before swine and giving holy things to dogs, and about asking for help regarding obedience to the Sermon on the Mount.

The second point of prayer Jesus mentions is seeking. The term *seek* has the idea of pursuing or hunting. We certainly need to be asking, but we also need to be seeking for the answer. For example, you might pray for God to change your heart regarding judging others falsely, but then you must also pursue putting off that sin and seek for ways in which you can do so. You might pray about when to stop giving truth to others, but you must also pursue them until it is clear that the time has come for you to stop casting pearls before swine. You might pray for the Lord to provide financially for you so that you can pay your bills, but you don't wait for gold dust to fall from heaven (like one church in Tulsa does); rather, you seek for ways in which you might earn that money. You ask, but you also seek for the answers. The Greek tense here indicates, again, that we keep on seeking, that we never let up on it. Jesus says that if we keep on seeking we *will find*. Recently, I was encouraged regarding something I've been praying about for years, and God graciously allowed me to have a conversation with someone that made me realize why He had not yet answered that prayer.

The third point of prayer is that we must knock. The term *knock* indicates perseverance. Luke 11:5-8 provides us a wonderful illustration of this: "And He said to them, 'Which of you shall have a friend, and go to him at midnight and say to him, "Friend, lend me three loaves; for a friend of mine has come to me on his journey, and I have nothing to set before him"; and he will answer from within and say, "Do not trouble me; the door is now shut, and my children are with me in bed; I cannot rise and give to you"? I say to you, though he will not rise and give to him because he is his friend, yet because of his persistence he will rise and give him as many as he needs.'" And then in the very next verse, verse 9, Jesus says, "So I say to you, ask, and it will be given to you; seek, and you will find; knock, and it will be opened to you." Just like the persistent friend did, you keep on knocking and you don't give up!

Jesus says here in the Matthew 7 that when we knock, it *will be opened* to us. One man helps us with this verse and says, "'Ask' implies asking for a conscious need. The word also suggests humility in asking, for it is commonly used of one asking a superior. The next step, 'seek,' involves asking but adds action. The idea is not merely to express one's need, but to get up and look around for help. It involves effort. 'Knock' includes asking, plus acting, plus persevering—like someone who keeps pounding on a closet door!"[85] As children of God, we all have asked for things, but sometimes we wait and nothing happens, so we seek the answers. Or, we find that God has answered but not in the way we had desired, so we keep seeking the answers. And we continue asking and seeking and knocking until He opens the door with the answer or the thing that we have asked for.

These are encouraging words. Yet, I fear that we are quick to keep on praying and asking and seeking for things we want but are not so quick to do so in regard to our sinful attitudes of judging or other sins we're dealing with. The context here appears to be asking, seeking, and knocking regarding the virtues Jesus has been teaching about. Many will come to the end of a study like this being thoroughly convicted and asking God to help them change, but sadly they will soon start doing the next study or the next thing and quickly forget about the changes they need to make. They're like the man James mentions in his epistle who looks in the mirror and goes away forgetting what he or she looked like. They fail to make any changes, because just glancing in the mirror does nothing to change one's looks. We have to do something about it (James 1:21-25)! Remember, Jesus has already said that we are to be perfect as He is perfect and, yet, in this life we know we won't ever attain perfection. But we keep striving for it; we keep asking, we keep seeking, and we keep knocking. The Christian life is a war, and in that war we daily beat our bodies into subjection. Jesus moves from the points of prayer to the promise of prayer in verse 8.

---

85 R. Kent Hughes, *The Sermon on the Mount: The Message of the Kingdom* (Wheaton: Crossway Books, 2001), 234.

The Promise of Prayer

Matthew 7:8

> For everyone who asks receives, and he who seeks finds, and to him who knocks it will be opened. (Matthew 7:8)

Ladies, God is a God who cannot lie and this is a promise for answered prayer especially regarding asking, seeking, and knocking about things in the Sermon on the Mount and obedience to those things. Jesus says that *everyone who asks receives*, that *he who seeks finds*, and that everyone *who knocks* will have the door *opened*. This promise begs us to examine our motives in praying and to make sure that we are not personally being a hindrance in any way to God answering our prayers. Many people pray for selfish reasons, some with bitter hearts, and some for their own personal gain and not for God's glory. All these and any other hindrances we would do well to examine so that we can be free to ask and receive, seek and find, knock and watch the door be opened! Living in Tulsa, we regularly hear well-meaning, professing believers claim that Jesus promised unconditionally to answer our every prayer. This isn't true! I like how John Stott corrects this mistaken assumption. He says,

> It is absurd to suppose that the promise "Ask, and it shall be given you" is an absolute pledge with no strings attached; that "Knock, and it will be opened to you" is an "Open, Sesame" to every closed door without exception; and that by the waving of a prayer wand any wish will be granted and every dream will come true. The idea is ridiculous. It would turn prayer into magic, the person who prays into a magician like Aladdin, and God into our servant who appears instantly to do our bidding like Aladdin's genie every time we rub our little prayer lamp.[86]

---

86 John Stott, *Sermon on the Mount* (Nashville: B & H Academic, 2011), 297.

As a matter of fact, let me further say that I am thankful that this is not a promise for unconditional answered prayer! You and I would become monsters if this were the case, because our prayers would be tools used to manipulate God into catering to our own indulgence and self-glory.

Again, I remind you that the context of this asking, seeking, and knocking is for right judging, along with the whole of the Sermon on the Mount. Do you pray for things more than you pray for your own heart to be right with God? Do you pray for others to be sanctified more than you pray for your own sanctification? This is Jesus' point here in the Sermon on the Mount; don't be like the Pharisees who think they are better than everyone else!

No doubt, some will take this verse completely out of its context and say that it's a blank check for whatever they want. If this verse really promised what it appears to be promising, it would be ludicrous, because then I could ask God for anything I want and He would be obligated to give it to me. That makes God my magician and me a monster! No parent in their right mind would give their child everything they asked for! "Can I have a cookie, Mom?" "Yes," Mom says. "Can I have the car?" "Yes, of course, and take it out all night." "Can I have all your money?" "Yes, and take your dad's too!" "Can I play video games all day?" "Yes." "Can I hit my sibling?" "Why, of course, honey." Do we see how ludicrous that is?! If we allowed our children such indulgence we would be like the spoiled teenaged boy I just read about, who killed four people in a drunken driving accident and got off scot-free. The story said that his parents gave him whatever he wanted with absolutely no consequences. He was going 70 miles an hour in a 40 mph zone and his blood-alcohol content was triple what it should be. Not only were four people killed but 11 others were injured, and some of them paralyzed. That is a perfect illustration of what you and I would be like in the spiritual realm if God gave us whatever we wanted. In fact, Jesus illustrates His promise with a human illustration that we can easily understand. So, we go from the promise of answered prayer to some important principles that we would do well to heed.

The Principles of Prayer

Matthew 7:9-10

> Or what man is there among you who, if his son asks for bread, will give him a stone? (Matthew 7:9)

If your *son asks for bread*, will you *give him a stone*? Perhaps you're wondering why Jesus uses such an illustration. In biblical times, loaves of bread and stones were similarly shaped. Their bread wasn't like the bread we typically buy at the store, nicely sliced and put in a plastic bag. Loaves of bread in biblical times were rounder and flatter than ours, and some were completely flat, much like tortillas or pita. The rounder loaf of bread could easily be mistaken for a stone. This is interesting, because when Satan tempted Jesus in the wilderness, one of Satan's tactics was to tempt Jesus to turn stone into bread. Matthew 4:1-4 states, "Then Jesus was led up by the Spirit into the wilderness to be tempted by the devil. And when He had fasted forty days and forty nights, afterward He was hungry. Now when the tempter came to Him, he said, 'If You are the Son of God, command that these stones become bread.' But He answered and said, 'It is written, "Man shall not live by bread alone, but by every word that proceeds from the mouth of God."'" The illustration is clear: A parent would not give a child a stone to eat unless he wanted a hefty dentist bill. That would be absurd, right?! Why would a loving parent give a hungry child a stone to eat? Jesus gives yet another illustration that is equally as ridiculous, in verse 10.

> Or if he asks for a fish, will he give him a serpent? (Matthew 7:10)

If your son *asks for a fish*, would you *give him a serpent*? The first illustration is weird enough, but the second one is even more bizarre. A stone won't hurt you unless you eat it, but a snake is dangerous. Why would you give a child a snake?! A fish is long and sometimes slimy, much like a snake is, and either of the two could easily be mistaken for the other. The idea here is that a parent isn't going to be deceptive with a child and trick them. A child asking for a fish is, more than likely, hungry for food; a parent isn't going to, instead, give that child a snake that would bite him!

Jesus' point is clear, and in these two verses there are two principles that we would do well to remember. First, when God answers prayer He never tricks or deceives us! Second, He may not answer when or how we desire but He will answer according to His will for us. Our loving heavenly Father knows what is best for us; He would never give us something that would harm us, even though we might wonder from time to time. Ladies, this should make us think— when God says no to our requests, or says to wait, it may be that the thing we are asking for will not be good for us. The following poem pens this truth well:

> I asked for health that I might do greater things;
> I was given infirmity that I might do better things.
> I asked God for strength that I might achieve;
> I was made weak that I might learn to obey.
> I asked for riches that I might be happy;
> I was given poverty that I might be wise.
> I asked for power and the praise of men;
> I was given weakness to sense my need of God.
> I asked for all things that I might enjoy life;
> I was given life that I might enjoy all things.
> I got nothing I asked for but everything I hoped for;
> In spite of myself, my prayers were answered—
> I am among all men most richly blessed.
> Yes, God always gives us what's best for us.[87]

The Provision of Prayer

Matthew 7:11

If you then, being evil, know how to give good gifts to your children, how much more will your Father who is in heaven give good things to those who ask Him! (Matthew 7:11)

---

87 Author unknown

Jesus now ends this section on prayer by giving us a wonderful provision of prayer, in verse 11. He says, *If you then, being evil*, if you being the depraved person that you are, if you who have selfish motives in your giving, *know how to give good gifts to your children*, do you not think that *your Father who is in heaven*, who is holy and without sin, will give you *good things*? As I sat writing these words it was one week till Christmas day. My husband and I were planning to spend the holiday with our daughter, son-in-law, and four grandchildren. I had enjoyed purchasing gifts for them, and as I wrapped the packages I thought about the glee and joy that they would have when they received those gifts. Now, I confess, I don't ever have as many gifts to give to my grandchildren as one lady I heard about, who had more than 300 gifts for her 3 children! The picture I saw online showed the gifts piled up almost to the top of the tree! As much as we like to give gifts—and hopefully we're not as indulgent as that lady—often our giving is tainted with selfish motives and even, sometimes, with strings attached. But not our God. He has no selfish motives in His giving and there are no strings attached. Our best gift-giving is tainted with sin, but it is not so with our Father. Jesus' half-brother James is clear in James 1:16-18: "Do not be deceived, my beloved brethren. Every good gift and every perfect gift is from above, and comes down from the Father of lights, with whom there is no variation or shadow of turning. Of His own will He brought us forth by the word of truth, that we might be a kind of firstfruits of His creatures." The Father gives good and perfect gifts, even if they might not seem like it to us. In fact, the context of these verses in James is one of trials, and, basically, James is saying even those trials that God allows us to go through are good and perfect gifts. It might seem like God has handed you a stone or a snake, but, in reality, He has handed you bread and fish. So what is the provision of answered prayer? It is that God gives us good gifts—even if they don't seem so good to us!

Jesus ends this section the same way He began it, and that is with the reminder to ask. He says the Father *gives good things to those who ask Him!* Jesus began in verse 7 by saying ask Me. Herein lies the failure among most kingdom citizens: they don't ask. We will spend oodles of time murmuring and complaining about what we don't have or what we think we need but little time asking God to help us. We will spend quite a bit of time complaining about the faults of others and little time confessing our own sins to God. We do not have because, quite frankly, we do not ask!

Summary

The Points of Prayer (v 7): As we consider the promise of answered prayer, we're reminded that Jesus gives three points regarding prayer—ask, seek, and knock. How often do you ask, seek, and knock? And how often do you ask, seek, and knock regarding obedience to the Sermon on the Mount? Can you honestly say that you are praying about everything? Can you honestly say that you are seeking for those answers to prayer? Can you honestly say that you are persevering in prayer by continuing to knock on the doors of heaven? One man has said, "We ask for what we wish; we seek for what we miss; we knock for that from which we feel ourselves shut out."[88]

The Promise of Prayer (v 8): Secondly, we have the wonderful promise that God will indeed answer our prayers. Has God answered your prayers? And has God answered your prayers specifically regarding changes you need to make because of this sermon we're studying? What prayers has He answered this week? If God doesn't answer your prayers, have you stopped long enough to examine why? Could it be that there are hindrances to your praying that you are unwilling to deal with? If God has never answered any of your prayers, then you might want to do some serious self-examination, making sure that you are a genuine kingdom citizen, because we know that God does not hear the prayers of the unrepentant.

The Principles of Prayer (vv 9-10): Thirdly, there are two principles of answered prayer. First, when God answers prayer, He never tricks or deceives us! Second, He may not answer when or how we desire,

---

88 From Jamieson, Fausset, and Brown Commentary, Electronic Database. Copyright © 1997, 2003, 2005, 2006 by Biblesoft, Inc. All rights reserved.

but He answers according to His will for us. When God answers prayers, but not quite as you expected, are you just as thankful and as excited as when He answers your prayers exactly as you had hoped? Do you really believe that He has a plan and that He knows the beginning from the end? Can you trust Him with whatever answers He gives, knowing that you are His child and that He would never give you something harmful, just as you would never give anything harmful to your child?

The Provision of Prayer (v 11): Finally, there is a wonderful provision in answered prayer: that God gives us good gifts. Those gifts might not always seem good to us, but we must bank on the promise that God does work everything out for our good, as He has promised in Romans 8:28. Some of those good things would fall under the category of progress in your walk due to obeying this wonderful Sermon on the Mount! Paul prayed three times for something he called a thorn in the flesh to be taken from him, but God did not answer the way Paul wanted Him to; instead, Jesus gave Him something better: His strength in place of Paul's weakness. David prayed for seven days that his baby would not die, and yet it did. Moses prayed to enter the Promised Land, but God did not let him. Instead, God gave David and Moses better gifts. God gave them the wonderful reminder that He is just, He is holy, and He is a God who cannot lie. God gave them the good gift of not going against the very nature of who He is! Even Jesus our Lord prayed that He would be spared the awful torment of crucifixion and separation from His Father; God said no and gave Him something better: redemption for mankind! Yes, the Father has gone on record to promise us that He will answer our prayers, but He has not gone on record promising to answer them according to our will (though many times He does); rather, He answers our prayers according to His will! And His will is always the best for His child!

Questions to Consider

The Promise of Answered Prayer
Matthew 7:7-11

1. (a) Read Matthew 7:7-11 along with Luke 11:9-13. What is different about these two passages? (b) Why do you think they are different?

2. Memorize Matthew 7:7.

3. (a) In what ways are Luke 11:5-8 and Luke 18:1-8 good illustrations of Matthew 7:7-8? (b) What should be our attitudes in prayer, according to Romans 12:12; Ephesians 5:20; 6:18; Colossians 4:2; and 1 Thessalonians 5:17? (c) Do these characterize your attitudes in prayer?

4. (a) Jesus says we are to ask and it will be given to us. His brother James says in his epistle that we ask but do not receive. According to James 4:1-5, what might be some of the reasons we do not receive what we ask for? (b) What is similar about Matthew 7:1-12 and James 4:1-11? (c) Why do you think prayer and judging others are both mentioned in such close proximity in the Matthew passage as well as the James passage?

5. (a) What would be some possible reasons God does not answer our prayers, according to Psalm 66:18; Matthew 6:7; Mark 11:25-26; Luke 18:1; James 1:5-7; 4:1-4; 1 Peter 3:7; 1 John 5:14; (b) Could any of these be the reasons God does not answer your prayers? (c) What will you do about it?

6. (a) What do you find the most difficult when it comes to praying? (b) What have been the most effective times of prayer in your own life? (c) Looking back over your life, what are some things that you prayed for that God did not answer but now you are thankful that He didn't? (d) Do you enjoy praying? Why or why not?

7. For what things do you need to be asking, seeking, and knocking? Write your needs in the form of a prayer request so others can pray for you!

Chapter 19

Living Out the Golden Rule

Matthew 7:12

As I sat writing this lesson, it was the year of yet another presidential election. Most of us found ourselves bombarded daily with ads, calls, and conversations regarding the candidates. We were inundated with news coverage of the candidate's remarks, which were often difficult to listen to in light of our Christian faith. Likely, not a day went by in which we didn't hear of some outlandish slander from one candidate regarding another. And if it wasn't slander, it was some catty remark that we all could have done without hearing. As kingdom citizens, we have to wonder how different election years would be if the men and women running for the office of the President of the United States considered and practiced Matthew 7:12? Such a thing would shock America, and yet we might begin to see once again the blessing of God on our nation.

But it's not just carnal politicians who seem to have difficulty following the golden rule. We seem to have a problem remembering it in the local church as well. If we seriously obeyed the principle set forth in Matthew 7:12, most of our sin would cease. If we really treated others the way we desire to be treated, we would stop lying, stealing, committing sexual immorality, gossiping, slandering, speaking flattery, getting angry, being arrogant, being bitter, having abortions, meddling in others' business, complaining, being rude, arguing, and a myriad of other sinful things. If we really started treating others the way we want to be treated, we would start honoring our parents, honoring our authorities, taking care of widows and orphans, disciplining our children as God says, being courteous to others, being hospitable, showing love by being joyful, merciful, compassionate, kind, longsuffering, gentle, good, self-controlled, and, again, a myriad of other godly things. If we really stopped long enough before every thought, word, and deed directed toward others to ask ourselves, "Is this how I would like to be treated? Is this how I would like others to speak to me? Is this how I would like others to think about me?" then we would see amazing things begin to happen in our personal and spiritual lives. We might see a glimpse of what Jesus has already spoken about in the Sermon on the Mount, that is, to be perfect as He is perfect (Matthew 5:48). So let's consider Matthew 7:12 as we contemplate living our lives in light of what many have called "The Golden Rule."

Matthew 7:12

> Therefore, whatever you want men to do to you, do also to them, for this is the Law and the Prophets.

In our last lesson, we looked at the wonderful promise of answered prayer and noticed three points of prayer: we are to ask, seek, and knock. We also learned the wonderful promise of prayer, that He will answer. (We considered hindrances to prayer, as well, along with answers we might not like so much!) We also learned two principles of prayer. First, when God answers prayer, He never tricks or deceives us! Second, He may not answer when or how we desire, but He answers according to His will for us. We ended with the provision of prayer, that God gives us good gifts. As we move on in our study of the Sermon on the Mount to examine how we are to be living out the golden rule, we need to consider four things:

> *We Need to Consider Ourselves* (v 12a)
> *We Need to Consider Others* (v 12b)
> *We Need to Consider the Law* (v 12c)
> *We Need to Consider the Prophets* (v 12d)

We Need to Consider Ourselves

Matthew 7:12a

Therefore, whatever you want men to do to you, (Matthew 7:12a)

Before we unpack this verse and its rich meaning, we need to be reminded that all too often we look at this verse and we quote it because we hope that others will treat us well, when, in reality, we need to look at this verse and then take a good, long look at ourselves. We ought to be examining ourselves to see if we treat others in the same ways that we would like to be treated.

Jesus begins this section of His sermon with the word *therefore*, which indicates that we need to look back. Now some believe that this refers to what Jesus has just said; in other words, because God answers our prayers and give us good things, then we ought to treat others with goodness. Since He is a loving and gracious God, then we are to be loving and gracious as we relate to our fellow man. While I certainly think those things are true, to be fair, it seems more likely that Jesus' words here really relate back to the whole teaching on the Sermon on the Mount. The *therefore* covers everything that Jesus has said thus far in His sermon, all the way back to chapter five. Because of what Jesus has already taught regarding our responsibility to our fellow man, then we therefore are to treat them as we would like to be treated.

As we think about living out the golden rule, we must first consider ourselves. Let's ask ourselves some questions as we think back on the whole of the Sermon on the Mount as it relates to our relationship to others. From Matthew 5:7, do you want others to be merciful to you, to show compassion, and to extend forgiveness? Then you show mercy by showing compassion and extending forgiveness to others! From Matthew 5:8, do you want others to have pure thoughts, motives, and actions in how they relate to you? Then you maintain pure thoughts, motives, and actions as you relate to others. From

Matthew 5:9, do you want others to make every effort to be at peace with you? Then you make every effort to be at peace with others, by pursuing peace and striving to solve conflicts and not to stir them up. From Matthew 5:21-26, do you desire that others would not lash out at you in anger? Then you don't lash out in anger at them. Do you desire that others reconcile with you when they are offended by you? Then you reconcile with others (and do it quickly!) when you are offended by them. From Matthew 5:27-30, do you want others to not lust after your spouse or commit adultery with your spouse? Then you don't lust after or commit adultery with their spouse. From Matthew 5:33-37, do you desire that others would keep the promises they've made to you? Then you keep the promises you've made to them. From Matthew 5:38-42, do you wish others would give up their rights for the sake of helping you out when you really need their help? Then you give up your rights for them when they need your help. From Matthew 5:43-48, would you like your enemies to make every effort to love you, bless you, do good to you, and pray for you? Then you make every effort to love your enemies, bless your enemies, do good to your enemies, and pray for your enemies! From Matthew 6:1-18, do you desire that others do their acts of righteousness (i.e., giving, praying and fasting) without hypocrisy? Then you do your acts of righteousness without hypocrisy. (Just in case you're wondering how this one relates to our fellow man, consider this: When we see others living in hypocrisy, we are tempted to have ill thoughts toward them; we might be tempted to gossip about them, avoid them, or simply dislike them.) From Matthew 6:19-24, do you desire that others be more sold out for Christ and less in love with the world? Then you be more sold out for Christ and less in love with the world.

From Matthew 6:25-34, do you desire that others would stop their needless worry, fears, and anxieties? Do people like that discourage you and weigh you down? Then you stop complaining to others about all your fears and worries. From Matthew 7:1-5, do you want those who confront sin in your life to be living a life of holiness and not be involved in blatant sin? Then you make sure before you confront others that you are living a life of holiness. From Matthew 7:6, do you like it when others keep nagging you about things that irritate you? Then you stop making religious comments to unbelievers who've made it clear that they've had enough! Now, obviously, these are not the only ways that we should examine ourselves as we consider how we want to be treated, but these are the areas that Jesus has mentioned thus far in the Sermon on the Mount. One man has said of this passage, "How we treat others is not to be determined by how we expect them to treat us or by how we think they should treat us, but how we want them to treat us. Herein is the heart of the principle, an aspect of the general truth that is not found in similar expressions in other religions and philosophies."[89]

We Need to Consider Others

Matthew 7:12b

do also to them, (Matthew 7:12b)

Having considered ourselves, we turn now to considering others. Taking the very same passages we just looked at, let's reword the questions so that we consider others, so that we consider whether we are doing unto them as we would like them to do unto us. From Matthew 5:7, do you stop to consider others when you fail to extend mercy, compassion, and forgiveness? Do you put yourself in their shoes and consider the hurt that you cause them? From Matthew 5:8, do you consider how your impure thoughts, motives, and actions affect others? Do you consider that you might be leading them down sinful paths by your actions? From Matthew 5:9, do you consider those with whom you refuse to make peace? Do you realize how that daily affects the hearts and lives of others? Do you stop to consider the turmoil you put them through because you refuse to be at peace with them? From Matthew 5:21-26, do you consider how your anger toward another person makes them feel? Do you consider that it is crippling to your relationship to them? Do you consider that they

---

89 John MacArthur, *The MacArthur New Testament Commentary: Matthew 5:1-7* (Chicago: Moody Press, 1985), 446.

often avoid you or walk on pins and needles around you because they fear your anger? Do you think about those with whom you are refusing to reconcile and how your actions affect their daily walk with the Lord? Do you consider the amount of time they may be putting into praying and hoping that one day you will be reconciled to them? From Matthew 5:27-30, do you consider the hurt that you inflict upon others when you lust or commit adultery with their spouse? Do you consider that the injured spouse will struggle the rest of their life with trusting their mate? Do you realize that the Word of God says the wound will never ever go away from that offended spouse? (Proverbs 6:32-35). They will always be plagued by the fact that they were sinned against by your moment of pleasure with their spouse. From Matthew 5:33-37, do you stop to consider your children, your grandchildren, your friends, your husband, or anyone else to whom you've made promises and yet failed to keep? Do you stop and think of the hurt that you cause them by your failure to keep your word, and how, if it's a repeated action on your part, they will struggle with believing anything you say because your word cannot be trusted?

From Matthew 5:42, do you consider the needs of others and how, for some, it is hard to even ask for help, but when they do ask, and you fail to lend a hand, how it not only mars your testimony with them but also blasphemes the very Word of God, which says that loving our brothers will be the preeminent way the world will know that we are believers? From Matthew 5:43-48, do you consider how it affects those you might call your enemies when you choose to avoid loving them, blessing them, doing good to them, and praying for them? Do you realize that your behavior may be a discouragement to them if they are at all hoping for reconciliation? From Matthew 6:1-18, do you consider trying to help others when they appear to be living hypocritically, instead of avoiding them or gossiping about them? Do you love them enough to lovingly confront them about the danger their soul is in even if it costs you the relationship? Do you consider that it is the Lord's testimony that is at stake among those who claim Christ but live in hypocrisy? From Matthew 6:19-24, do you consider those who are caught in the deception of loving the world and its idols? Do you see them as being in desperate need of a Savior, and do you love them enough to share with them the danger they are in? From Matthew 6:25-34, do you desire to help those who are caught up in needless worry, fear, and anxiety? Or are you willing to just let them go their sinful way, discouraging not only you but all those who are subject to their constant murmuring? From Matthew 7:1-5, do you consider others when you have the sobering task of confronting them and go with a spirit of humility, making sure that you are getting the 2x4's of sin out of your life first? Do you love them enough and consider them enough to follow through long-term, to make sure they're making the changes needed to truly get the speck out of their eye? From Matthew 7:6, do you consider how it affects others when you hound them with the gospel day after day after day? Perhaps, it is your unsaved husband whom you so desperately want to know the Lord, so you put Scripture verses up all over the mirror or have Christian music playing when he walks in the door? Do you consider that these things might be driving him further away, instead of endearing him to Christ? Obviously, these are not the only ways we should consider others as we think about living out the golden rule, but these are the areas Jesus has mentioned in the Sermon on the Mount.

We Need to Consider the Law

Matthew 7:12c

... for this is the Law ... (Matthew 7:12c)

We have considered ourselves and we have considered others. Now, Jesus says, *for this is the Law and Prophets*. Before we consider the law and the prophets, we need to define what Jesus is saying. By this statement, Jesus is saying that the golden rule is basically the sum of what is written in the Old Testament. Remember, He already said in the Sermon the Mount, "Do not think that I came to destroy the Law or the Prophets. I did not come to destroy but to fulfill" (Matthew 5:17). Loving others and doing to them as we want done to us is not something new; it is clearly found in the law and the prophets. Jesus' half-brother James reiterates this idea in James 2:8-13; he says, "If you really fulfill the royal law according to the Scripture, 'You shall love your neighbor as yourself,' you do well; but if you show partiality, you commit sin, and are convicted by the law as transgressors. For whoever shall keep the whole law, and yet stumble in one point, he is guilty of all. For He who said, 'Do not commit adultery,' also said, 'Do not murder.' Now if you do not commit adultery, but you do murder, you have become a transgressor of the law. So speak and so do as those who will be judged by the law of liberty. For judgment is without mercy to the one who has shown no mercy. Mercy triumphs over judgment." Even Paul, in Romans 13:8-10, says, "Owe no one anything except to love one another, for he who loves another has fulfilled the law. For the commandments, 'You shall not commit adultery,' 'You shall not murder,' 'You shall not steal,' 'You shall not bear false witness,' 'You shall not covet,' and if there is any other commandment, are all summed up in this saying, namely, 'You shall love your neighbor as yourself.' Love does no harm to a neighbor; therefore love is the fulfillment of the law."

The term *law* is a reference to the first five books of Moses, which are Genesis, Exodus, Leviticus, Numbers, and Deuteronomy. The *prophets* includes all the writings of the major and minor prophets that are recorded in the Old Testament. And, if you want to get technical about it, most of the Word of God can be summed up in loving our neighbors as ourselves. Even the Proverbs are filled with doing unto others as we would like done to us. Consider Proverbs 25:21: "If your enemy is hungry, give him bread to eat; and if he is thirsty, give him water to drink." This is certainly doing to our enemy as we would like done to us, right? And Proverbs 25:17, "Seldom set foot in your neighbor's house, lest he become weary of you and hate you." This is how we want to be treated, right? They say that both fish and company stink after three days. So, how do I treat those with whom I am staying? Like I would want to be treated? We also have Proverbs 25:8-10, which says, "Do not go hastily to court; for what will you do in the end, when your neighbor has put you to shame? Debate your case with your neighbor, and do not disclose the secret to another; lest he who hears it expose your shame, and your reputation be ruined." This sounds like loving my neighbor as myself, doesn't it? In fact, it's quite similar to something we've already studied in the Sermon on the Mount; in Matthew 5:25-26, where Jesus said, "Agree with your adversary quickly, while you are on the way with him, lest your adversary deliver you to the judge, the judge hand you over to the officer, and you be thrown into prison. Assuredly, I say to you, you will by no means get out of there till you have paid the last penny." And yet another proverb, Proverbs 25:11, deals with how we speak to others in a proper way: "A word fitly spoken is like apples of gold in settings of silver." We could go on and on, and perhaps it would be a good study, when you read your Bible through, to make note from Genesis to Revelation on how the Golden Rule is lived out or not lived out.

Let's consider the law as we live out the golden rule. Now, no worries, I do not plan to cover all the first five books of Moses, but I just want to give you an idea of how this might be fleshed out. The classic text would be, of course, a portion of the Ten Commandments. Exodus 20:12-17 says, "Honor your father and your mother, that your days may be long upon the land which the Lord your God is giving you. You shall not murder. You shall not commit adultery. You shall not steal. You shall not bear false witness against your neighbor. You shall not covet your neighbor's house; you shall not covet your neighbor's wife, nor his male servant, nor his female servant, nor his ox, nor his donkey, nor anything that is your neighbor's." Taking those few verses alone, we might ask, do you want your kids to honor you as their parents? Then you don't provoke your kids to wrath, and you set the example by honoring your own parents. We've dealt with murder and adultery already, so I won't address that. Do you want others to steal your stuff? Then don't steal their stuff, and that would include not just material possessions, but other things as well, such as their time, or not returning the things you've borrowed from them. Do you want others to tell you the truth? Then you tell them the truth. Do you want people to covet after your belongings? Your house, your husband, or anything else that belongs to you? Then you don't covet after their belongings.

We also have a passage you've probably noticed me use often, Leviticus 19:17-18, "You shall not hate your brother in your heart. You shall surely rebuke your neighbor, and not bear sin because of him. You shall not take vengeance, nor bear any grudge against the children of your people, but you shall love your neighbor as yourself: I am the Lord." Do you want people to love you enough to confront you when needed? Then you love others enough to confront them when needed. Also consider Exodus 23:4-5: "If you meet your enemy's ox or his donkey going astray, you shall surely bring it back to him again. If you see the donkey of one who hates you lying under its burden, and you would refrain from helping it, you shall surely help him with it." If something of yours is lost and your neighbor or someone else finds it, wouldn't you like for them to return it to you? Well, then you also, when you find something that doesn't belong to you, endeavor to find its rightful owner. One last example from the law, in Deuteronomy 15:7-8: "If there is among you a poor man of your brethren, within any of the gates in your land which the Lord your God is giving you, you shall not harden your heart nor shut your hand from your poor brother, but you shall open your hand wide to him and willingly lend him sufficient for his need, whatever he needs." If you were destitute and had nothing to eat or nowhere to live, would you be thankful for someone who was willing to help you? Then you, when you see those who don't have food or shelter, do not harden your heart but help them.

We Need to Consider the Prophets

Matthew 7:12d

… and the Prophets. (Matthew 7:12d)

Do you see what Jesus is saying? As we live out the golden rule, we consider ourselves, we consider others, we consider the law, and we also consider the prophets. Again, no worries, we won't go through all of the prophets—that wouldn't even be feasible! But let's take a few passages. For example, Isaiah, one of the major prophets, states this in Isaiah 58:6-7: "Is this not the fast that I have chosen: To loose the bonds of wickedness, to undo the heavy burdens, to let the oppressed go free, and that you break every yoke? Is it not to share your bread with the hungry, and that you bring to your house the poor who are cast out; when you see the naked, that you cover him, and not hide yourself from your own flesh?" Again, these things are similar to others we've looked at. We might ask ourselves, do I want others to help me with heavy burdens, to feed me, or to clothe me if I need it? Then I ought to help others with heavy burdens or those who might need food or clothing. Jeremiah, also a major prophet, says in Jeremiah 7:5-7, "For if you thoroughly amend your ways and your doings, if you thoroughly execute judgment between a man and his neighbor, if you do not oppress the stranger, the fatherless, and the widow, and do not shed innocent blood in this place, or walk after other gods to your hurt, then I will cause you to dwell in this place, in the land that I gave to your fathers forever and ever." Do I want others to oppress me when I am less fortunate than they are? Then I should not oppress others who are less fortunate than I am. One example from the Minor Prophets is Micah; in Micah 2:1-2, we read, "Woe to those who devise iniquity, and work out evil on their beds! At morning light they practice it, because it is in the power of their hand. They covet fields and take them by violence, also houses, and seize them. So they oppress a man and his house, a man and his inheritance." Do I want others to plan evil toward me as they lay in their beds at night and then carry out that evil the next day? Do I want others to covet after my things or oppress me in any way? Then I should not plan evil toward others, or covet after things or people that are not mine to have, or oppress others in any way.

We can see from what Jesus is saying in Matthew 7:12 that the Sermon on the Mount is not the only gauge of how we fulfill the golden rule; in reality, the whole of Scripture is. In Matthew 22:35-40, Jesus reiterates this point: "Then one of them, a lawyer, asked Him a question, testing Him, and saying, 'Teacher, which is the great commandment in the law?' Jesus said to him, 'You shall love the Lord your God with all your heart, with all your soul, and with all your mind.' This is the first and great commandment. And the second is like it: 'You shall love your neighbor as yourself.' On these two commandments hang all the Law and the Prophets." No wonder Jesus says it is by loving others that people will know we are His disciples (John 13:35). In fact, it's interesting to note that, in a similar fashion, "The sentiment was in use among the Jews. Hillel, an ancient Rabbi, said to a man who wished to become a proselyte, and who asked him to teach him the whole law, 'Whatever is hateful to you, do not do to another.' Something of the same sentiment was found among the ancient Greeks and Romans, and is found in the writings of Confucius."[90]

The golden rule is simple to understand but difficult to obey. What you would like others to do for you, you do for them. Practically speaking, as we go about our daily living, we can ask ourselves questions that will help us to obey his important command. Questions like: Is this the tone of voice I would like for my husband or friend to use when talking to me? Then I shouldn't talk to them in an unkind tone of voice. Would I like someone to be habitually late when they meet with me? Then I shouldn't be late with others. Would I like someone to ignore my phone call or text? Then I shouldn't ignore their phone calls or texts. Would I like someone to gossip and slander about me? Then I must not gossip and slander about others. Would I like my house guests to clean up after themselves? Then I ought to clean up after myself when I am a guest in someone else's home. Would I like my husband to give me his full attention when I am talking to him? Then I must give him my full attention when he's talking to me. [91]

---

90 Albert Barnes, *Barnes' Notes*, Electronic Database Copyright © 1997, 2003, 2005, 2006 by Biblesoft, Inc. All rights reserved.

91 This is the golden rule for righteous relationships. J.C. Ryle said, "This truth settles a hundred different points … it prevents the necessity of laying down endless little rules for our conduct in specific cases" (J.C. Ryle, Matthew: Expository Thoughts on the Gospels (Wheaton: Crossway, 1993), 51). William Barclay called this the "Mount Everest of ethics." Here Jesus, through the eye of omniscience, scans the whole of the Old Testament law and prophets, and summarizes those 39 books into one pregnant positive command. As matter of fact, Jesus was simply rephrasing a popular, well-known Jewish saying. Rabbi Hillel, about 10 years before Jesus, said these words, when challenged by a Gentile to summarize the law in the short time he could stand on one leg, and the rabbi responded, "What is hateful to yourself, do not do to someone else. This is the whole law; all the rest is commentary. Go and learn it." Jesus simply rephrased it in the positive and so removed the negative, self-serving element from it. We must ever keep in mind that our central problem is selfishness.

Summary

If the golden rule was obeyed among our nation's politicians, can you imagine how it would affect our entire world? As I mentioned at the beginning of this chapter, we might once again see God's blessing on our nation. If the golden rule was obeyed in our homes, can you imagine how it would affect our families? It might be just a touch of heaven at home. Can you imagine if the golden rule was lived out in our schools? We'd no longer have school bullies, school shootings, and all the other numerous problems that plague our school systems. If the golden rule were lived out in the work place, can you imagine how businesses would be affected? We would do away with lying in the workplace, cheating in the workplace, laziness in the workplace, sexual immorality in the workplace, etc. And what about driving? Can you imagine the result, if the golden rule were practiced in traffic? No longer would people cut others off in traffic and honk their horns in anger. And can you imagine if we obeyed the golden rule in our churches? How would it affect the Body of Christ? We would no longer have church splits, gossip and slander among church members, and jealousy and envy among those who profess Christ; instead, we'd have brothers and sisters in the Lord who love each other, consider each other as more important than themselves, and do unto others what they would like done to themselves! In all likelihood, we can all quote the golden rule; but can we live it? Let's endeavor, with the Lord's help, to do so!

Questions to Consider

Living Out the Golden Rule
Matthew 7:12

1. (a) Why do you think Jesus' exhortation in Matthew 7:12 comes immediately after His admonition on prayer in verses 7-11? (b) Why does Jesus say that doing to others as we would like done to us "is the Law and Prophets"?

2. Memorize Matthew 7:12.

3. (a) Read the following passages from the *law* and write down the ways in which they instruct us to treat others like we would like to be treated. Exodus 20:12-17; Leviticus 19:18; and Deuteronomy 22:1-4. (b) How does this help you to better understand what Jesus means in Matthew 7:12?

4. (a) Read the following passages from the *prophets* and write down the ways in which they instruct us to treat others as we would like to be treated? Isaiah 1:16-17; Jeremiah 7:5-6; Ezekiel 18:7-8; Amos 5:14-15; Micah 6:8; Zechariah 8:16-17. (b) How does this help you to understand more thoroughly what Jesus means in Matthew 7:12?

5. (a) In the following passages, who is being commanded or admonished to treat others like they would like to be treated? 1 Samuel 30:21-25; Job 16:1-5; Galatians 5:14-15; Ephesians 6:5-9; 1 Peter 5:1-4. (b) If it is mentioned in the text, note why the individual is to treat others in the manner they would like to be treated.

6. (a) What are some ways in which we can live out Matthew 7:12? (b) In what ways can we teach our children the principle in Matthew 7:12?

7. Do you think that you treat others the way you would like to be treated? How about your husband? Your children? Your friends? The people in your church? Your neighbors? Your enemies? Write a prayer request where you know you are in need of help in this matter.

Chapter 20

Heaven is for Real and Hell is For Real!

Matthew 7:13-14

Perhaps you glanced at the title of this lesson, *Heaven is for Real and Hell is for Real*, and thought that sounded somewhat familiar, and indeed it does! *Heaven is for Real*[92] is the title of a book written in 2010, a New York Times bestseller that sold more than 10 million copies. This book, along with several like it, make up the "heavenly tourism" book category that has plagued Christians for the past several years. Their stories been proven to be hoaxes, many of the authors having admitted to making up the stories of their journeys to heaven and making lots of money for doing so. I find it interesting that we're not plagued with titles like *Hell is for Real*, *90 Minutes in Hell*, *The Boy Who Came Back from Hell*, *Waking Up in Hell*, or *To Hell and Back*.[93] Books with titles like those, along with their fabricated stories, might do more to prompt people to consider eternity than all the flowery, fake books on heaven. Of course, such books probably wouldn't make the New York Times bestseller list, nor would Hollywood make movies out of them. But while the book *Heaven is for Real* is a scam, hell *is* for real and it's not a scam. Jesus makes that clear in the few verses we will consider in this lesson. Jesus wants His audience listening on the mount to know that heaven is indeed for real—but so is hell! We will consider two of the most sobering verses in all of Scripture, in my opinion; let's consider what Jesus says in Matthew 7:13-14.

Matthew 7:13-14

> Enter by the narrow gate; for wide is the gate and broad is the way that leads to destruction, and there are many who go in by

---

92 Todd Burpo, *Heaven is for Real* (Nashville: Thomas Nelson Publishers, 2010).

93 These are all puns, based on the titles of books that have been written on heaven.

it. ¹⁴Because narrow is the gate and difficult is the way which
leads to life, and there are few who find it.

On our journey through our last lesson, we considered *Living out the
Golden Rule*, and as we did we considered four things: the need to
consider ourselves, consider others, consider the law, and consider
the prophets. In this lesson, we'll consider that *Heaven is for Real
and Hell is for Real*, and because they both are real places, we want
to make clear several things:

> There are *Two Doors* (v 13)
> *Two Directions* (vv 13-14)
> *Two Destinations* (vv 13-14)
> *Two Decisions* (vv 13-14)

That will be our outline for this lesson.

Perhaps you are wondering what the golden rule has to do with what
Jesus is saying next. How does obeying the golden rule determine
my destination? Think about what Jesus is saying: if we are not
doing unto others as we want them to do to us, isn't this an indicator
of a bigger problem? Jesus says it is by our love for each other that
others will know that we belong to Him (John 13:35). Genuine
children of God love each other, consider each other, and do unto
others as they want done unto them. The apostle John is clear when
he says in 1 John 3:14, "We know that we have passed from death to
life, because we love the brethren. He who does not love his brother
abides in death." So, the one who does not do unto others as she
would have others do unto her, (which we learned last time was
the whole of the Sermon on the Mount, and also the Law and the
Prophets, and really the whole of Scripture) is manifesting that she
is not a genuine kingdom citizen.

Two Doors

Matthew 7:13

> Enter by the narrow gate; for wide is the gate and broad is the
> way that leads to destruction, and there are many who go in by
> it. (Matthew 7:13)

Let's consider, first, the two doors in verse 13. Jesus begins by saying *enter by the narrow gate*. And we might wonder, "Why does Jesus say this at this time in His sermon?" When we consider that He has been making clear all throughout His sermon that there are two types of people—the religious hypocrite and the kingdom citizen—His words make sense. He is now drawing a conclusion to make it clear to His listeners that there are only two ways. Jesus is winding down His sermon, and in doing so, He speaks boldly about the two ways (vv 13-14), the two trees (vv 15-20), the two professions (vv 21-23) and the two builders (vv 24-27). Many of us would like there to be a third option. We would like to keep one foot in the church and one foot in the world, but that is not what kingdom citizens look like, nor is it what their hearts desire. The Scriptures say absolutely nothing about a third option.

Jesus is also doing what most preachers do even today when they preach a sermon. Having finished presenting the content of a sermon, a preacher then draws his thoughts to a conclusion and leaves his audience with a decision which must be made. Will those in the audience obey what they have just heard taught, or will they leave making no change whatsoever? Are they going to look into the mirror and see that they need to make some changes, or are they going to look into the mirror of God's Word and go on about their daily business, forgetting all the spiritual imperfections in their lives which need to be changed? God is sovereign, but, my friend, we are responsible for what we hear.

Jesus calls us to enter in. The word *enter* demands an action; we have to do something about it. I know that God is sovereign in salvation and that He has chosen some before the foundation of the world, yet man is responsible and we must make a choice. Jesus says enter in. His words remind me of a song that was sung years ago by Steve Green. A part of it goes like this: "Enter in, enter in; surrender to the Spirit's call, to die and enter in. Enter in, find peace within; the holy life awaits you, enter in. The conflict still continues, raging deep within my soul. My spirit wars against my flesh, in a struggle for control. My only hope is full surrender, so with each borrowed breath, I inhale the Spirit's will for me, to die a deeper death."[94]

So, where do we enter? Jesus says *the narrow gate*, the narrow door. The word *narrow* indicates that this door is hard to get through; it is restrictive, cramped, and not very inviting. We've all traveled down roads that are narrow, so narrow sometimes that we fear we might not make it. Jesus is referring here to a door—a gate—which is narrow like that. No wonder Jesus compels His audience to agonize to get in; in Luke 13:24, He says, "Strive to enter through the narrow gate, for many, I say to you, will seek to enter and will not be able." We know there is only one way to get through this door. Jesus clearly says in John 10:9, "I am the door. If anyone enters by Me, he will be saved, and will go in and out and find pasture." And in John 14:6, He says, "I am the way, the truth, and the life. No one comes to the Father except through Me."

Notice that Jesus does not encourage us to enter *the wide gate*, the wide door. The term *wide* means spread out and spacious; this gate is clearly more inviting because there's more room to get in. But, Jesus says, the reason that we should enter in by the narrow gate is because the other choice, the wide gate, will lead us to destruction.

---

94 Words and Music by Jon Mohr, Steve Green and Greg Nelson Copyright 1986 Jonathan Mark Music/Birdwing Music (ASCAP)/Bug and Bear Music.

Two Directions and Two Destinations

Matthew 7:13-14

> Enter by the narrow gate; for wide is the gate and broad is the way that leads to destruction, and there are many who go in by it. (Matthew 7:13)

There are two doors, the narrow one and the wide one. But there are also two directions. The first one Jesus mentions in verse 13 and He calls it the *broad* way. It's the direction that makes the most sense because it has so much room and there are so many people following it. There are truly a lot of people going down that road, and the longer I live the more I realize how true that is. Proverbs 16:25 wisely says, "There is a way that seems right to a man, but its end is the way of death." It seems like the logical direction to go; it's the direction that most of my neighbors, most of my family, and most of my co-workers are going; why, it's even the direction many religious people are going! So, why not go that direction? Jesus says, because that direction, that way, that road has an ending: it *is the way that leads to destruction. Destruction* means ruin, both spiritual and eternal. And while not many books have been written about it, it is a horrible place. One man had the boldness many years ago to write an article that greatly sobered me the first time I heard it read. Here is a portion of it:

> Hell is a place of darkness (Matthew 8:12). Imagine the person who has just entered hell—a neighbor, relative, co-worker, friend. After a roar of physical pain blasts him, he spends his first moments wailing and gnashing his teeth. But after a season, he grows accustomed to the pain, not that it's become tolerable, but that his capacity for it has enlarged to comprehend it, yet not be consumed by it. Though he hurts, he is now able to think, and he instinctively looks about him. But as he looks, he sees only blackness.

In his past life he learned that if he looked long enough, a glow of light somewhere would yield definition to his surroundings. So he blinks and strains to focus his eyes, but his efforts yield only blackness. He turns and strains his eyes in another direction. He waits. He sees nothing but unyielding black ink. It clings to him, smothering and oppressing him. Realizing that the darkness is not going to give way, he nervously begins to feel for something solid to get his bearings. He reaches for walls or rocks or trees or chairs; he stretches his legs to feel the ground and touches nothing. Hell is a "bottomless pit" (Revelation 20:1, 2 KJV); however, the new occupant is slow to learn. In growing panic, he kicks his feet and waves his arms. He stretches and he lunges. But he finds nothing. After more feverish tries, he pauses from exhaustion, suspended in black. Suddenly, with a scream he kicks, twists, and lunges until he is again too exhausted to move. He hangs there, alone with his pain. Unable to touch a solid object or see a solitary thing, he begins to weep. His sobs choke through the darkness. They become weak, then lost in hell's roar. As time passes, he begins to do what the rich man did—he again starts to think. His first thoughts are of hope. You see, he still thinks as he did on earth, where he kept himself alive with hope. When things got bad, he always found a way out. If he felt pain, he took medicine. If he were hungry; he ate food. If he lost love, there was more love to be found. So he casts about in his mind for a plan to apply to the hope building in his chest.

Of course, he thinks, Jesus, the God of love, can get me out of this. He cries out with a surge, "Jesus! Jesus! You were right! Help me! Get me out of this!" He waits, breathing hard with desperation. The sound of his voice slips into the darkness and is lost. He tries again. "I believe, Jesus! I believe now! Save me from this!" Again the darkness smothers his words. Our sinner is not unique. Everyone in hell believes. When he wearies of appeals, he does next what anyone would do—assesses his situation and attempts to adapt. But then it hits him—this is forever. Jesus made it very clear. He used the same words for "forever" to describe both heaven and hell. Forever, he thinks, and his mind labors through the blackness until he aches. "Forever!" he whispers in wonder. The idea deepens, widens, and towers over him. The awful truth spreads before him like endless, overlapping slats: When I put in ten thousand centuries of time here, I will not have accomplished one thing. I will not have one second less to spend here. As the rich man pleaded for a drop of water, so, too, our new occupant entertains a similar ambition. In life he learned that even bad things could be tolerated if one could find temporary relief. Perhaps even hell, if one could rest from time to time, would be more tolerable. He learns, though, that "the smoke of [his] torment goes up forever and ever; and [he has] no rest day and night" (Revelation 14:11 NASB). No rest day and night—think of that.[95]

Sadly, Jesus says of this way that *there are many who go in by it*. The Greek word for *many* is shocking; it means most. In other words: most go in that way. A large amount of people, a majority of people, go in that way. No wonder we read at the end of the sermon that they were struck dumb! Jesus has mentioned two doors, the narrow one and the wide one. He's mentioned one direction, the broad one, and one destination, destruction. In verse 14, He tells us of the other direction and the other destination. He says,

> Because narrow is the gate and difficult is the way which leads to life, and there are few who find it. (Matthew 7:14)

---

95 John Thomas, *Moody Monthly*, September 1985.

Jesus repeats what He said in verse 13, reminding His listeners that the gate is *narrow*. Repetition in Scripture is always intended as a means of emphasizing something. It's as if Jesus is reminding them not to forget this. Some will forget, of course, and they will continue on the broad way and forget that there is only one other option, the hard one, and not a third option.

In addition to this direction being narrow, Jesus also adds that it is difficult. It is not like the broad direction. *Difficult* means that this way has trouble, this way has tribulation, this way has suffering. It is not lovely and it is not popular. It is well put in Acts 14:22: "We must through many tribulations enter the kingdom of God." Lest anyone misunderstand, I want to be clear that those going down the broad road don't have a life of ease and comfort. Oh, they might enjoy the pleasures of sin for a season, but the Bible says that the way of the transgressor is hard (Proverbs 13:15, KJV). But kingdom citizens are sure to have tribulations and difficulties—persecution, suffering for righteousness' sake, hatred from others, rejection from family members, ridicule, and, for some, even physical persecution and death. But, oh, it's a glorious way, even with all its troubles! Isaiah puts in well in Isaiah 35:8, "A highway shall be there, and a road, and it shall be called the Highway of Holiness. The unclean shall not pass over it, but it shall be for others. Whoever walks the road, although a fool, shall not go astray."

There are two directions. The first one is mentioned in verse 13, the broad direction, the broad way; and the second one is also mentioned in this verse, the difficult direction, the difficult way. But unlike the broad way that leads to destruction, this difficult way *leads to life.* Way back in Deuteronomy 30:19, Moses told the Israelites, "I call heaven and earth as witnesses today against you, that I have set before you life and death, blessing and cursing; therefore choose life, that both you and your descendants may live." Choose life; don't choose death. Choose blessing; don't choose cursing.

It's sad to say that not many will go this way; Jesus says *there are few who find it. Few* is a word which in the Greek means puny. Only a few will go this way. Most will go the broad way; few will go the narrow way. In Luke 13:22-28, Jesus makes this clear to another audience: "And He went through the cities and villages, teaching, and journeying toward Jerusalem. Then one said to Him, 'Lord, are there few who are saved?' And He said to them, 'Strive to enter through the narrow gate, for many, I say to you, will seek to enter and will not be able. When once the Master of the house has risen up and shut the door, and you begin to stand outside and knock at the door, saying, 'Lord, Lord, open for us,' and He will answer and say to you, 'I do not know you, where you are from,' then you will begin to say, 'We ate and drank in Your presence, and You taught in our streets.' But He will say, 'I tell you I do not know you, where you are from. Depart from Me, all you workers of iniquity.' There will be weeping and gnashing of teeth, when you see Abraham and Isaac and Jacob and all the prophets in the kingdom of God, and yourselves thrust out." In Matthew 20:16, Jesus states, "So the last will be first, and the first last. For many are called, but few chosen." One song writer penned it well: "There's a great, broad road through the meadow, and many travel there. But I have a gentle Shepherd, I would follow anywhere. Up a narrow path, through the mountains, to the valley far below, to be ever in His presence, where He leads me I will go. There is a great, broad road to nowhere, and so many travel there, but I have a gentle Shepherd, I would follow anywhere. Though the journey take me far away, from the place I call my home, to be ever in His presence, where He leads me I will go."[96] One commentator, Albert Barnes, writes very clearly regarding these two verses,

> Christ here compares the way to life to an entrance through a gate. The words "straight" and "strait" have very different meanings. The former means "not crooked;" the latter, "pent up, narrow, difficult to be entered." This is the word used here, and it means that the way to heaven is "pent up, narrow, close," and not obviously entered. The way to death is open, broad, and thronged. The Saviour here referred probably to ancient cities. They were surrounded with walls

---

96 Words by Twila Paris

and entered through gates. Some of those, connected with the great avenues to the city, were broad and admitted a throng; others, for more private purposes, were narrow, and few would be seen entering them. So, says Christ, is the path to heaven. It is narrow. It is not "the great highway" that people tread. Few go there. Here and there one may be seen-traveling in solitude and singularity. The way to death, on the other hand, is broad. Multitudes are in it. It is the great highway in which people go. They fall into it easily and without effort, and go without thought. If they wish to leave that and go by a narrow gate to the city, it would require effort and thought. So, says Christ, "diligence" is needed to enter life. See Luke 13:24. None go of course. All must strive, to obtain it; and so narrow, unfrequented, and solitary is it, that few find it. This sentiment has been beautifully versified by Watts: "Broad is the road that leads to death, and thousands walk together there; but wisdom shows a narrower path, with here and there a traveler."[97]

The Pharisees were heading down the broad path, the path that leads to hell. Jesus even pronounces woes on them in Matthew 23 and talks about how great their damnation will be. Kingdom citizens, on the other hand, are heading down the narrow path, the one Jesus teaches about; it's a difficult one, but it leads to life. And, contrary to popular opinion, there is not a third option.

Summary: Two Decisions

Matthew 7:13-14

Enter by the narrow gate; for wide is the gate and broad is the way that leads to destruction, and there are many who go in by it. [14]Because narrow is the gate and difficult is the way which leads to life, and there are few who find it.

97 Albert Barnes, *Barnes' Notes*, Electronic Database Copyright © 1997, 2003, 2005, 2006 by Biblesoft, Inc. All rights reserved.

Clearly, there are *Two Doors* (v 13): the narrow one and the wide one. Entering the narrow door results in what the apostle John says in Revelation 22:14, "Blessed are those who do His commandments, that they may have the right to the tree of life, and may enter through the gates into the city." Entering through the wide door results in what John says in Revelation 20:15, "And anyone not found written in the Book of Life was cast into the lake of fire."

There are also *Two Directions* (vv 13-14): one is broad and one is difficult. The broad one reminds me of Proverbs 14:12: "There is a way that seems right to a man, but its end is the way of death." And Psalm 1:6, which says, "But the way of the ungodly shall perish." The difficult direction reminds me of the 23rd Psalm, where there are dangers and difficulties along this way, this direction, yet the Psalmist ends with these words in verse 6: "Surely goodness and mercy shall follow me all the days of my life; and I will dwell in the house of the Lord forever."

There are also *Two Destinations* (vv 13-14): one leads to destruction, and the other leads to life. One leads to hell; the other to heaven. One leads to eternal fire; the other leads to eternal freedom. One leads to eternity with God and all the saints; the other to eternity with Satan and all the sinners. One leads to eternal light; the other to eternal darkness. One leads to no more tears or sorrows; the other leads to weeping and gnashing of teeth.

I have mentioned the two doors, the two directions, the two destinations, but I have not yet mentioned the *Two Decisions* (vv 13-14). Yes, there are two. You, my friend, have one of two decisions you can make. You can follow the crowd, the majority, and go the broad way, or you can make the other decision to follow the few, the puny, and go the narrow way. I can't make that decision for you. The person sitting next to you can't make that decision for you; neither can a friend or a spouse. Only you. What will be your decision? Or, what decision have you already made? Consider this:

William Pope was a member of the Methodist Church in England for most of his life. He made a pretense of knowing Christ and served in many capacities. His wife died a genuine believer. Soon, however, he began to drift from Christ. He had companions who believed in the redemption of demons. He began going with them to the public house of prostitution. In time, he became a drunkard. He admired Thomas Paine and would assemble with his friends on Sundays when they would confirm each other in their infidelity. They amused themselves by throwing the Bible on the floor and kicking it around. Then he contracted tuberculosis. Someone visited him and told him of the great Redeemer. He said Pope could be saved from the punishments of his sins.

But Pope replied, "I have no contrition; I cannot repent. God will damn me! I know the day of grace is lost. God has said to such as me, 'I will laugh at your calamity, and mock when your fear cometh.' I have denied him; my heart is hardened." Then he cried, "Oh, the hell, the pain I feel! I have chosen my way. I have done the horrible damnable deed; I have crucified the Son of God afresh; I have counted the blood of the covenant an unholy thing! Oh that wicked and horrible thing of blaspheming the Holy Spirit, which I know that I have committed; I want nothing but hell! Come, oh devil and take me!"98

Pope had spent most of his life in the church, but his end was infinitely worse than his beginning. Every man and woman has the same choice. You can choose the narrow gate and receive eternal life, or you can choose the broad gate which leads to destruction. It doesn't seem like a difficult choice, does it? Yet, millions of people

98 John MacArthur, *The Upper Room* (The Woodlands: Kress Biblical Resources, 2014), 179-180. The last paragraph has been reworded for this particular lesson, but the ideas have been taken from the last paragraph on page 180.

resist God's gift of salvation. Perhaps, you know people like that; perhaps, you are like that yourself. Time is short, and I lovingly remind you that there are only two doors, two directions, and two destinations. But there are also two decisions; which one will you make?

Questions to Consider

Heaven is for Real and Hell is For Real!
Matthew 7:13-14

1. (a) As you read Matthew 7:13-14, write down as many contrasts as you can find. (b) Which gate are you going to enter?

2. Memorize Matthew 7:13-14.

3. (a) As you read Psalm 1 and Psalm 73, what do you notice in those psalms that stands out to you as being similar to Matthew 7:13-14? (b) How does the Psalmist describe each of the ways of the godly and the ungodly? (c) How does the Psalmist describe each of their destinations?

4. (a) Read Matthew 25:31-46. What are the two destinations that Christ mentions in this passage? (b) What determines one's destination, according to this text? (c) In what ways is this passage similar to what we have studied in the Sermon on the Mount? (d) Why do you think some say there are more than two destinations, heaven or hell?

5. (a) According to Romans 8:18; 2 Corinthians 5:8; Philippians 3:20-21; Revelation 21:3-4, 27; and Revelation 22:3-5, what awaits those who go through the narrow gate? (b) According to Daniel 12:2; Matthew 18:8; Matthew 25:41, 46; 2 Thessalonians 1:9; and Revelation 20:10, what awaits those who go through the wide gate? (c) Why do you think few travel the narrow way while many travel the broad way?

6. (a) As you prayerfully reflect on this lesson, are you sure of which road you are traveling down? (b) Is there anyone you know who professes to be going down the narrow road, but you fear is going down the wide road instead? (c) Will you lovingly share with them the danger they are in?

7. Write a prayer request—which pertains to this lesson—for yourself or for someone else (please be discreet).

Chapter 21

Jesus' Warning Regarding False Teachers!

Matthew 7:15-20

In one of his books, pastor and author Charles Swindoll recalls a time when he was invited to an elegant party at a physician's home. The hostess had served up dog food on crackers, with cheese, bacon, olive, and a sliver of pimento on top, and he called it "hors d'oeuvres a la Alpo." There was one guest who simply could not get enough of this particular hors d'oeuvre and kept coming back for more. The hostess finally broke the news to her guest, and Swindoll goes on to say he can't quite recall what happened next, but that the guest probably barked and bit the hostess on the leg! Swindoll's account, he says, is intended to illustrate an important truth regarding religious fakes, or false teachers. He says, "I'm referring to religious fakes … professional charlatans … frauds … counterfeit Christians who market their wares on shiny plates of deceit, they serve up delectable dishes camouflaged by logical-sounding phrases. A glance at the silver platter and everything looks delicious: 'apostles of Christ … angels of light … servants of righteousness.' Through the genius of disguise, they not only look good, they *feel* good, and they *smell* good! The media serves them under your nose."[99]

Such words are pointed and true, especially as we think of the false teachers of our day. False prophets and false teachers certainly aren't a new thing; they're as old as the beginning of time. Jesus dealt with them in His day, too. And He has much to say about them as He warns His audience on the mount regarding these religious fakes! Let's listen in.

---

99 Charles R. Swindoll, *Growing Strong in the Seasons of Life* (Portland: Multnomah Press, 1983), 147-148.

Matthew 7:15-20

Beware of false prophets, who come to you in sheep's clothing, but inwardly they are ravenous wolves. [16]You will know them by their fruits. Do men gather grapes from thornbushes or figs from thistles? [17]Even so, every good tree bears good fruit, but a bad tree bears bad fruit. [18]A good tree cannot bear bad fruit, nor can a bad tree bear good fruit. [19]Every tree that does not bear good fruit is cut down and thrown into the fire. [20]Therefore by their fruits you will know them.

As we consider Jesus' words in this passage of Scripture, we'll see:

The Warning of False Teachers (v 15a)
The Wardrobe of False Teachers (v 15b)
The Works of False Teachers (vv 16-18)
The Woe of False Teachers (v 19)
The Wrap-Up Statement Regarding False Teachers (v 20)

In our last lesson, we learned that there are two doors, the narrow one and the wide one; there are also two directions, the broad one and the difficult one; there are two destinations, one which leads to life and the other which leads to destruction; there are also two decisions, one which follows the mob to hell and the other which follows the few to heaven. I'm trusting that all of us are with the latter group. But just because we might be going down the narrow way, the right direction, heading for eternal glory, doesn't mean we can let our guard down. There are dangers out there and we'd best watch out for them! They're called "sheep in wolves' clothing." So, Jesus begins this section of His sermon with a warning about false teachers.

The Warning of False Teachers

Matthew 7:15a

Beware of false prophets, who come to you in sheep's clothing,
but inwardly they are ravenous wolves. (Matthew 7:15)

Jesus' warning regarding false prophets starts with the word *beware*, a term that means to be cautious, to pay attention; it also has the idea of holding our minds away from them. We should not expose ourselves to false teachers. That's why I find it odd when people ask me what I think of so and so (a potential false teacher); I'll try to listen to or read a little of so and so's teaching and then I'll think to myself, "I don't want to expose myself to this garbage!" Why should we waste our time on such nonsense when we can feed on the truth?! I fear that many of us don't give thought to this at all, and yet, my friend, we should! There are so many false teachers out there and they are on the increase, as Jesus said they would be; yet many will drink in whatever these false teachers say without measuring it with the Word of God. Oh, beware, my friend!

Jesus calls these guys *false prophets*. A *false prophet* is someone who is a pretender, a religious imposter, someone who teaches incorrect doctrine. In the Old Testament, there were prophets who prophesied falsely, and they were condemned and sometimes put to death. There were also false prophets and false teachers in the New Testament. To the particular audience Jesus is addressing, He would more than likely be referring to the Scribes and Pharisees. We've already learned that the Scribes and Pharisees were outwardly religious but inwardly full of hypocrisy and deceit. In fact, Jesus tells the disciples in Matthew 16:12 to beware of the doctrine of the Pharisees and Sadducees. Their teachings were dangerous. But Jesus is not the only one who warned about them, as you see in the Questions to Consider. The apostle Paul also has a warning about false teachers in Colossians 2:8, and he actually uses the same word Jesus does here in Matthew: "Beware lest anyone cheat you through philosophy and empty deceit, according to the tradition of men, according to the basic principles of the world, and not according to Christ." Consider also Titus 3:10, where Paul commands us to get away from heretics after a first and second admonition. The warning regarding false teachers is to beware.

The Wardrobe of False Teachers

Matthew 7:15b

> Beware of false prophets, who come to you in sheep's clothing, but inwardly they are ravenous wolves. (Matthew 7:15)

Jesus moves on to now describe their wardrobe. He says: *who come to you in sheep's clothing, but inwardly they are ravenous wolves.* My dear sister, these words are frightening because Jesus says these false teachers look the opposite of what we think they should look like. They look like the real thing! They look just like kingdom citizens, just like sheep. To be more precise, they look like true prophets who, like Elijah, wear sheep's clothing. In other words, they appear as ministers of righteousness when, in reality, they are fake. Both *sheep* and *wolves* would have been common animals to Jesus' audience, much like cats and dogs are common animals to us. Many in the biblical world had the occupation of shepherd. They would tend to the sheep, and as they did, one of their jobs would be to protect the sheep from ravenous wolves. So, Jesus' imagery is perfect for His audience. These false prophets are dressed outwardly like sheep; they're cute, woolly, and innocent-looking. This is a fascinating analogy because throughout His sermon Jesus has been condemning the outward works of the Scribes and Pharisees. They look great on the outside, just like soft, woolly sheep do.

And notice that Jesus says these false teachers *come to you.* This is significant; it conveys the idea that they are on the lookout to prey on you. They're energized by Satan, who also is on the look out to prey on you (see Job 1:6-2:8 and 1 Peter 5:8). They look innocent on the outside, but don't be fooled by them. Jesus warns in Mark 12:38 that the false teachers of His day literally looked like the real thing in their long robes: "Then He said to them in His teaching, 'Beware of the Scribes, who desire to go around in long robes, love greetings in the marketplaces.'" One man has said it well, "The false prophet is a man who has no 'strait gate' or 'narrow way' in his gospel. He has nothing which is offensive to the natural man; he pleases all. He is in 'sheep's clothing', so attractive, so pleasant, so nice to look at. He has such a nice and comfortable and comforting message. He pleases everybody and everybody speaks well of him. He is never persecuted for his preaching, he is never criticized severely. He is praised by the Liberals and Modernists, he is praised by the Evangelicals, he is praised by everybody. He is all things to all men in that sense; there is no 'strait gate' about him, there is no 'narrow way' in his message, there is none of the 'offense of the cross'."100

Jesus continues by saying that outwardly these false teachers look great but *inwardly they are ravenous wolves*. This means they are greedy savages looking for something to devour, just like a wolf attacks a sheep. The apostle Paul has a sobering warning regarding this in Acts 20:29-31, when he is telling the elders at Ephesus good-bye; he says, "For I know this, that after my departure savage wolves will come in among you, not sparing the flock. Also from among yourselves men will rise up, speaking perverse things, to draw away the disciples after themselves. Therefore watch, and remember that for three years I did not cease to warn everyone night and day with tears." Paul says these savage wolves will be men on the elder board, and they will not spare the flock, and they will draw men after them. "Beware!" Paul says, "I have warned you for three years!" In 2 Corinthians 11:13-15, Paul warns: "For such are false apostles, deceitful workers, transforming themselves into apostles of Christ. And no wonder! For Satan himself can transform into an angel of light. Therefore it is no great thing if his ministers also transform themselves into ministers of righteousness, whose end will be according to their works." My dear friend, we should not be surprised at this. These guys are greedy wolves, and Peter says they are so greedy that they want to make merchandise of us (2 Peter

---

100 D. Martyn Lloyd-Jones, *Studies in the Sermon on the Mount* (Grand Rapids: Eerdmans Publishing Co., 1959, 1960), 500-501.

317

2:3). Jesus speaks vividly of their wardrobe in Matthew 23:27-28, "Woe to you, Scribes and Pharisees, hypocrites! For you are like whitewashed tombs which indeed appear beautiful outwardly, but inside are full of dead men's bones and all uncleanness. Even so you also outwardly appear righteous to men, but inside you are full of hypocrisy and lawlessness."

What is the wardrobe of false teachers? They look just like kingdom citizens; they look just like sheep. Perhaps that is frightening to you and you are wondering how in the world you are going to know a false teacher. Well, Jesus lets us know how to discern a false teacher by letting us know what the works of a false teacher are, in verses 16-18.

The Works of False Teachers

Matthew 7:16-18

> You will know them by their fruits. Do men gather grapes from thornbushes or figs from thistles? (Matthew 7:16)

So often we hear that we are not to judge. Is this really what Jesus teaches? Well, yes and no. Yes, we are to judge according to Matthew 7, making sure that we remove the plank out of our own eye and that we judge according to what Jesus says here. We cannot judge a person's heart, but we can judge with righteous judgment; Jesus makes this clear in John 7:24: "Do not judge according to appearance, but judge with righteous judgment." Jesus is also clear here in Matthew 7 that *we will know them by their fruits*. The word *know* means to become fully acquainted with them. Ladies, we cannot do this by looking at a false teacher's outward appearance because, remember, they look like the real thing. Instead, we have to look at their *fruits*, their works. Jesus says *Do men gather grapes from thornbushes or figs from thistles? Grapes* and *figs* obviously have value; thorns and thistles do not. From a distance, however, you might not be able to see that thorns and thistles are not grapes or figs, but as you get closer you can obviously see the difference. So it is with false teachers. From a quick glance, you might think they're the real thing, but as you get closer to them and examine their life, you clearly see a difference. We must carefully examine the fruit.

Perhaps you are wondering how we do that, how we carefully examine a teacher's fruit. First, we must consider the fruit of a teacher's life. Do their lives demonstrate the fruit of the Spirit? Do they possess the love, joy, peace, longsuffering, kindness, goodness, faithfulness, gentleness, and self-control Paul mentions in Galatians 5:22-23? What about the fruit of righteousness that is mentioned numerous times in Scripture? You could almost just take the Sermon on the Mount to examine their lives. Do they possess the qualities we've studied in this book? Do they possess humility and love, which are the two pillars of the Christian's life? Does their life reflect holy living? Are their actions at home the same as they are out in public? (You might have to ask family members to answer that question. I remember one lady telling me she had asked a pastor when the last time was that he had looked at pornography—now, that takes boldness—but what a great question to ask!) What about the fruit of their lips? What is their speech like? Is it wholesome or unwholesome? Kind or harsh? What about the fruit of the gospel? Are they actively sharing the good news of Jesus Christ and the power of the gospel? What about the fruit of their labors, those who follow after these teachers? Are the lives of their followers pure and Christ-like? Jesus says in Matthew 23:15, "Woe to you, Scribes and Pharisees, hypocrites! For you travel land and sea to win one proselyte, and when he is won, you make him twice as much a son of hell as yourselves." Their "converts" are an aspect of their fruit. As Jesus says in Luke 6:39, when the blind lead the blind, the only plausible outcome is that they'll both fall into a ditch.

We also must consider the fruit of a teacher's lips. What do they teach? That is a fruit! One man has said that he thinks there are four doctrinal tests of false teachers: "First, the false prophet avoids preaching on such things as the holiness, righteousness, justice and wrath of God. Second, he avoids preaching on the doctrine of the final judgment. Third, false prophets fail to emphasize the fallenness and depravity of mankind. Fourth, false prophets de-emphasize the substitutionary death and atonement of Christ."[101]

One important thing to keep in mind as we examine the fruit of others is that it takes time for fruit to grow. It might be that a teacher is like Apollos, who is mentioned in Acts 18: "Now a certain Jew named Apollos, born at Alexandria, an eloquent man and mighty in the Scriptures, came to Ephesus. This man had been instructed in the way of the Lord; and being fervent in spirit, he spoke and taught accurately the things of the Lord, though he knew only the baptism of John. So he began to speak boldly in the synagogue. When Aquila and Priscilla heard him, they took him aside and explained to him the way of God more accurately. And when he desired to cross to Achaia, the brethren wrote, exhorting the disciples to receive him; and when he arrived, he greatly helped those who had believed through grace; for he vigorously refuted the Jews publicly, showing from the Scriptures that Jesus is the Christ" (Acts 18:24-28). Apollos was far from being a false teacher, even though some in our day would be quick to label him as such! He was fervent in spirit and taught accurately the doctrine he was acquainted with, but he was uneducated regarding baptism; he only knew of the baptism of John. So, Priscilla and Aquila took him aside privately and helped him. Perhaps, after examination, you might realize that the person you're concerned about just needs a more thorough understanding of the Scriptures. If so, take that person aside privately and talk to them with gentleness and you will help them. This is the reason it's important that teachers and preachers be older in the faith, that they have had time to grow and learn in order to pass down good things to others. It is imperative that we don't rush people into the office of teaching, as James 3:1 says, and that they are not novices, as 1 Timothy 3:6 states. And, in verse 17 of our passage, Jesus goes on to emphasize the works of false teachers again.

> Even so, every good tree bears good fruit, but a bad tree bears bad fruit. (Matthew 7:17)

---

101 R. Kent Hughes, *The Sermon on the Mount: The Message of the Kingdom* (Wheaton: Crossway Books, 2001), 250-251.

There is no exception here. *Every good tree bears good fruit. Good* means that this fruit is valuable. I'm reminded by this of the godly man in Psalm 1:3 where it says, "He shall be like a tree planted by the rivers of water, that brings forth its fruit in its season, whose leaf also shall not wither; and whatever he does shall prosper." This guy is so in love with the Word of God that he meditates on it night and day and he brings forth fruit. A good tree will bear good fruit. But, the opposite is true as well, *a bad tree bears bad fruit. Bad* means it is rotten and worthless. Also in Psalm 1, it talks about the ungodly man and his fruit; it says in Psalm 1:4-5, "The ungodly are not so, but are like the chaff which the wind drives away. Therefore the ungodly shall not stand in the judgment, nor sinners in the congregation of the righteous." Religious imposters bring forth bad fruit, kingdom citizens bring forth good fruit, and there are no exceptions. How shocking it will be on that day when Jesus says, "Depart from me; I never knew you!" And yet, the ones He'll be talking to will be those claiming to have done marvelous works in His name, claiming to have produced fruit in His name (as we'll see in our next lesson, in Matthew 7:21-23). Jesus goes on in verse 18 and says,

> A good tree cannot bear bad fruit, nor can a bad tree bear good fruit. (Matthew 7:18)

A good tree cannot bear bad fruit. And, equally true, *nor can a bad tree bear good fruit.* Why? It's impossible! In Matthew 12:33-37, Jesus rebukes the false teachers of His day when He says, "Either make the tree good and its fruit good, or else make the tree bad and its fruit bad; for a tree is known by its fruit. Brood of vipers! How can you, being evil, speak good things? For out of the abundance of the heart the mouth speaks. A good man out of the good treasure of his heart brings forth good things, and an evil man out of the evil treasure brings forth evil things. But I say to you that for every idle word men may speak, they will give account of it in the day of judgment. For by your words you will be justified, and by your words you will be condemned." These are stinging words, but they are true! The heart is revealed by the mouth and the life. If you are evil, you will produce evil things. If your heart is good, it will produce good things. And, just in case some think they can get by with it, Jesus says they can't, because they will be either justified or condemned on that day by their works.

What will happen to those trees that don't produce good fruit? In the physical realm, you would get rid of them; you'd cut them down and burn them. That's exactly what happens in the spiritual realm, as well. Jesus now turns from the false teacher's works to their woe, and a dreadful one it is indeed.

The Woe of False Teachers

Matthew 7:19

> Every tree that does not bear good fruit is cut down and thrown into the fire. (Matthew 7:19)

The words *every tree* indicate that there are no exceptions. Every single one *that does not bear good fruit is cut down and thrown into the fire*. When writing about false teachers, Jude says, "These are spots in your love feasts, while they feast with you without fear, serving only themselves. They are clouds without water, carried about by the winds; late autumn trees without fruit, twice dead, pulled up by the roots" (Jude 1:12). These false teachers are dead and are pulled up by the roots. In Hebrews 6:8, we read, "but if it bears thorns and briers, it is rejected and near to being cursed, whose end is to be burned." Those that are not genuine believers, those who are false teachers, are cut down and thrown into the fire and burned. Second Peter 2:17 says that the blackness of darkness is reserved for them forever. Even Jesus, pronouncing woes of the religious imposters of His day, says in Matthew 23:33, "Serpents, brood of vipers! How can you escape the condemnation of hell?" In other words: they won't! The false teacher's woe is eternal damnation. And it is the woe of all who do not call upon the name of the Lord Jesus Christ to be saved. Jesus now ends His words regarding false prophets with a wrap-up statement regarding them in verse 20.

The Wrap-Up Statement Regarding False Teachers

Matthew 7:20

Therefore by their fruits you will know them. (Matthew 7:20)

Therefore, because of what Jesus has just said, *by their fruits you will know them.* You don't have to guess about false teachers; you will know. Just as you don't have to guess whether a tree is bad or good when you closely examine its fruit, so it is with false teachers. You will know. In fact, 1 John 4:1-4 promises that all believers will overcome false teachers. This doesn't mean that we should be out witch-hunting and looking for the bad in every teacher or preacher, but it does mean that we must be on guard. We should believe the best until we can prove otherwise.

Summary

What is *The Warning of False Teachers* (v 15a)? Beware; watch out! My friend, are you on the lookout for false teachers? Are you entertaining yourself by listening to their garbage? Beware, and remember that if the blind lead the blind, they will both fall into the ditch. A disciple will become like his teacher!

What is *The Wardrobe of False Teachers* (v 15b)? Herein lies the difficulty with their wardrobe: because they wear the same thing you do, they look like the real thing. It behooves us to be discerning and to make sure that we know the biblical marks of a false teacher so that we will not be led away by their ravenous ways!

What are *The Works of False Teachers* (vv 16-18)? What kind of fruit do they produce? Bad fruit! Again, this means that you and I must know the Word of God and what God says is good fruit. We must be willing to do careful examination of a teacher's life and teaching. This does not mean that once I find out the truth, that a particular teacher is a false teacher, that I keep listening to them.

It does mean that I lovingly warn others to stay away from them. I think we can look at the life, the lips, and the love. The life: Is it holy, or is it sinful, greedy, and sensual? The lips: Do they teach sound doctrine, or do they use their mouth for flattery and to draw people after them? The love: Do they love God, or do they deny His attributes and use others to make merchandise of them?

What is *The Woe of False Teachers* (v 19)? Eternal hell fire. Blackness of darkness forever. These are serious words! Do you love those who are false teachers enough to warn them? Do you pray for them? There are three ladies that I pray for often, whom I believe are false teachers. I pray that they would consent to wholesome words. I'm grieved for the women they lead astray.

What is *The Wrap-Up Statement Regarding False Teachers* (v 20)? By their fruits, by their works, you will know them. Do you know them? If I were to ask you who the false teachers are in our day, could you tell me? How did you discern who they are?

Charles Swindoll ends his masterful illustration regarding false teachers with these words: "They may have a 'new' look—feel and taste like the real thing—but they are not. As Screwtape once quoted to Wormwood their father's couplet: 'Old error in new dress is ever error nonetheless.' Which is another way of saying, 'Dog food is dog food, no matter how you decorate it.' Or as Paul put it so pointedly, 'They are false ... deceitful ... disguising themselves as apostles of Christ.' They may not look like it, but they are as phony as a yellow three-dollar bill. Unfortunately, as long as there are hands to pick from the platter, there will be good-looking, sweet-smelling tidbits available. But some day, some dreadful day, the final Judge will determine and declare truth from error. There will be a lot of gagging and choking ... and it will no longer taste good. Nothing tastes good in hell."[102]

---

102 Swindoll, *Growing Strong in the Seasons of Life*, 148.

Questions to Consider

Jesus' Warning Regarding False Teachers!
Matthew 7:15-20

1. (a) According to Matthew 7:15-20, how does one recognize a false teacher? (b) How do you recognize a false teacher? (c) How would you define a false teacher?

2. Memorize Matthew 7:20.

3. (a) What are the marks of a false teacher, according to Deuteronomy 18:17-22; Jeremiah 23:14-22; Ezekiel 13:16; Matthew 24:4-11; Romans 16:17-18; 1 Timothy 4:1-3; 2 Timothy 4:3-4; 2 Peter 2; 1 John 4:1-4; and Jude? (b) Looking at these Scriptures, along with the Matthew 7:15-20 passage, write a summary sentence about how to discern a false teacher.

4. (a) Jesus says in Matthew 7:19 that trees which don't produce good fruit are hewn down and cast into the fire and are burned. With that in mind, read John 15:1-6 and write down anything you see that is similar to the Matthew verse. (b) What do you think it means that the branches are burned? Prove your answer biblically.

5. (a) What does Jesus say in Luke 3:7-14 that is similar to what He says in Matthew 7:15-20? (b) What fruit is mentioned in the Luke passage? (c) How is the fruit in the Luke passage similar to some of the content of what we have studied in the Sermon on the Mount?

6. (a) What biblical methods do you use to discern false teachers? (b) What practical methods do you use to discern false teachers? (c) What are some of the false teachings that we hear in our day?

7. (a) Are you currently being led away by false teaching? (b) Do you know someone who is? (c) Please write a request for yourself or someone else, asking God to help you in the area of discernment, or a request for someone you know who is a false teacher.

Chapter 22

Profession Minus Possession Equals Perdition

Matthew 7:21-23

An interesting poll came out not long ago reporting that 79 percent of Americans claim to be Christians. Yet, only 40 percent of Americans go to church; only 26 percent read their Bibles; and only 21 percent pray on a daily basis. However, a whopping 77 percent of professing Christian men view pornography monthly; 45 percent of professing Christians admit to doing something sexually immoral; and 23 percent of professing Christians admit to having had sex with someone other than their spouse. On and on we could go with statistics about American Christians, and we would probably find it most discouraging and alarming. But there's something even more alarming than these statistics, and that is the alarming message Jesus will give in the few short verses we will study in this lesson. Jesus will make it clear that profession minus possession equals perdition. Consider these words from Jesus:

Matthew 7:21-23

Not everyone who says to Me, "Lord, Lord," shall enter the kingdom of heaven, but he who does the will of My Father in heaven. ²²Many will say to Me in that day, "Lord, Lord, have we not prophesied in Your name, cast out demons in Your name, and done many wonders in Your name?" ²³And then I will declare to them, "I never knew you; depart from Me, you who practice lawlessness!"

In our last lesson, we learned several things regarding false teachers. First, the warning of false teachers: beware! Second, their wardrobe: it looks just like the real thing, a sheep's wardrobe; in reality, they are nothing more than wolves dressed in sheep's clothing. Third, their works: they produce bad fruit. Fourth, their woe: eternal hell-fire. Lastly, the wrap-up statement Jesus gives regarding them: by their fruits we will know them! In this lesson, *Profession Minus Possession Equals Perdition*, we will consider a three-fold outline:

Profession without Possession (v 21)
Passion without Possession (v 22)
Perdition without Possession (v 23)

As we saw in our last lesson, there are people who are false teachers, who look like the real thing but are not. Jesus ended that portion of His sermon by saying that by their fruits we will know them. This is the case not just for false teachers but also for all who profess the name of Christ. All those who profess Christ should have certain characteristics about them. Let's consider those who profess Christ but do not possess Him, in verse 21.

Profession without Possession

Matthew 7:21

Not everyone who says to Me, "Lord, Lord," shall enter the kingdom of heaven, but he who does the will of My Father in heaven. (Matthew 7:21)

Jesus begins with an absolute negative. He says *not everyone who says to Me, "Lord, Lord," shall enter the kingdom of heaven*. In other words, *not everyone* who says they know Me does know Me. There are some who profess Him as Lord but do not possess Him as Lord. And notice, it is what they *say*. This is very similar to what John says in 1 John 2:4-5, "He who says, 'I know Him,' and does not keep His commandments, is a liar, and the truth is not in him. But whoever keeps His word, truly the love of God is perfected in him. By this we know that we are in Him." John and Jesus are saying the same thing. You can say you know Jesus all you want to, but if you are not doing His will, if you are not keeping His commandments, then you are not His child. In fact, the book of 1 John is loaded with these types of verses from what I call the "if-we-sayers." They love to say, but they don't love to do. Listen to the "if-we-sayers" in 1 John 1:6-10: "*If we say* that we have fellowship with Him, and walk in darkness, we lie and do not practice the truth. But if we walk in the light as He is in the light, we have fellowship with one another, and the blood of Jesus Christ His Son cleanses us from all sin. *If we say* that we have no sin, we deceive ourselves, and the truth is not in us. If we confess our sins, He is faithful and just to forgive us our sins and to cleanse us from all unrighteousness. *If we say* that we have not sinned, we make Him a liar, and His word is not in us" (all emphases mine). Oh, my friend, we can say all the right stuff—"I know God," "I have fellowship with God," "I this," "I that"—but if we are not doing His will, then we are mouthing empty words.

Jesus goes on here in Matthew to let us know what these people say; they say *Lord, Lord. Lord* means one who is supreme in authority, one who is Master, and who has absolute authority over my life. He is one I can never say no to. I delight to do His will! To call Him Lord without possessing Him as Lord is no Lordship. These who merely say this *shall not enter the kingdom of heaven.* You might think that is unfair because the Word does say that I just need to call on the name of the Lord and I will be saved (Romans 10:13). But listen to what Jesus says as He explains why these professors He's addressing on the mount won't be saved, why they won't enter into heaven. He says you can call Me Lord all you want to, *but* only *he who does the will of my Father in heaven* will enter into His kingdom. Interestingly, there are two Greek words for the term *but*, alla and de. Alla is the stronger of the Greek words and it is the one used here. Jesus is making a point, and He's making a strong point by the Greek word He uses. Many will believe that profession alone is enough to enter into the kingdom of heaven, but Jesus makes it clear that will not happen. It is only those who do the will of His Father. He says the same thing in Luke 6:46, "But why do you call Me 'Lord, Lord,' and not do the things which I say?" James, the Lord's brother, gives us this warning as well in his epistle; he says in James 1:22-25, "But be doers of the word, and not hearers only, deceiving yourselves. For if anyone is a hearer of the word and not a doer, he is like a man observing his natural face in a mirror; for he observes himself, goes away, and immediately forgets what kind of man he was. But he who looks into the perfect law of liberty and continues in it, and is not a forgetful hearer but a doer of the work, this one will be blessed in what he does." James says if you are a hearer but not a doer, then you have deceived yourself into thinking you are a Christian when you are not. In case you're wondering if that is really what he is saying, he goes on to say it's only those who continue in the word and do the work that are blessed. In fact, he goes on to say that real religion is taking care of orphans and widows and keeping ourselves unspotted from the world. These things are what? Things that we do, acts of obedience! It is very clear from Revelation 22:14-15 that only those who do the will of God will enter heaven: "Blessed are those who do His commandments, that they may have the right to the tree of life, and may enter through the gates into the city. But outside are dogs and sorcerers and sexually immoral and murderers and idolaters, and whoever loves and practices a lie."

Just to be clear: Jesus doesn't condemn calling Him Lord, and indeed we should call Him Lord. But calling Him Lord without obeying Him as Lord is nothing but hypocrisy. Profession without possession is dangerous. But so is passion without possession, as Jesus makes clear in verse 22.

Passion without Possession

Matthew 7:22

> Many will say to Me in that day, "Lord, Lord, have we not prophesied in Your name, cast out demons in Your name, and done many wonders in Your name?" (Matthew 7:22)

Jesus begins with that frightening word *many*. This is the same word He used in verse 13 when He spoke of many going down the broad road. The term *many* means most, so when He says *many will say to Me in that day*, He means, "most will say to Me in that day." *That day* is a reference to the Day of Judgment. The reason we know this is because He has just spoken about those who will not enter into the kingdom of heaven. How sobering it will be when the events of Revelation 20:11-15, the Day of Judgment, happen: "Then I saw a great white throne and Him who sat on it, from whose face the earth and the heaven fled away. And there was found no place for them. And I saw the dead, small and great, standing before God, and books were opened. And another book was opened, which is the Book of Life. And the dead were judged according to their works, by the things which were written in the books. The sea gave up the dead who were in it, and Death and Hades delivered up the dead who were in them. And they were judged, each one according to his works. Then Death and Hades were cast into the lake of fire. This is the second death. And anyone not found written in the Book of Life was cast into the lake of fire." Again note, it is those who do, those who work. We are not saved by works, but our works and our obedience prove our salvation. As James says, faith without works is dead (James 2:20-26).

Notice that they are still saying *Lord, Lord*; they are still calling Him *Lord*. But with their verbal profession, they seem to also have passion, as evidenced by all that they claim to have done for Him. On the Day of Judgment, they are going to try to convince the Lord of their genuineness. And here is what they will claim to have done: First, they will claim they have *prophesied* in His name. We know that there are two types of prophecy. In the Old Testament, there were individuals called prophets, whom God used as His mouthpieces to warn others of impending judgment. These things came to pass because God said that they would. These prophets would foretell events and speak divine inspiration, revelation received directly from God. There is also another meaning of the word prophecy, which seems to be the spiritual gift that we see in the New Testament (Ephesians 4:11). In this case, the prophet is someone who is an inspired speaker, who heralds God's Word, that which has already been spoken and is now recorded in the written Word of God, the Bible. (I have the gift of prophecy, in the sense of heralding God's Word, but not in the sense of foretelling the future!)

So, these professors Jesus is talking about will plead with the Lord on that day, by reminding Him of all the prophesying they've done in His name, all the preaching they've done in His name.

Second, they will remind Him that they have *cast out demons* in His name. We know that the apostles were given this ability, because of what we read in Mark 3:13-15, "And He went up on the mountain and called to Him those He Himself wanted. And they came to Him. Then He appointed twelve, that they might be with Him and that He might send them out to preach, and to have power to heal sicknesses and to cast out demons." Interestingly enough, in this account, when Mark lists the 12 apostles, he lists Judas Iscariot in verse 19, the one who betrayed Christ (Mark 3:16-19): "Simon, to whom He gave the name Peter; James the son of Zebedee and John the brother of James, to whom He gave the name Boanerges, that is, 'Sons of Thunder'; Andrew, Philip, Bartholomew, Matthew, Thomas, James the son of Alphaeus, Thaddaeus, Simon the Canaanite; and Judas Iscariot, who also betrayed Him. And they went into a house." Jesus gave Judas the power to cast out demons and yet Judas was not a child of God. Jesus says in Matthew 26:24 that it would have been good for him (Judas) if he had not been born. And in John 17:12, Jesus calls Judas the son of perdition.

Third, these professors claim that they have also *done many wonders* in Jesus' name. This would imply that they had miraculous powers and were able to do supernatural works. These people have passion for the Lord's work; they've done all these things in His name. You might wonder as I did when I studied this passage: If our salvation is evidenced by our works, then why are these works, which they so passionately claim to have done, not evidence of their salvation? How could they have miraculous powers? Are they energized by demons? Let's consider a couple of passages that will help us. Exodus 7:8-13, "Then the Lord spoke to Moses and Aaron, saying, 'When Pharaoh speaks to you, saying, "Show a miracle for yourselves" then you shall say to Aaron, "Take your rod and cast it before Pharaoh, and let it become a serpent."' So Moses and Aaron went in to Pharaoh, and they did so, just as the

Lord commanded. And Aaron cast down his rod before Pharaoh and before his servants, and it became a serpent. But Pharaoh also called the wise men and the sorcerers; so the magicians of Egypt, they also did in like manner with their enchantments. For every man threw down his rod, and they became serpents. But Aaron's rod swallowed up their rods. And Pharaoh's heart grew hard, and he did not heed them, as the Lord had said." Pharaoh's men could do the same things God's men could do. But Pharaoh's men were sorcerers and magicians. Paul states in 2 Thessalonians 2:9-10, concerning the work of Satan: "The coming of the lawless one is according to the working of Satan, with all power, signs, and lying wonders, and with all unrighteous deception among those who perish, because they did not receive the love of the truth, that they might be saved." Paul also warns us in 2 Corinthians 11:13-15, "For such are false apostles, deceitful workers, transforming themselves into apostles of Christ. And no wonder! For Satan himself transforms himself into an angel of light. Therefore it is no great thing if his ministers also transform themselves into ministers of righteousness, whose end will be according to their works." Jesus warns us in the Olivet Discourse that as the end of the age winds down we will see an increase in these oddities. Consider Matthew 24:23-25, which says, "Then if anyone says to you, 'Look, here is the Christ!' or 'There!' do not believe it. For false christs and false prophets will rise and show great signs and wonders to deceive, if possible, even the elect. See, I have told you beforehand."

There are many people living today who, more than likely, will find themselves in the camp of those Jesus is talking about here in Matthew 7:23. We see much of this sensationalism going on today, and it is nothing but bogus. This is why Jesus just said that it is by their fruits that we will know them. We must test the spirits to see if they are of God, as John says in 1 John 4:1. Also, Deuteronomy 13:1-3 helps us: "If there arises among you a prophet or a dreamer of dreams, and he gives you a sign or a wonder, and the sign or the wonder comes to pass, of which he spoke to you, saying, 'Let us go after other gods'—which you have not known—'and let us serve them,' you shall not listen to the words of that prophet or that dreamer of dreams, for the Lord your God is testing you to know whether you love the Lord your God with all your heart and with all your soul." The test of whether it is of Satan or of God, according to what Moses tells the Israelites in this passage, is whether it lines up with God's Word. If it doesn't, then run—don't walk—away from such a person! Also, as we saw in our last lesson, we must examine the life to make sure it matches up with the profession. So, these people have professions without possession, they have passion without possession, but they also have perdition without possession. These are some of the most frightening words in all of God's Word and they should make us shudder!

Perdition without Possession

Matthew 7:23

And then I will declare to them, "I never knew you; depart from Me, you who practice lawlessness!" (Matthew 7:23)

They have been calling Him Lord. They've been saying all the things they've done in His name. But now Jesus has something to say to them, and these will be the final words they will hear Him say. He puts it this way: *and then I will declare to them*. The word *declare* means to fully and plainly tell. What will He tell them? The first thing He will tell them is *I never knew you*. Now, what does that mean? The word *know* is a word that describes an intimate relationship. In the Old Testament, it was often used to describe the sexual relationship between a man and a woman. So, here, the word would indicate the personal, intimate relationship between God and those whom He knows. He never had a personal relationship with these professors. In fact, the words *I never* mean not even at any time, never at all, never for a moment have I known you. Of course, Jesus knows them in the sense that He is omniscient and He created them; but He never knew them in the sense of having a personal relationship with them. This is similar to what He says to the 5 foolish virgins in the parable of the 10 virgins in Matthew 25:11-12: "Afterward the other virgins came also, saying, 'Lord, Lord, open to us!' But he answered and said, 'Assuredly, I say to you, I do not know you.'" Paul also speaks plainly about this in 1 Corinthians 8:3; he says, "But if anyone loves God, this one is known by Him."

Let me give you an illustration that might help you further understand what Jesus is saying. For example, I might tell you that I know President Donald Trump. What I mean is that I know a lot of things about him: he is our 45th president; he has a wife named Melania; he has five children; he likes to golf; he's a billionaire; and a myriad of other things I could tell you about him because I've read facts about him. But do I know him personally? Do I have a relationship with him? No! I've never even met him! We must be so careful about saying we know God if we don't know God! We must also be careful when people say they believe in God. What does that mean? The demons believe in God, according to James 2:19, and yet even the demons have enough sense to tremble before Him, which is more than most humans do!

Then, Jesus tells them *depart from Me*. *Depart* means to go away. And then He calls them those *who practice lawlessness*, those who violate the law of God. The works they claimed to have done in His name were nothing more than deeds of lawlessness. In the context of the Sermon on the Mount, we would have to wonder if this is a reference to the Scribes and Pharisees, whom He has been contrasting throughout this whole sermon with those who are truly His. Those who have professed to know God but have lived lives of hypocrisy. Those who loved to be admired, who have made sure that all their works were done to be seen of men. To those He will say depart from me *you workers of iniquity*! Chilling words! In this same spirit, Paul says in 2 Timothy 2:19, "Nevertheless the solid foundation of God stands, having this seal: 'The Lord knows those who are His,' and, 'Let everyone who names the name of Christ depart from iniquity.'"

Summary

Before we conclude, I want to say this: we have one more lesson to finish this study, but, oh, my friend, this one is most important as it is a matter of life of death. Please do not treat this lesson as more knowledge that you can add to your knowledge bank, but look at it through the lens of serious self-examination. As Paul begged the church at Corinth to do in 2 Corinthians 13:5-6, "Examine yourselves as to whether you are in the faith. Test yourselves. Do you not know yourselves, that Jesus Christ is in you?—unless indeed you are disqualified. But I trust that you will know that we are not disqualified." Oh, my friend, please test yourself! I don't want any of you—not one of you, including myself—to be disqualified. I do not want any of us to hear those awful and terrifying words, "Depart from Me; I never knew you!"

Let's consider what we have learned in this lesson and ask ourselves some vital questions. What about *Profession without Possession* (v 21)? Do you profess that Jesus is Lord? Have you confessed Him as Lord? If so, are you now doing His will? All of it? Are there any areas in your life where you are resisting what He has asked you to do? Do you know His Word well enough to know what He requires of you? How sad it will be to do mouth confession in this life, only to come to the Day of Judgment and realize that it was only mouth mercy. Then you will find yourself with the many who are only then bowing their knees to His Lordship and confessing Him as Lord, as Paul mentions in Philippians 2:9-11: "Therefore God also has highly exalted Him and given Him the name which is above every name, that at the name of Jesus every knee should bow, of those in heaven, and of those on earth, and of those under the earth, and that every tongue should confess that Jesus Christ is Lord, to the glory of God the Father." I would rather call Him Lord now than wait till that day, when it will be too late and the only words I could possibly hear would be, "Depart from Me; I never knew you!"

What about *Passion without Possession* (v 22)? What good works are you doing in His name? Teaching a class? Ministering to the needs of others? Working in the nursery? Cleaning the church? Discipling others? Using your spiritual gifts? Are you passionate about these things you do? That is good! And we should be passionate! But we must make sure in our zeal that we are not doing these works like the Pharisees. Paul mentions this in Romans 10:1-4, when he says, "Brethren, my heart's desire and prayer to God for Israel is that they may be saved. For I bear them witness that they have a zeal for God, but not according to knowledge. For they, being ignorant of God's righteousness, and seeking to establish their own righteousness, have not submitted to the righteousness of God. For Christ is the end of the law for righteousness to everyone who believes." These Jews had passion but not according to knowledge; they did not know God, and He never knew them.

What about *Perdition without Possession* (v 23)? If we are professing and passionate but without possessing genuine faith, then Jesus says we will perish; we will succumb to perdition without possession. Oh, my friend, let's not be like those of Proverbs 30:12: "There is a generation that is pure in its own eyes, yet is not washed from its filthiness." Let's carefully examine ourselves in light of what Jesus has said here and, in fact, in light of what He has said all throughout His Sermon on the Mount, beginning in Matthew 5. Does your life look like that of a genuine kingdom citizen?

Those American "Christians" whom I spoke of at the beginning of this lesson would do well to open that Bible they rarely read, attend that church they rarely attend, and pray to that God they claim to know. Maybe, just maybe, instead of "profession plus passion minus possession equals perdition," they might find themselves with "profession plus passion plus possession equals paradise."

I know these are sobering words to consider. Perhaps we should all have the attitude of John Newton, who once said, "If I ever reach Heaven I expect to find three wonders there: first, to meet some I had not thought to see there; second, to miss some I had thought to meet there; and third, the greater wonder of all, to find myself there."[103]

---

103 *"John Newton Quotes"Quotes.net.* STANDS4 LLC, 2017. Web. November 5, 2017

Questions to Consider

Profession Minus Possession Equals Perdition
Matthew 7:21-23

1. (a) Read Matthew 7:21-23 along with Romans 10:9-13. (b) How do you reconcile these two passages?

2. Memorize Matthew 7:21.

3. (a) Jesus says that those who call Him Lord without doing the things He says do not belong to Him. According to Matthew 18:3; Mark 3:35; John 3:5; Romans 2:13; Titus 1:15-16; James 1:22-27; and James 2:20-26, what things indicate that we belong to Him? (b) What other Scriptures come to your mind when you think of those who profess Christ without obedience to Christ? (c) What things can we do to combat the false idea in many churches today that we can be on our way to heaven without a life of obedience?

4. (a) Why is it imperative that we do God's will, according to Matthew 7:21-23; 12:50; Luke 11:28; and Romans 2:13? (b) How have you sought to teach others the importance of obedience? (c) Is obedience to the Lord a joy for you? (d) What practical things have you learned in your own life, regarding obedience to the Lord, that you can pass on to others?

5. (a) To whom will the Lord say, "Depart from Me," according to Matthew 25:31-46; Luke 13:24-30; Revelation 20:15; and 22:15? (b) What do you think Jesus means in Matthew 7:23 by the words "practice lawlessness"?

6. (a) Who called Jesus Lord in Matthew 25:1-13? (b) Did they go to glory? (c) Who else in Scripture comes to mind as someone who professed to know Christ but proved to be false in the end? (d) What things do you learn from these examples?

(www.quotes.net/quote/16032).

7. (a) *Please* examine your life in light of Matthew 7:21-23 and the other Scriptures we've considered in this lesson; it is a matter of your eternal destiny. Do you call Jesus Lord without living a life of obedience? (b) Do you know anyone in your circle of influence who calls Jesus Lord without living in obedience to Him? (c) With these things in mind, come with a prayer request for yourself or another (please, be discreet).

Chapter 23

Wise Man, Foolish Man: Which are You?

Matthew 7:24-29

Growing up in a minister's home gave me numerous opportunities to learn children's songs, many of which I can still remember today. One song, in particular, I'm sure was taken from the end of the sermon we've been studying, the Sermon on the Mount. The words to the song go like this:

> The wise man built his house upon the rock;
> The wise man built his house upon the rock;
> The wise man built his house upon the rock;
> And the rain came tumbling down.
>
> Oh, the rain came down, and the floods came up;
> The rain came down, and the floods came up;
> The rain came down, and the floods came up;
> And the wise man's house stood firm.
>
> The foolish man built his house upon the sand;
> The foolish man built his house upon the sand;
> The foolish man built his house upon the sand;
> And the rain came tumbling down.
>
> Oh, the rain came down, and the floods came up;
> The rain came down, and the floods came up;
> The rain came down, and the floods came up;
> And the foolish man's house went "splat!"[104]

As catchy as the words to that children's song may be, the words from Jesus' sermon are far from catchy—more like astounding! He

---

104 Words by Ann Omley, 1948 (public domain)

fills in a bit more detail than the catchy song; let's listen to what He says:

Matthew 7:24-29

"Therefore whoever hears these sayings of Mine, and does them, I will liken him to a wise man who built his house on the rock: [25]and the rain descended, the floods came, and the winds blew and beat on that house; and it did not fall, for it was founded on the rock. [26]But everyone who hears these sayings of Mine, and does not do them, will be like a foolish man who built his house on the sand: [27]and the rain descended, the floods came, and the winds blew and beat on that house; and it fell. And great was its fall." [28]And so it was, when Jesus had ended these sayings, that the people were astonished at His teaching, [29]for He taught them as one having authority, and not as the Scribes.

In this lesson, *Wise Man, Foolish Man: Which are You?* we will see:

Three Similarities between the Wise Man and the Foolish Man

Three Differences between the Wise Man and the Foolish Man

In our last lesson, we saw that there are those who have a profession or passion for Christ without having possession of Christ; which results in everlasting punishment, eternal hell. Their ending is not because they don't have profession or passion, but because they do not possess the living Christ, evidenced by the fact that they have not done the will of God—they have not obeyed Him.

Jesus is still drawing His sermon to a conclusion and these are His final words on the Mount. Matthew 8:1 tells us that after this sermon He came down from the mountain and the crowds followed Him. Let's begin as Jesus does by examining the wise man.

Therefore whoever hears these sayings of Mine, and does them, I will liken him to a wise man who built his house on the rock: (Matthew 7:24)

Jesus begins with the word *therefore*, which points back to everything He has said in His Sermon on the Mount. Therefore, because of everything He has said in this sermon, then *whoever hears* has a choice: do what He says, or don't do what He says. The *whoever* here is universal; it does not matter who you are. You can be among those sitting upon the mount during Jesus' sermon or you can be among those who are reading these words right now! You can be rich or poor, educated or uneducated, Jew or Gentile, male or female; whoever you are, it doesn't matter. What does matter is your response to what has been spoken. Jesus says if you hear these things He has said and you do them, then you are wise. And notice, my friend, Jesus is clear that *these sayings* are His, as evidenced by the word *Mine*. We must be careful to make sure that everything we hear taught by anyone other than our Lord is backed up by His sayings and no other.

This hearing is essential, but there is something that is even more essential, and this is where the wise man is very different from the foolish man. The wise man does what Jesus says. Jesus says this person who *hears* and *does* is like *a wise man who built his house on the rock.* If it is your desire to be in the category of wise women, then you must do what Jesus says. Paul states this very clearly in Romans 2:13: "For not the hearers of the law are just in the sight of God, but the doers of the law will be justified." Jesus says in Luke 11:28, "… blessed are those who hear the word of God and keep it!" Jesus, again, says in John 14:15, "If you love Me, keep My commandments." And then in John 15:14, "You are My friends if you do whatever I command you." And in the last book of the Bible, John says, "Blessed are those who do His commandments, that they may have the right to the tree of life, and may enter through the gates into the city" (Revelation 22:14).

The word *wise* refers to one who is discreet, one who is a man or woman of understanding. We know there is a way to acquire wisdom; Job 28:28 says, "And to man He said, 'Behold, the fear of the Lord, that is wisdom, and to depart from evil is understanding.'"

In my lifetime, I have noticed that the people who possess the most wisdom are the ones who are most obedient to the Word, whereas the people who are the most foolish are the ones who are not obedient to the Word.

Jesus says this wise man has *built his house on the rock*. The word for *rock* here indicates that it is a massive rock, and it actually refers to a rocky formation like a mountain or a cliff. It also indicates that this rock is immovable. This is interesting terminology, especially since Jesus is sitting on a mount as He's preaching these words. A passage that we would do well to consider is 1 Corinthians 3:9-11: "For we are God's fellow workers; you are God's field, you are God's building. According to the grace of God which was given to me, as a wise master builder I have laid the foundation, and another builds on it. But let each one take heed how he builds on it. For no other foundation can anyone lay than that which is laid, which is Jesus Christ." Notice that Paul uses the same word Jesus uses, the word *wise*. A wise builder builds on a solid foundation. My friend, if your house is not built on the solid foundation of Jesus Christ, you are not only unwise but you are also in great trouble, as we will see in a moment. However, if your life is built on Christ, the solid rock, then you will have no fear of what is to come. And Jesus speaks of that which is to come in verse 25.

> and the rain descended, the floods came, and the winds blew and beat on that house; and it did not fall, for it was founded on the rock. (Matthew 7:25)

If you live in a place like Oklahoma, where I live, then you understand what Jesus is describing here when He speaks of rain, floods, and winds. Torrential storms can have a serious impact on one's home. We've all seen videos of floods and homes floating down the river or falling off a slope somewhere. It's devastating. But a physical storm does not seem to be what Jesus is referring to, because even those homes that have been built upon rock—massive rock—are just as susceptible to destruction if they fall off that rock. Neither is Jesus talking about the storms of life, as some have advocated. When we consider the context of what Jesus has been saying as He's winding down His sermon, then it's fairly simple to understand what He's saying here. He is keeping with the theme of the ending: two persons and two destinations. This would not be a new thought to the Jewish audience listening on the mount; they would, more than likely, be thinking back to Ezekiel 13. They would know that Jesus is referring to the final judgment. Listen to Ezekiel 13:8-16:

> Therefore thus says the Lord God: "Because you have spoken nonsense and envisioned lies, therefore I am indeed against you," says the Lord God. "My hand will be against the prophets who envision futility and who divine lies; they shall not be in the assembly of My people, nor be written in the record of the house of Israel, nor shall they enter into the land of Israel. Then you shall know that I am the Lord God. Because, indeed, because they have seduced My people, saying, 'Peace!' when there is no peace—and one builds a wall, and they plaster it with untempered mortar—say to those who plaster it with untempered mortar, that it will fall. There will be flooding rain, and you, O great hailstones, shall fall; and a stormy wind shall tear it down. Surely, when the wall has fallen, will it not be said to you, 'Where is the mortar with which you plastered it?'" Therefore thus says the Lord God: "I will cause a stormy wind to break forth in My fury; and there shall be a flooding rain in My anger, and great hailstones in fury to consume it. So I will break down the wall you have plastered with untempered mortar, and bring it down to the ground, so that its foundation will be uncovered; it will fall, and you shall be consumed in the midst of it. Then you shall know that I am the Lord. Thus will I accomplish My wrath on the wall and on those who have plastered it with untempered mortar; and I will say to you, 'The wall is no more, nor those who plastered it, that is, the prophets of Israel who prophesy concerning Jerusalem, and who see visions of peace for her when there is no peace,'" says the Lord God.

Jesus has been saying the same thing in the Sermon on the Mount that God said to those in Ezekiel's day. There are the true and the false; there are the false prophets and the true prophets; there are the Scribes and Pharisees and there are the true kingdom citizens. But one thing both will face is eternity; both will face the final storm; the storm of judgment. Some will fall; some will not. Only those who have built carefully on a strong foundation will stand. Proverbs 3:35 states, "The wise shall inherit glory, but shame shall be the legacy of fools." Remember, the end is what Jesus has been speaking about in the Sermon on the Mount as He is winding down His message. Two trees, two fruits, two gates, two ways, two roads, and two destinations.

So the end comes, the final storm of life, so to speak. The wise person, whose foundation is built upon the rock of Christ, can go through that final judgment and he or she will not fall. Why? Because they are founded on the rock, the solid rock of Christ. But notice that the house was saved because of the rock, not because of anything that the man (or woman) did. Jesus is the only one who can save. The songwriter put it well: "On Christ the solid rock I stand, all other ground is sinking sand."[105] Brother Peter understood this well, as he writes in 1 Peter 2:4-8, "Coming to Him as to a living stone, rejected indeed by men, but chosen by God and precious, you also, as living stones, are being built up a spiritual house, a holy priesthood, to offer up spiritual sacrifices acceptable to God through Jesus Christ. Therefore it is also contained in the Scripture, 'Behold, I lay in Zion a chief cornerstone, elect, precious, and he who believes on Him will by no means be put to shame.' Therefore, to you who believe, He is precious; but to those who are disobedient, 'The stone which the builders rejected has become the chief cornerstone,' and 'a stone of stumbling and a rock of offense.' They stumble, being disobedient to the word, to which they also were appointed." Jesus will now contrast the foolish man with the wise man and we will begin to see their similarities as well as their differences.

---

105 Words by Edward Mote, 1834.

> But everyone who hears these sayings of Mine, and does not do them, will be like a foolish man who built his house on the sand: (Matthew 7:26)

But is a word of contrast. In contrast to the wise, we have the foolish. The foolish also hear the sayings of Christ. *This is the first thing that is similar about the wise man and the foolish man—they both hear the same sayings.* However, the wise man does something about what he hears; he obeys what he hears, while the foolish man does not. *This is the first difference between them—they have different responses: one does what he hears, and one does not.* But didn't Jesus say that already in Matthew 5:19-20? "Whoever therefore breaks one of the least of these commandments, and teaches men so, shall be called least in the kingdom of heaven; but whoever does and teaches them, he shall be called great in the kingdom of heaven. For I say to you, that unless your righteousness exceeds the righteousness of the Scribes and Pharisees, you will by no means enter the kingdom of heaven." The phrase *does not* here in Matthew 7:24 means an absolute denial; in other words, they do not do them. The rabbis taught that it was essential to hear the law, but they would argue as to whether it was just as essential to obey the law. They were hearers but not necessarily doers. In John 14:23-24, Jesus, again, reiterates this point: "Jesus answered and said to him, 'If anyone loves Me, he will keep My word; and My Father will love him, and We will come to him and make Our home with him. He who does not love Me does not keep My words; and the word which you hear is not Mine but the Father's who sent Me.'"

Jesus calls foolish those who do not obey His words. *Foolish* means moral blockhead, stupid, absurd. The Greek word is moros, from which we get our English word moron. "Now, wait a minute," you might be saying, "Jesus just told us not to call anyone a fool or we will be in danger of hell fire, and yet He calls these guys fools. I don't get it." We must always remember context! The context of Matthew 5:22 was that of getting angry without a cause and harboring an unresolved offense with someone. The context here in Matthew 7:26 is that of not obeying what Jesus says. As Psalm 14:1 tells us, the fool in his heart says no to God. (In our English translations, Psalm 14:1 is often rendered, "The fool has said in his heart, 'There is no God,'" but a literal translation would render it, "No God!")

This fool builds his house not on the rock but on the sand. *Sand is defined as a loose granular substance composed of rock. This is the second difference between the wise man and foolish man: they not only have different responses to Jesus' words but they also have different foundations.* One is a solid mass; the other is sand. One is solid; the other is a bunch of little itty-bitty rocks. One is solid; the other is mushy. But there's still more that these two have in common, as we see in verse 27.

> and the rain descended, the floods came, and the winds blew and beat on that house; and it fell. And great was its fall. (Matthew 7:27)

The second thing the wise man and the foolish man have in common is that they not only hear the same sayings but they also encounter the same storm. Both the wise man and the foolish man will stand before God; neither will be exempt. The writer to the Hebrews is clear in Hebrews 9:27: "And as it is appointed for men to die once, but after this the judgment." And Paul in Romans 14:10, says "… we shall all stand before the judgment seat of Christ."

Jesus is clear that the foolish man's house *fell*, which means that it crashed. But Jesus doesn't end there; He says *and great was its fall*. The word *great* means mega in the Greek, which means that it was big, it was huge. *The third difference between the wise man and the foolish man is that, in addition to having different responses and having different rocks for foundations, they also have different results—one falls; one stands.* Dear one, hearing the teachings of Christ without doing the teachings of Christ is dangerous. In fact, it's eternally dangerous, because it can send you to hell. The only ones who will be able to stand in judgment will be those whose names are written in the Lamb's Book of Life, those who have bowed the knee, those who have traveled the narrow road, those who have agonized to enter in. In the physical sense, sand is easier to get ahold of than a massive rock. It weighs less and it's easier to maneuver than a big rock. But Jesus has already said one way is easy and one way is hard. It is only those who do what Jesus says who will be able to stand, it is only those whose house is built upon the rock who will not fall.

The very first Psalm in the Psalter, Psalm 1, contrasts the godly with the ungodly, the wise with the foolish. Consider these words and notice the similarities between this Psalm and Jesus' final words on the mount: "Blessed is the man who walks not in the counsel of the ungodly, nor stands in the path of sinners, nor sits in the seat of the scornful; but his delight is in the law of the Lord, and in His law he meditates day and night. He shall be like a tree planted by the rivers of water, that brings forth its fruit in its season, whose leaf also shall not wither; and whatever he does shall prosper. The ungodly are not so, but are like the chaff which the wind drives away. Therefore the ungodly shall not stand in the judgment, nor sinners in the congregation of the righteous. For the Lord knows the way of the righteous, but the way of the ungodly shall perish." Did you notice what the Psalmist said? The same thing Jesus said! The ungodly will not stand in the Day of Judgment. They will fall. Why? Because they have been foolish by not being obedient. Another song writer put it well, "In times like these you need a Savior. In times like these you need an anchor. Be very sure, be very sure, your anchor holds and grips the Solid Rock! This Rock is Jesus, yes, He's the One. This Rock is Jesus, the only One! Be very sure, be very sure, your anchor holds and grips the Solid Rock!"[106] Jesus' brother James is very clear in James 1:22-25, "But be doers of the word, and not hearers only, deceiving yourselves. For if anyone is a hearer of the word and not a doer, he is like a man observing his natural face in a mirror; for he observes himself, goes away, and immediately forgets what kind of man he was. But he who looks into the perfect law of liberty and continues in it, and is not a forgetful hearer but a doer of the work, this one will be blessed in what he does." John also is clear in his epistle, in 1 John 2:3-6, "Now by this we know that we know Him, if we keep His commandments. He who says, 'I know

106 Words by Ruth Caye Jones, 1944.

Him,' and does not keep His commandments, is a liar, and the truth is not in him. But whoever keeps His word, truly the love of God is perfected in him. By this we know that we are in Him."

This is the end of Jesus' Sermon on the Mount, but it is not the end of what Matthew says, as he ends with these poignant words in verses 28-29. And here we will see our third similarity between the wise man and the foolish man.

> And so it was, when Jesus had ended these sayings, that the people were astonished at His teaching, (Matthew 7:28)

The sermon is over. Jesus has ended what He has to say. But the people are astonished at His teaching—and rightly so. You and I have been studying this sermon for some time now, and you, like me, have probably been astonished at its teaching. I've had the Sermon on the Mount memorized for years, but I have been astonished and convicted all over again as I have studied and taught it. What does it mean that they were *astonished*? It means that they were struck with astonishment, they were amazed; they were dumbfounded. *The third similarity between the wise man and the foolish man is, in addition to hearing the same sayings and encountering the same storm, but that they also have the same response to the Lord's words— they're struck dumb!* Matthew doesn't divide the audience into two categories here; he simply says they (all of them) were struck dumb. And why were they astonished? Because, as verse 29 says,

> for He taught them as one having authority, and not as the Scribes. (Matthew 7:29)

Jesus *taught* like no one else, because Jesus taught with *authority*. He did *not* teach *as the Scribes*. The Scribes were professionals. They were the taught ones, the ones who had been to school, we might say. They knew all the right stuff; they followed the law to its letter. But they had no power because they did not have the Spirit of God. That certainly describes a lot of ministers in our day, doesn't it? There sure are a lot of professional preachers out there, but there are few who speak with power and authority. In fact, scholars tell us that there are copies of parts of the teachings of the rabbis and they are dull and boring. Their teaching had no life because they themselves had no eternal life—they had no power. One man has said, "They had heard many sermons before from the regular rabbis in the synagogues. We have specimens of these discourses preserved in the Mishna and Gemara, the Jewish Talmud when both were completed, the driest, dullest collection of disjointed comments upon every conceivable problem in the history of mankind. The Scribes quoted the rabbis before them and were afraid to express an idea without bolstering it up by some predecessor. Jesus spoke with the authority of truth, the reality and freshness of the morning light, and the power of God's Spirit. This sermon which made such a profound impression ended with the tragedy of the fall of the house on the sand like the crash of a giant oak in the forest. There was no smoothing over the outcome."[107]

Summary

There are *Three Similarities between the Wise Man and the Foolish Man*: they hear the same sayings of Christ; they encounter the same storm, and they have the same sobering response, being struck dumb. We also, whether foolish or wise, have heard the sayings of Christ, during this study and throughout our lives. We also, will all stand in the last judgment before we step into heaven or hell. We all are struck dumb not only at this particular sermon we have studied but at so much of God's Word that leaves us speechless. The similarities we share are hard factors in determining whether we are foolish or wise.

But there are also *Three Differences between the Wise Man and the Foolish Man*: they have different responses to Jesus' sayings—one does them, while the other does not; they have different rocks—one is massive and solid, while the other is sandy and shifting; and they have different results—one stands and enters into eternity with Christ, while the other falls, and the fall is very great and results

107 *Robertson's Word Pictures in the New Testament*, Electronic Database. Copyright © 1997, 2003, 2005, 2006 by Biblesoft, Inc. Copyright © 1985 by Broadman Press.

in those frightening words, "Depart from me, you who practice lawlessness" (Matthew 7:23). These differences help us to determine what category we fall under, foolish or wise.

It is true that we may not know whether our foundation is rock or sand until we face the judgment; we may not know if we will stand or fall on the Day of Judgment because some of us will remain self-deceived right unto the end. But the issue of obedience is something we can tangibly measure. We must remember that Jesus is not just comparing the saved with the lost; He is comparing those who are saved and those who think they are saved. They both hear Jesus' sayings; we might say they both come to church and hear sermons; they look the same externally; they both know the religious songs and the religious words; they both teach Sunday School classes; they both tithe; but, in reality, they each make a different choice. My friend, you have heard the sayings of Jesus on the mount, but have you obeyed His teachings?

One man says, "We sometimes admire the response of those who listened in amazement to Jesus' sermon—and there is something admirable about it. But there is also something inadequate about it: Matthew pointedly refrains from telling us that the people *obeyed* it. They thought it was the most admirable sermon they had ever heard. Indeed, it is the most admired sermon in human history. But Jesus did not preach it in order to be admired for His homiletical skills. He preached it to produce obedience. He preached it so that the authority people *recognized* in His preaching might be *realized* in their lives. You have seen the authority in His sermon. Now, will you submit to it?"[108]

There is an interesting passage in Deuteronomy, in which Moses is giving some of his final words to the Israelites before he dies. He even tells them that he knows that after he dies they will fall back into their evil ways and not obey the Lord (Deuteronomy 31:29). He basically leaves them with the choice of choosing eternal life

---

108 Sinclair B. Ferguson, *The Sermon on the Mount* (Carlisle: Banner of Truth Trust, 1987), 171.

or choosing eternal death. This is the same thing our Lord has been stressing to us on the mount. With Moses' words, I'll close.

> See, I have set before you today life and good, death and evil, in that I command you today to love the Lord your God, to walk in His ways, and to keep His commandments, His statutes, and His judgments, that you may live and multiply; and the Lord your God will bless you in the land which you go to possess. But if your heart turns away so that you do not hear, and are drawn away, and worship other gods and serve them, I announce to you today that you shall surely perish; you shall not prolong your days in the land which you cross over the Jordan to go in and possess. I call heaven and earth as witnesses today against you, that I have set before you life and death, blessing and cursing; therefore choose life, that both you and your descendants may live; that you may love the Lord your God, that you may obey His voice, and that you may cling to Him, for He is your life and the length of your days; and that you may dwell in the land which the Lord swore to your fathers, to Abraham, Isaac, and Jacob, to give them. (Deuteronomy 30:15-20)

Questions to Consider
Wise Man, Foolish Man, Which Are You?
Matthew 7:24-29

1. (a) What is similar and what is different about the wise man and the foolish man in Matthew 7:24-29? (b) Which category do you fall under, wise or foolish? (c) How do you know?

2. Memorize Matthew 7:24-29.

3. (a) The wise man and foolish man are also contrasted in Deuteronomy 28. What are the blessings of obedience and the curses of disobedience, according to this chapter? (b) In what ways are Deuteronomy 28 and Matthew 7:24-29 similar?

4. (a) When Jesus ends His sermon, Matthew says the people were astonished at his doctrine. According to the following passages, at what other times were the people astonished at His teaching and what happened as a result (if it's mentioned)? Matthew 13:54-58; Mark 1:21-22; Mark 6:1-6; Luke 4:31-37; John 7:14-31; and John 7:40-53. (b) Has Jesus' teaching in the Sermon on the Mount astonished you? In what ways? (c) What has happened in your life as a result of His astonishing sermon?

5. In lesson 1 of our study, the following question was asked: "Read Matthew 5-7 and write down at least 10 things you don't understand from these chapters. (Save this for the last lesson in hopes that you will understand them by then!)" Since with this lesson we are completing our study of the Sermon on the Mount, would you say that you now understand those "things" that you did not understand then?

6. (a) Glance over the Sermon on the Mount, Matthew 5-7. Have you made any changes due to this study? (b) If you haven't, what would Jesus say to you from Matthew 7:24-29? (c) What is your biblically-informed strategy to press on toward maturity in Christ, now that you've completed this study?

7. (a) Have you ever listened to a sermon or read the word of God without obeying it? (b) What is the danger of doing that? (c) Have you ever listened to a sermon or read the word of God and obeyed it? (d) What is the delight of doing so?

8. Write a prayer of thanksgiving to the Lord for this sermon we have studied. Please include specific changes you have made or challenges that you have benefited from through the study of this particular passage.

About the Author

Susan Heck, and her husband Doug have been married for over 40 years. She has been involved in Women's Ministries for over 30 years. This includes teaching Bible Studies, counseling, and leading Ladies with the Master women's ministry at Grace Community Church in Tulsa, Oklahoma. (www.gccoftulsa.net)

Susan is a certified counselor with the Association of Certified Biblical Counselors (ACBC, formerly NANC). She is the author of "With The Master" Bible Study Series for women. Previously published books in that series are,

- With the Master in the School of Tested Faith:
    A Ladies' Bible Study of the Epistle of James

- With the Master in Heavenly Places:
    A Ladies' Bible Study on Ephesians

- With the Master on our Knees:
    A Ladies' Bible Study on Prayer

- With the Master in Fullness of Joy:
    A Ladies' Bible Study on the Book of Phillipians

- With the Master Before the Mirror of God's Word:
    A Ladies' Bible Study on First John

She is also the author of five published booklets:
- Putting Off Life Dominating Sins
- A Call to Scripture Memory
- A Call to Discipleship
- Assurance: Twenty Tests for God's Children
- The Liberating Gospel: A Call to Salvation

Susan's teaching ministry is an outgrowth of her memorization work on the Bible. She has personally memorized 23 books of the New Testament word-for-word (The Gospel of Matthew, The Gospel of John, Romans, Second Corinthians, Galatians, Ephesians, Philippians, Colossians, First and Second Thessalonians, First and Second Timothy,

Titus, Philemon, Hebrews, James, First and Second Peter, and First, Second, and Third John, Jude, Revelation), one book of the Old Testament (Jonah), and several other portions of Scripture.

Susan and her husband have two grown children and seven grandchildren. Both children and their spouses are in full-time ministry. Because of the enthusiasm of ladies who attended Susan's Bible studies, she has been invited to speak to ladies' groups both nationally and internationally. (www.withthemaster.org)